WALKS AND TREKS IN CROATIA

About the Author

Rudolf Abraham (www.rudolfabraham.co.uk) is an award-winning travel writer and photographer specialising in Croatia, Central and Eastern Europe. He is the author of more than 10 books, and his work is published widely in magazines. He first visited Croatia in the late 1990s, returned to live in Zagreb for two years, and continues to make several trips a year to his favourite country in Europe.

Other Cicerone guides by the author
St Oswald's Way and St Cuthbert's Way
The Islands of Croatia
The Mountains of Montenegro
The Peaks of the Balkans Trail
Torres del Paine

Acknowledgements

For this third edition of *Walks and Treks in Croatia*, thanks are due to Tanja Augustinović at the Kvarner Tourist Office, Marinko Jakovljević at the Fužine Tourist Office, Silvija Sobol at the Risnjak National Park Office, Dragica Jović of the Paklenica National Park Office, Dajana Tepšić at the Istrian Tourist Office, Dubravko Primorac at Lobagola in Zagreb, Griet and Anri at Kuća Baijlo in Zadar, Ulrich Teitz at Deutsche Bahn, Jakov Žarko for his company on Dinara, and members of the HGSS and Dinaridi. Finally, for her advice, and company on a number of these routes, and for her help with the language section I must thank my wife Ivana – with whom I first discovered Velebit, and to whom this book is dedicated.

WALKS AND TREKS IN CROATIA

MOUNTAIN TRAILS AND NATIONAL PARKS, INCLUDING VELEBIT, DINARA AND PLITVICE

by Rudolf Abraham

JUNIPER HOUSE, MURLEY MOSS,
OXENHOLME ROAD, KENDAL, CUMBRIA LA9 7RL
www.cicerone.co.uk

© Rudolf Abraham 2019
Third edition 2019
ISBN: 978 1 85284 769 2
Second edition 2010
First edition 2004

Printed by KHL Printing, Singapore
All photographs are by the author unless otherwise stated.
A catalogue record for this book is available from the British Library.

Route mapping by Lovell Johns www.lovelljohns.com
Contains OpenStreetMap.org data © OpenStreetMap
contributors, CC-BY-SA. NASA relief data courtesy of ESRI

for Ivana

Updates to this Guide

While every effort is made by our authors to ensure the accuracy of guide-books as they go to print, changes can occur during the lifetime of an edition. Any updates that we know of for this guide will be on the Cicerone website (www.cicerone.co.uk/769/updates), so please check before planning your trip. We also advise that you check information about such things as transport, accommodation and shops locally. Even rights of way can be altered over time.

The route maps in this guide are derived from publicly available data, databases and crowd-sourced data. As such they have not been through the detailed checking procedures that would generally be applied to a published map from an official mapping agency, although naturally we have reviewed them closely in the light of local knowledge as part of the preparation of this guide.

We are always grateful for information about any discrepancies between a guidebook and the facts on the ground, sent by email to updates@cicerone.co.uk or by post to Cicerone, Juniper House, Murley Moss, Oxenholme Road, Kendal, LA9 7RL.

Register your book: To sign up to receive free updates, special offers and GPX files where available, register your book at www.cicerone.co.uk.

Front cover: Hiker on Premužićeva staza, Northern Velebit National Park (Route 16, Stage 2)

CONTENTS

Knin castle

Mountain safety

Every mountain walk has its dangers, and those described in this guidebook are no exception. All who walk or climb in the mountains should recognise this and take responsibility for themselves and their companions along the way. The author and publisher have made every effort to ensure that the information contained in this guide was correct when it went to press, but, except for any liability that cannot be excluded by law, they cannot accept responsibility for any loss, injury or inconvenience sustained by any person using this book.

International distress signal *(emergency only)*
Six blasts on a whistle (and flashes with a torch after dark) spaced evenly for one minute, followed by a minute's pause. Repeat until an answer is received. The response is three signals per minute followed by a minute's pause.

Helicopter rescue
The following signals are used to communicate with a helicopter:

Help needed:
raise both arms
above head to
form a 'Y'

Help not needed:
raise one arm
above head, extend
other arm downward

Emergency telephone numbers
Police: 92;
Fire: 93;
Ambulance: 94;
Emergency services can also be contacted on: 112;

Mountain rescue can be very expensive – be adequately insured.

Symbols used on route maps

route
alternative route
start point
finish point
start/finish point
alternative start
alternative finish
route direction
spring
woodland
urban areas
regional border
international border
station/railway
peak
manned/unmanned refuge
building
church/monastery/cross
castle
pass
water feature
viewpoint
cave

Relief
in metres

5000 and above
4800–5000
4600–4800
4400–4600
4200–4400
4000–4200
3800–4000
3600–3800
3400–3600
3200–3400
3000–3200
2800–3000
2600–2800
2400–2600
2200–2400
2000–2200
1800–2000
1600–1800
1400–1600
1200–1400
1000–1200
800–1000
600–800
400–600
200–400
0–200

SCALE: 1:50,000

0 kilometres 0.5 1
0 miles 0.5

Contour lines are drawn at 25m intervals
and highlighted at 100m intervals.

9

AUSTRIA

ITALY

SLOVENIA

Skrad

Samobor

Zagr

MEDVE

SAMOBORS
GORJE

GORS
Risnjak
NP

Opatija
Delnice

Delnice

Karlovac

Poreč

Rijeka

Fužine

Ogulin

ISTRIA

Pazin

KAPELA

Rovinj

KRK

Brijuni
Islands NP

Pula

CRES

Senj

Plitvička
jezera NP

RAB

LOŠINJ

Sjeverni Velebit NP

Karlobag

Gospic

PAG

Paklenica NP

Starigrad-Paklenica

Zadar

Knin

DINAR

Kornati
Islands NP

Krka NP

Šibenik

ITALY

KOZ

Trogir

Sp

ADRIATIC SEA

HVAR

VIS

4 Walk
9 Trek

Part 1: Walks around Zagreb
Part 2: Istria and the Opatija Riviera
Part 3: Gorski kotar
Part 4: Velebit
Part 5: The Dalmation Hinterland
Part 6: Central Dalmatia
Part 7: Southern Dalmatia

Varaždin

HUNGARY

N

0   25 miles

0   50 km

1:3 000 000

Bjelovar

NICA

CROATIA

SLAVONIA

PAPUK

Sisak

Osijek

Vukovar

Slavonski Brod

Ilok

SERBIA

BOSNIA-
HERZEGOVINA

23

MOSOR

25

RAČ

Makarska

BIOKOVO

T

27

PELJEŠAC

A

KORČULA

Mljet

NP MLJET

SNIJEŽNICA

MONTENEGRO

Dubrovnik

26

KOSOVO

Old Austrian packhorse track, Snježnica (Route 26)

INTRODUCTION

Viewpoint overlooking the Velika Paklenica gorge from just below Manita peć, Paklenica National Park (Route 18)

My love affair with Croatia began some 20 years ago, when I first visited Velebit, in the middle of winter. It turned out to be a rather wonderful place, snow-bound, unfamiliar, and yet unspeakably beautiful. Within a year I had moved to Zagreb where I lived and worked for two years, making frequent trips into the mountains, which formed the basis of the first edition of this guide, published in 2004. I have been returning to Croatia ever since.

The past decade or so has seen a huge increase in the number of people visiting Croatia – mainly the coast and islands, more recently with a *Game of Thrones*-induced twist to things – and Zagreb appears to have

suddenly been 'discovered' thanks in part to its enormous Christmas market, voted one of the best in Europe.

This is not to say that the Croatian coastline is busier than any other attractive and sunny part of Europe during the summer months – indeed, it remains less crowded in many places, and comparatively unspoilt. And while most visitors head straight for the coast – the lovely Dalmatian towns and villages and the glittering isles of the Croatian archipelago – the mountains remain largely untouched.

Croatia's rugged mountains rise up suddenly, often spectacularly, beyond the narrow ribbon of coastal cities and rocky beaches. It is these mountains – the limestone massifs of Velebit, Gorski kotar, Mosor and Biokovo, extending in furrowed ranges from Slovenia in the north to Montenegro in the south – which so dramatically divide the Adriatic from the continental interior, contributing as much to the particular character of the country as the more celebrated coastline. More significantly, from the point of view of this guide, they provide a superb, and as yet remarkably unspoilt arena for the mountain walker, whether you're after an easy day walk or an extended mountain trek.

Often only a few hours from the coast by way of steep and rocky trails, these mountains have much to commend them as a walking destination. Ranging from gently sloping, forested hills to rugged tops and limestone crags, they form a landscape of outstanding beauty; at their most spectacular they are a karst labyrinth of domed peaks and cavernous sink-holes, sun-bleached ridges and rocky dells. They are not a wilderness experience in the traditional sense (then again, little in Europe is). Trails are for the most part well-established and clearly marked, mountain huts are plentiful and local walkers abound. But the scenery is as lovely as it is varied, the terrain rewarding, and the views often breathtaking. And despite their modest elevation – Velebit rises to less than 1800m – there is still plenty to be found that is challenging. Furthermore, in contrast to many of the mountain areas in neighbouring Slovenia, Velebit and Gorski kotar remain well within the capabilities of the well-equipped walker during the winter months, despite heavy snowfall.

Diocletian's Palace, Split – a UNESCO World Heritage Site

KEY FACTS AND FIGURES

Country name:	Republika Hrvatska
Capital:	Zagreb
Population:	4.29 million (2011 census)
Language:	Croatian
Main religion:	Roman Catholic (86.3%)
Currency:	kuna (Kn or HNK)
Land surface area:	56,594km²
Length of coastline (including islands):	5,835km
Number of islands, islets and reefs:	1185
Time zone:	GMT +1 (CET)
International telephone code:	+385
Electricity:	220V/50Hz

Finally, the very proximity of these areas to the coastal scenery and islands, and to historic cities such as Dubrovnik, Split and Zadar, is a considerable attraction in itself. These cities boast some stunning Roman and medieval architecture – Dubrovnik often being touted, with considerable justification, as the best-preserved medieval city on the Mediterranean.

To complement these better-known features of the country, the walks in this guide provide a more intimate view of Croatia and its people, and a counterbalance to the bustle of its coastline during the summer months (after which the coast largely reverts to its sleepy Dalmatian self). And while the walls of Dubrovnik heave with sightseers, the hiker can still follow a sinuous ridge without seeing another soul, or sit comfortably on a high pass below Zavižan, and take in a dazzling sunset across the Croatian archipelago.

GEOGRAPHY AND GEOLOGY

Croatia, my Croatian friends told me long before I first visited their beautiful country, is like a bird in flight. Look at a map and you'll see this quite clearly: the great wings spread back across Slavonia, poised between beats; the head hanging low in Istria, and protruding out into the Adriatic; the body and tail stretching down through Lika and Dalmatia; the belly splintering into the myriad isles of the Croatian archipelago. It is an attractive image, and one which has stayed with me ever since (certainly it is more poetic than the comparison between Croatia's rather peculiar shape and a boomerang).

From a hiking perspective, the most interesting areas are the successive ranges of mountains running parallel to the Adriatic coast – the belly and tail of the bird, to take the analogy further. Collectively known as the Dinaric Alps, these mountains

15

rise steeply from the narrow band of settlements along the coast, frequently to 1500m and in some cases to over 1700m, forming a dramatic natural barrier between the rocky coastline and the continental interior.

The Dinaric Alps are simultaneously the longest mountain chain in Croatia and its most spectacular area for hiking. Stretching southeast some 700km from the Slovenian border, these mountains run the length of Croatia, through Montenegro and into Albania, from where they continue as the Pindos Mountains in Greece. Their steep western slopes present an almost impenetrable barrier towards the Adriatic, and with only a few exceptions (such as the Krka and the Cetina rivers, which break through the mountains as impressive canyons on their way to the Adriatic) their drainage is almost entirely eastwards into the Danube.

The Dinaric Alps are composed of a series of distinct massifs or ranges, some higher or more extensive than others. From north to south in Croatia these are Gorski kotar, Velebit, Mosor and Biokovo, with various smaller areas in between, and behind them the Dalmatian hinterland and the Lika basin; Dinara (which includes the highest peak in Croatia) lies slightly further inland, along the border with Bosnia. To their west is the rocky, highly indented coastline for which Croatia is best known. Croatia's islands, which like the mountains run in a general northwest–southeast

direction, effectively constitute low-lying outer ranges of the Dinaric Alps, their valleys long ago submerged beneath the waters of the Adriatic.

Croatia's mountains are formed primarily of Cretaceous limestone – laid down on the seabed in the form of shells and other marine life when the Adriatic, along with the rest of this part of central and eastern Europe, was submerged beneath a shallow tropical sea some 66–145 million years ago. The Croatian Adriatic had become a coastal plain by the Pleistocene Era (2.5 million–11,700 years ago), with the gradual flooding of this coastal plain during the Holocene leading around 7000 years ago to the creation of the islands and the Adriatic Sea as we now know it.

Croatia is karst country. Karst is formed by the gradual dissolving of the limestone rock by rainwater – or, more specifically, by the combination of rainwater and carbon dioxide from the earth's atmosphere and the soil, which results in a weak solution of carbonic acid. Over millennia this process gradually enlarges surface drainage holes, as well as horizontal and vertical cracks and fissures in the rock, as the water percolates downwards, creating distinctive surface features such as vertical fluting (karren), solution pans, limestone pavement and sinkholes (doline), while beneath the surface it leads to the formation of an extensive network of caves and underground drainage channels, with all rainwater rapidly disappearing

Karst features on Bojinac (Route 19, Stage 1), Paklenica National Park, Southern Velebit

underground, re-emerging later as karst springs, either in the foothills of the mountains or as submarine springs (*vrulja*). Collapses in the roof of these subterranean voids leads to the formation of larger sinkholes and cenotes. *Polje* – large, level- floored depressions up to several kilometres in size, where a thin layer of alluvial soil has gradually accumulated – often form the only suitable areas for growing vegetables and the cultivation of crops.

Many of Croatia's caves and sinkholes (*špilja* or *peć*, and *jama*, respectively) reach astonishing depths – Lukina jama on Velebit is among the 15 deepest sinkholes in the world, and contains a single, stomach-churning vertical drop of over 500m.

Although in many places now denuded and bare, and typified by poor vegetation, the Dinaric Alps were once heavily forested. Progressive deforestation (both by foreign powers and the local population) and overgrazing since well before the Middle Ages led to extensive soil erosion, exposing the underlying rock to chemical and mechanical weathering. (The Republic of Venice, in particular, is frequently singled out for its role in the process, drawing much of the timber for its fleet from Dalmatian forests.) Local restrictions on the sale of timber to foreign powers (in the case of the Republic of Dubrovnik, as early as the 13th century) failed to check the process, and archives from the town of Zadar, dating from 1803, state that the forests of the surrounding mountains were by then so devastated that not even a piece of firewood could be found.

Kozjak (Route 24)

The Croatian archipelago encompasses a mind-boggling number of islands of various shapes and sizes – some 1185 of them, bringing the total length of the already very indented coastline to well over 5500km. Generally elongated, they follow the northwest–southeast orientation of the coastal ranges, and represent all that remains above sea level of a low, outlying range of hills once part of the Dinaric Alps. Beaches are typically rocky or of fine shingle, although there are a few sandy beaches too.

Slavonia, by contrast, is an extensive plain, and is extremely fertile. (It was the fertility of the land which, in the aftermath of World War 2, encouraged many people from Dalmatia to move to Slavonia.) Its eastern border meets Serbia on the Danube, and its northern and southern borders are defined by the Drava and the Sava, respectively. Low, wooded hills dot various areas such as that north of Požega, while the landscape becomes progressively flatter towards the eastern border with the Danube and to the northeast, where it stretches off into the Hungarian plains.

Croatia's geographical position places it on the fringe of that rather ill-defined territory known in the West as the Balkans, though most Croatians prefer not to attach that label to their country – and may politely inform you that the Balkans begin somewhere southeast of the River Sava.

HISTORY

The earliest evidence of human habitation in Croatia dates back to the Palaeolithic era, most famously in the

18

form of humanoid bones and stone tools unearthed in a cave at Krapina, north of Zagreb, and dated to around 65,000BC. Evidence of the presence of Neolithic man is widespread: these early fishing and farming communities were characterised by the cultivation of cereals and the domestication of livestock, the development of 'tell' settlements and the introduction of copper working. Finds from the later Vučedol culture, which flourished around 2800–2500BC, include some remarkably beautiful pottery objects – the most famous of which figures on the reverse of the modern 20Kn note. Finds from the Bronze Age include axe-heads discovered in Slavonia and on Hvar, datable to around 2000BC. From the middle of the second millennium BC the Dalmatian coast was joined by sea routes to Italy and the Aegean, leading to an increase in trade and an expansion of external contacts; and from the end of the Iron Age we gradually enter the realm of recorded history.

The Illyrians

The precise origin of the Illyrians remains a matter of conjecture, but from about 800BC they come to dominate the history of the eastern Adriatic. An Indo-European people, the Illyrians were in effect composed of numerous tribes scattered throughout the region from the Veneto to Albania, some perhaps more deserving of the title 'Illyrian' than others. Among the most important of these

were the Liburni (famed pirates, who originally controlled the coast from Istria to the River Krka); the Delmatae (inhabiting the coast and hinterland, including the Dinaric mountains, and noted for their near unassailable hill forts); and the Japodes (inhabiting the area behind the Liburni, north to the Sava and west to Velebit, whom Strabo describes as living on Mount Albion – perhaps Velebit). A number of them (Histri, Delmatae, Ardiaei) were to leave their names in the region (Istria, Dalmatia, Adriatic), and by the early 3rd century BC the Ardiaei had formed a powerful kingdom in the south, centred around Lake Shkodër in modern Albania.

From the sixth century BC, Greek settlements and trading posts began to be established on the Adriatic coast and on the islands, notably at Korkyra meliana ('black Korčula'), Issa (Vis), Pharos (Hvar) and Tragurion (Trogir), which assured the spread of Greek culture on the islands and along the coast. The fourth century BC also saw the arrival of the Celts, who subjugated the Illyrians in Pannonia (an area roughly corresponding to modern Slavonia) and settled around the middle Danube and in the Sava and Drava valleys.

The Illyrian kingdom reached the height of its power during the third century BC under King Agron and, following his death, Queen Teuta, with the defeat of the Aetolian Greeks. Teuta then despatched enormous plundering expeditions against Epirus, and particularly the city of Phoenice, which was then emerging as a centre of commerce and trade with Rome. It was perhaps Illyrian interference with this trade, combined with the murder of a Roman envoy sent to complain against Illyrian piracy, which prompted the Romans to launch their attack on Illyria in 229BC, with 200 ships and a massive contingency of infantry and cavalry. Thereafter a Roman protectorate was established over the Greek coastal cities and islands.

The Roman period
The Romans conducted a succession of campaigns against the Illyrians. The Roman province of Illyricum was placed under senatorial control in 27BC, and passed to imperial control upon the full conquest of the Pannonian tribes during 13–11BC, which extended Roman territory to the Danube. Following the great Illyrian revolt of AD6–9, Pannonia became a separate province and Upper Illyria was renamed Dalmatia.

Establishing their capital at the old Illyrian stronghold of Salona (Solin, near Split), the Romans built roads and cities and developed trade, exploiting the wealth of minerals and timber offered by the territory as well as the agriculturally rich farmland of Pannonia. Among the most important Roman settlements were Jadera (Zadar), Parentium (Poreč) and Polensium (Pula), while a defensive boundary (the Roman limes) was established across the interior. The late third century emperor Diocletian's Palace still graces the city of Split.

Byzantine influence on the coast was to become increasingly prominent following the dedication of Constantinople in 330 as the new capital of the Roman, and later the Byzantine, empire.

Invasions
The fourth and fifth centuries were marked by a succession of Hunnish and Gothic invasions. The Visigoths swept into the region during the period 379–401, while in 450 the Huns appeared in northern Pannonia,

Roman forum, Church of St Donatus and bell tower of Cathedral of St Anastasia, Zadar

Ivan Meštrović's sculpture 'History of the Croats' (Povijest Hrvata), in front of the Faculty of Law in Zagreb

followed by the Ostrogoths. The Slavs, originally from Ukraine and the steppes north of the Black Sea, began migrating into the valleys of the Danube and the Sava some time after the year 500, and from there later expanded into the Dinaric mountains and along the Adriatic. In the second half of the sixth century the Avars, a nomadic people of Turkic and Mongol stock, swept south into the region, sacking Salona and laying siege to Constantinople.

In the chaotic wake of the Slavic and Avar invasions, a people known as the 'White Croats' were invited by the Emperor Heraclius to move into the region and fight against the Avars in 626. A Slavic (or at least Slavicised) people, these White Croats were at that time living in an area north of the Carpathians. Moving south-west as requested, they successfully defeated the Avars, after which they settled in the region to which they would eventually give their name: Croatia. They were followed by the Serbs, who migrated from their home (known as 'White Serbia', also north of the Carpathians), and settled east of the Croats. Although the historical accuracy of this account has been questioned, the existence of a 'White Croatia' north of the Carpathians is confirmed by medieval sources.

The arrival of Charlemagne at the close of the eighth century brought first Pannonian and then Dalmatian Croatia under Frankish sovereignty, with all of Dalmatia save some key cities and islands being formally ceded by Byzantium to the Franks in 812. These campaigns were followed by a gradual and more widespread conversion of the local population to Christianity. Byzantium regained its control of Dalmatia in 868–878, when it became one of a number of Byzantine themes, with its capital at Zadar.

Croatia's golden age

The second half of the ninth century saw a gradual increase in power and autonomy, which would lead to Croatia's brief but much vaunted golden age. This was reflected in a move towards religious autonomy and the appearance of local Croatian dukes in a position of rule.

After successfully repelling the first of many Hungarian attacks, Tomislav became the first king of Croatia in 925. However, power struggles within the ruling class followed his death, and it was not until the reign of Petar Krešimir IV (1058–1074) that Dalmatia was regained from Byzantine control, and Dalmatian and Pannonian Croatia unified for the first time into a single state. Petar was succeeded by Zvonimir (1075–1089), who had the title King of Croatia and Dalmatia conferred upon him by the Pope. However, the country once more fell into disunity after his death, which effectively marked the end of the Croatian royal house. Popular legend tells that Zvonimir was actually murdered by his own people, and that his dying curse upon them was that they should be forever ruled

by foreign powers. Indeed, Croatia would see some 900 years of foreign rule before regaining its independence in the 1990s.

Hungarian and Austrian rule

In 1091 Hungary, under King Ladislav, invaded northern Croatia, finally defeating the last pretender to the throne on Mount Gvozd (the modern Petrova gora). In 1102, a treaty was signed between the 12 Croat tribes and the Hungarian King Koloman, with the Hungarian Arpad dynasty inheriting the rights of the Croatian kings, and a Hungarian *ban* (governor) being installed. The Dalmatian nobility accepted Koloman's rule, but this was to be limited by Venice's increasing power in the Adriatic.

It was during this period that the city of Dubrovnik (or Ragusa) rose to prominence. Founded in the first half of the seventh century by refugees from Epidaurus (Cavtat), a city recently devastated by the Avars and the Slavs, Dubrovnik soon grew rich on maritime trade, and in the 12th century developed into an independent republic. In 1190, Dubrovnik signed treaties against external enemies, in particular Venice, as well as trading agreements with the pirates at Omiš. In the 14th century its territory stretched from the Bay of Kotor in the south to the northern tip of the Pelješac peninsula, and included the islands of Lastovo and Mljet.

In the 12th century, Venice launched a series of attacks on the

coastal cities of Dalmatia, as well as on a number of its islands. In 1202 the Venetian Doge Dandolo enlisted the support of the armies of the Fourth Crusade to capture Zadar – following which an infuriated Pope excommunicated the entire expedition. In 1205 Dubrovnik also fell to Venice. The Mongol invasions of the 13th century saw them pursue King Bela of Hungary to the Adriatic coast, which they ravaged before being recalled to their homeland on the death of Genghis Khan. The power struggles that followed the death of Bela in 1270 were used by Venice as an opportunity to take Šibenik and Trogir. Between 1342 and 1382 King Ludovik I of Hungary reestablished control over Croatia, but the country slid into anarchy on his death. Following this, the Croatian nobility misguidedly turned to Ladislas of Naples, who was crowned king of Zadar in 1403. Ladislas soon sold Zadar to Venice for a miserable 100,000 ducats, and by 1420 Venice controlled the whole of Dalmatia, a grip it would not relinquish until the arrival of Napoleon.

The Ottomans

The overwhelming defeat of Serbian, Croatian and Bosnian forces by the Ottomans at the battle of Kosovo in 1389, together with the fall of Constantinople in 1453, saw the Balkan peninsula opened up to Turkish invasion. Bosnia was conquered in 1463 and Herzegovina in 1482, and thousands of refugees trekked north. In 1493 the Croatian nobility were decimated at the battle of Krbavsko polje in Lika, and city after city fell to the Ottoman advance. In 1526 the Hungarian forces under Ludovik II were defeated at the battle of Mohács, and 1529 saw the

23

Ottomans lay siege to Vienna. The Austrian Archduke Ferdinand was elected king of Croatia by its parliament under the proviso that he would help defend the country against the Ottomans; but by the end of the century only a small area around Zagreb, Karlovac and Varaždin remained under Austrian control. Austria established the military frontier across the war-ravaged and largely depopulated Croatian hinterland, and settled the area with large numbers of Vlachs (mountain inhabitants of both Orthodox and Catholic faiths), who were granted a degree of independence in return for their services as frontier soldiers. The Croatian parliament objected furiously to their settlement on Croatian soil and to their exemption from the system of feudal taxes imposed on the rest of the population. Yet the Vlachs were to remain in the Krajina for more than 450 years, until their descendents were expelled at the close of the war in the 1990s.

During the 16th century the Uskoks, fugitives from the Ottoman advance based in Senj, turned to a phenomenally successful career of piracy and conducted a long reign of terror against the Turks, with refugees joining them as partisans. The rout of the Ottoman forces at the second siege of Vienna in 1683 marked a reversal of Ottoman fortunes in the Balkans, and in 1699 the Treaty of Sremski Karlovci saw all Turkish claims to Croatia and Hungary renounced.

The 19th century

The arrival of Napoleon at the end of the 18th century brought new changes to the region, as well as renewed hopes of Croatian unity. However, although Dalmatia was transferred to Austria upon the disintegration of the Venetian republic in 1797, the administrative division of Dalmatia and Slavonia was maintained, much to Croatian disgust. In 1805 Napoleon's victory over the Austrian forces at Austerlitz resulted in Dalmatia being ceded to France, and in the creation of the Illyrian Provinces. Dubrovnik was occupied by Napoleon's troops the following year, following which the Republic of Dubrovnik was dissolved and became part of the new Illyrian Provinces.

Zagreb old town

Napoleon instigated a number of positive reforms in Dalmatia to counteract the years of neglect suffered by the region. These included a tree plantation programme, in an attempt to restore the denuded forests; the establishment of schools and the University of Zadar to combat illiteracy; the draining of the marshes to combat rampant malaria; the construction of new roads and hospitals; and the introduction of new crops. Yet these reforms remained largely unpopular, due in part to French opposition to the clergy, and to the fact that new taxes were introduced to pay for the reforms.

The 1815 Congress of Vienna returned Dalmatia to Austria, while placing the rest of Croatia under Austria's Hungarian province. This saw a restoration of power to the former-Italian elite in Dalmatia, and the imposition of Hungarian language and culture upon Croatia as a whole. The reaction to all of this was the Illyrian Movement, which surfaced in the 1830s and marked the beginning of a national awakening, or national revival, in Croatia. Typically at this time, upper-class Dalmatians spoke Italian, while German and Hungarian were spoken in northern Croatia. Perhaps not surprisingly then, the Illyrian Movement centred on a revival of the Croatian language.

During the revolutions of 1848, Croatia agreed to intervene against a Hungarian revolutionary movement on the side of the Hapsburgs in return

for greater autonomy, and 40,000 troops were despatched under the command of governor Josip Jelačić. This celebrated figure (whose statue stands in Zagreb's main square, the eponymous Trg bana Jelačić) was both a loyal officer in the Austrian army and a firm supporter of the Illyrian Movement. However, the battles were indecisive, and ultimately Jelačić was not the only component of the force which finally broke Hungarian resistance. Opposition to any form of revolutionary regime grew in Austria: the emperor revoked all revolutionary and constitutional changes, and the Croatian parliament was closed.

Against this background two schools of political thought developed within 19th-century Croatia, both directed towards the emancipation of the country from foreign rule. The old Illyrian Movement became the National Party, led by the charismatic Bishop Josip Juraj Strossmayer. Strossmayer, who also supported the cause of Serbian independence, believed (with considerable justification) that the differences between Croats and Serbs were being magnified by foreign manipulation, and that this could be combated only by south Slavic unity, although he felt that this should be within the framework of the Austro-Hungarian Empire, rather than complete independence. The opposing movement was the Party of Rights, led by Ante Starčević. Militantly anti-Serbian, he promulgated the idea of an independent Croatia consisting of Slavonia, Dalmatia, the Krajina, Slovenia, Istria and part of Bosnia and Herzegovina.

During this period, the Orthodox church encouraged Serbs to form a national identity based upon their religion, which together with the attacks of Starčević, led to a gradual polarisation of the two populations and an increasing sense of a separate, Orthodox identity within largely Catholic Croatia. The Hungarians exploited the situation by supporting the Serbian cause, dividing the country still further.

Organised resistance to Austro-Hungarian rule first erupted in Dalmatia, and in 1905 Croat representatives in Rijeka and Serbian representatives in Zadar joined forces to call for a unification of Dalmatia and Slavonia, with a guarantee of Serbian equality.

The Kingdom of Serbs, Croats and Slovenes

With the collapse of the Austro-Hungarian Empire at the end of World War 1, Croatia feared that it might be further dissected by foreign powers (certainly the Treaty of London, signed in 1915, seemed to suggest that an Allied victory would be followed by Croatia effectively being carved up between Italy and Serbia). Pula, Rijeka and Zadar were quickly gobbled up by Italy, and to prevent further territory being lost, a Croatian delegation persuaded the Serbian government to agree to the establishment of a parliamentary monarchy ruling over the two countries. On 1 December 1918 the first communal Yugoslav state, the Kingdom of Serbs, Croats and Slovenes, was founded. It was to last until 1941, although it was never recognised by the Treaty of Versailles.

However, problems with the new regime soon became apparent: currency reforms benefited Serbia at the expense of Croatia; a treaty with Italy gave Istria, Zadar and a number of islands to Italy; and a new constitution abolished the Croatian parliament and centralised power in Belgrade. Opposition was spearheaded by Stjepan Radić, the leader of the Croatian Peasant Party – until he was murdered in parliament, in 1928. Following this the constitution was suspended, and what amounted to a military dictatorship ensued under King Alexander.

Almost immediately the Croatian Liberation Movement, better known as the Ustaša, was set up under Ante Pavelić, with the stated aim of establishing an independent Croatian state, by force if necessary. Having fled to Italy, where he established training camps under the auspices of Mussolini, Pavelić masterminded the assassination of Alexander on a state visit in Marseilles, following which he was imprisoned and the training camps closed. Alexander's successor, his cousin Prince Paul, attempted to advance the cause for Croatian autonomy, but progress was cut short by the events of World War 2.

World War 2

Germany invaded Yugoslavia on 6 April 1941, installing the Ustaša as rulers of the Nezavisna Država Hrvatska or NDH (Independent State of Croatia), headed by Pavelić, and ushering in what is arguably the darkest chapter of Croatian history. Between 1941 and 1945 a range of decrees issued by Pavelić were implemented against the 'enemies' of the regime: primarily Jews, Gypsies and Serbs. These took the form of horrific local pogroms, with almost 80 per cent of the Jewish population sent to extermination camps in Nazi Germany, and Serb extermination camps set up to carry out the unwritten Ustaša demand that one-third of the Serbian population should be killed, one-third expelled and one-third converted to Catholicism. The estimated number of Serb deaths varies enormously, but is possibly as high as 80,000.

However, the Ustaša drew their support from only a minority of the population, centred around Lika and western Herzegovina, and owed their authority to the support of Hitler and Mussolini. That their support would remain minimal in Dalmatia was guaranteed by an agreement to cede large chunks of the coast and islands to Italy. Armed Četnik (Serbian nationalist) resistance to the Ustaša began under General Dražo Mihailović, but soon degenerated into massacres of Croats and Bosniaks in eastern Croatia and Bosnia. The National Liberation Partisans under Josip Broz Tito, with their notions of 'Brotherhood and Unity' and a unified Yugoslav state, attracted both Croats and Serbs appalled by the cycle of reciprocal

27

massacres, as well as anti-fascists in general. The initial Allied support for the Četniks was re-channelled to the Partisans, who by 1943 controlled much of Croatia.

The Federal Peoples' Republic of Yugoslavia

Following the end of World War 2, the Federal Peoples' Republic of Yugoslavia was established on 29 November 1945, consisting of six republics and two autonomous provinces. Tito initiated a number of constitutional reforms, but the channelling of money from the wealthier Croatia and Slovenia to Belgrade and to the less prosperous republics, combined with the suppression of organised religion (due to the perception that it had played its part in polarising the population, leading to the bloody inter-ethnic fighting of World War 2) and the over-representation of Serbs in government positions and the security forces, led to increasing dissatisfaction in Croatia, which culminated in the 'Croatian Spring' of 1971. Croatia's increasingly vocal criticism of Belgrade's policies and calls for greater autonomy and constitutional reform were swiftly answered with purges, jail sentences and repression. Following Tito's death in 1980, the Serb and Croat nationalist aspirations, which he had largely driven underground in 1971, slowly rose to the surface again.

Against a background of sweeping change and the collapse of communism in eastern Europe and the former Soviet Union, free elections were held in April 1990, which saw Franjo Tuđman and the Croatian Democratic Union elected to power with 40 per cent of the vote. Mass dismissals of Serbs from the public service sector, combined with a Serbian media campaign heralding the rebirth of the Ustaša, prompted Croatia's 600,000-strong Serb community in the Krajina and in eastern Slavonia to demand autonomy, while Serb extremists within Croatia staged provocations intended to draw federal military intervention. In March 1991, a Serb unit took over the headquarters of Plitvička jezera National Park, and the resultant fighting between them and the Croatian police claimed the first victims (on both sides) of the war in Croatia.

Independence

In May 1991, following the deaths of 12 Croatian policemen near Osijek, a referendum was held, with more than 90 per cent voting in favour of Croatian independence. Independence was formally declared on 25 June 1991. In response, the Krajina Serbs held their own referendum and voted to remain part of Yugoslavia. In June 1991 heavy fighting broke out in the Krajina and eastern Slavonia, after which the Serb-dominated Yugoslav People's Army (JNA) increasingly intervened on its own authority in support of Serbian irregulars.

European Community mediation persuaded Croatia to freeze its declaration of independence to prevent the country spiralling into further bloodshed, but in the three months following 25 June, one-quarter of Croatian territory fell to Serb militias and the JNA. The United Nations (UN) declared an arms embargo on all republics of the former Yugoslavia. In October, the JNA and Montenegrin militia positioned themselves on the hills above Dubrovnik, beginning a siege that would last until June the following year and draw widespread international media attention. In November Vukovar finally fell, having been almost razed to the ground by relentless air and artillery bombardment, and many of the surviving inhabitants were massacred. By December, thousands of people had died in the fighting in Croatia, and more than half a million fled their homes.

Early in 1992, UN negotiations were followed by the deployment of a 12,000 member UN Protection Force. The ceasefire declared in January 1992 largely held, and was accompanied by the withdrawal of the JNA, although significantly it did not mark a return to pre-war borders or provide for their future settlement. Moreover, for the Krajina it only temporarily froze the existing situation, without offering a permanent solution. In January the European Community caved to pressure from Germany and recognised Croatian independence. A few months later, the storm that had been brewing over Bosnia finally broke, plunging the country into a war of almost unimaginable barbarity.

In January 1993 the Croatian army launched an offensive in the south Krajina, recapturing large tracts of territory. In May 1995 Croatian forces entered occupied western Slavonia, quickly regaining control of the area; the Krajina Serbs responded by shelling Zagreb. Some 15,000 Serbs fled Slavonia, despite assurances of their safety from the Croatian government. In August Croatia launched a massive military offensive on the Serb stronghold of Knin. The Serb army fled northward, together with over 100,000 civilians whose roots in the area stretched back some four-and-a-half centuries. Attacks followed on the few who stayed.

In December 1995 the Dayton Accord was signed in Paris, and Croatia's international borders were recognised (although a small UN mission remained to oversee the demilitarisation of the Prevlaka peninsula – the southernmost tip of Croatia, which was disputed by Croatia and Montenegro – until 2002). The years following the war saw a gradual trickle of refugees returning to Slavonia, and a massive increase in tourism in Dalmatia. In recent years, tourism has skyrocketed. Croatia was accepted into the Council of Europe in 1996, achieved candidate status in its bid for European Union (EU) membership by 2004, and finally became a member of the EU in July 2013.

Today Croatia is a quiet place, where the level of political excitement does not rise much higher than a dispute over fishing rights with neighbouring Slovenia. The economy is improving, though prices remain comparatively high when measured against an average local salary.

ARCHITECTURE, ART AND CULTURE

Croatia's coastal and island towns are a wonderfully seductive amalgamation of Romanesque, Renaissance, Venetian and Baroque architecture – Dubrovnik, Korčula, Rab, Trogir and Zadar, to name just a few. Baroque architecture is at its richest in Varaždin and Osijek, while nobody can claim to have really seen Croatia without spending some time in its capital, Zagreb, the centre of which is a lovely assortment of Secessionist and neo-Baroque styles.

The country's finest Roman ruins are to be found in Split and Pula: the complex of Diocletian's Palace at the former, and the incredibly well-preserved amphitheatre at the latter (the sixth largest in the world). Other important Roman sites include Zadar and Salona (Solin, in Split), while numerous smaller finds are on display at the archaeological museums in Split, Zagreb and elsewhere. In Poreč, the Euphrasian Basilica (commissioned by Bishop Euphrasius in 535–550) contains some astonishingly beautiful Byzantine mosaics.

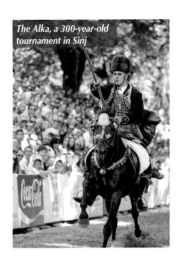

The Alka, a 300-year-old tournament in Sinj

Several of these sites (the Euphrasian Basilica, Diocletian's Palace, Trogir, Dubrovnik) are UNESCO World Heritage Sites. Croatia has also maintained many traditional crafts and festivals, several of which are inscribed on the UNESCO list of Intangible Cultural Heritage.

WILDLIFE AND PLANTS

Croatia has an incredibly rich bio-diversity for a country its size, with more than 38,000 known species of plants and animals, including around 1000 that are endemic, and many that are threatened or endangered. These include large and smaller mammals, a profusion of reptiles and invertebrates, and an extraordinarily rich plant life, while the waters of the Adriatic are inhabited by a wealth of marine life.

Mammals

Croatia's mountains and forests play host to a wide range of mammals including in small numbers Europe's three large carnivores: the brown bear, grey wolf and lynx.

The brown bear (*Ursus arctos*) inhabits the forests of Gorski kotar and highland Velebit, although your chances of seeing more than the odd track in the snow are slim indeed. (After two decades of hiking in Croatia, I have yet to see anything more than just this in the wild.) Sadly, the brown bear is still hunted for sport in Croatia (and overseas visitors pay top dollar to slaughter them), and you will see hunting and baiting towers in some parts of the country. Croatia's brown bear population is estimated at around 400. The grey wolf (*Canis lupus*) inhabits some of the more remote parts of the Dinaric Alps, its population currently lying somewhere around 200 – although again, sightings are extremely rare, and the huge distances covered by wolf packs makes it hard to give an accurate assessment of numbers. Although the grey wolf is protected in Croatia, more than half of recorded deaths are by illegal shooting. The Eurasian lynx (*Lynx lynx*) is present on Risnjak and Velebit but, again, sightings are extremely rare.

Wild pig (*Sus scrofa*) roam the forests, as do somewhat less reclusive species such as red deer (*Cervus elaphus*) and roe deer (*Capreolus capreolus*). Mouflon, or wild mountain sheep (*Ovis aries musimon*), are particularly common on Biokovo. Other mammals include the wild cat (*Felix silvestris*), chamois (*Rupicapra rupicapra*),

Eurasian lynx (Lynx lynx) at the zoo in Maksimir park, Zagreb

red squirrel (*Sciurus vulgaris*), pine marten (*Martes martes*) and common dormouse (*Glis glis*). Incidentally, Croatia's currency (the kuna) is named after the marten – *kuna* in Croatian – the pelts of which were used as a unit of trade and measure of currency in the Middle Ages, and are recorded in this context as early as 1018.

Numerous species of bat inhabit the karst caves and forests of Croatia (18 species in Krka, 16 in Paklenica, for example).

Greater and Mediterranean horseshoe bat (*Rhinolophus ferrumequinum* and *Rhinolophus euryale*), Savi's pipistrelle (*Hypsugo savii*), Greater mouse-eared bat (*Myotis myotis*) and Long-fingered bat (*Myotis capaccinii*), the latter classified as vulnerable on the IUCN Red List (Krka National Park has one of the largest colonies of this species in Europe).

*A dice snake (*Natrix tessellata*) in Plitvička jezera National Park (Route 22)*

Reptiles and amphibians

The rocky limestone of Croatia's coastal ranges and islands provides an ideal habitat for reptiles, of which Croatia has 41 species (nine of them endemic), with the greatest concentration of these being on the Dalmatian coast and islands.

Croatia's reptiles include an impressive number of species of snake – most of them completely harmless – and in the summer your chances of seeing one are fairly high. The two venomous species of snake to be alert for in Croatia are the nose-horned viper (*Vipera ammodytes*), known locally as *poskok*; and the common viper or adder (*Vipera berus*), known locally as *šarka* or *šarulja*. The former grows up to 60cm in length, and sometimes to 95cm; it is either light grey or brownish copper, with a dark-black zigzag pattern along its back, and is recognisable by the soft horn at the end of its snout. It can jump a fair distance, hence its name in Croatian (from *skočati*, which means 'to jump'). There is a well-preserved specimen at the hut PD Zavižan.

Both these snakes are likely to be found on rocky hillsides, under low bushes and around dry-stone walls;

the nose-horned viper sometimes wraps itself along tree branches, too, while the adder may also be found in forest clearings. The Meadow viper (*Vipera ursinii macrops*), a subspecies of Orsini's viper, which is listed as Vulnerable on the IUCN Red List, has been recorded in the higher reaches of Paklenica National Park; it is also venomous, although less so and more docile than either of the above species.

While the nose-horned viper is Europe's most venomous snake, it's worth pointing out that it's also found in plenty of other, well-visited parts of Europe including Italy and Greece, while the adder is found in the UK. In any case, walking boots and hiking poles will usually alert a snake to your approach and give it time to slither off, and snakes will usually only bite in self-defence.

Non-poisonous species of snake include the following:

- The Four-lined snake (*Elaphe quatuorlineata*), one of the largest European snakes, although completely harmless and easily recognisable by the yellowish-brown stripes along the back of adult specimens.
- The Leopard snake (*Elaphe situla*), which has distinctive brownish-red, dark-edged markings.
- The Balkan whip snake (*Hierophis gemonensis*), one of the most common species of snake.
- Dahl's whip snake (*Platyceps najadum*), which is particularly fast moving.

- The Montpellier snake (*Malpolon monpessulanus*). Technically speaking the Montpellier snake is also venomous (although much less so than the nose-horned viper or the adder), however the fangs are at the back of its jaws rather than the front, so it is extremely unlikely for a human to be bitten unless the snake is actually picked up.
- And, the Grass snake (*Natrix natrix*) and Dice snake (*Natrix tessellata*), which can be found around lakes, rivers and wetland areas.

A number of lizards are also common, in particular the Common wall lizard (*Podarcis muralis*) and Italian wall lizard (*Podarcis sicula*) – which are quite hard to tell apart, both having brownish or greenish stripes along their bodies – and the Dalmatian wall lizard (*Podarcis melisellensis*), more easily recognised by its bright red or orange underside. The sand lizard (*Lacerta agilis*), Horvath's rock lizard (*Lacerta horvathi*) and Mosor rock lizard (*Lacerta mosorensis*) are found at slightly higher altitudes than the previous three species. The Dalmatian algyroides (*Algyroides nigropunctatus*) is unmistakable, with its bright blue throat; as is the Balkan green lizard (*Lacerta trilineata*), from its sheer size (up to 16cm long) as much as its vivid green colouring, and the only slightly smaller Green lizard (*Lacerta viridis*). Other reptiles include the glass lizard (*Ophisaurus apodus*) and Hermann's tortoise (*Testudo hermanni*).

Amphibians include the fire sala-mander (*Salamandra salamandra*) and the less common alpine salamander (*Salamandra atra*), moor frog (*Rana arvalis*), marsh frog (*Rana ridibunda*), edible frog (*Rana kl. esculenta*) and Balkan stream frog (*Rana graeca*). Krka National Park constitutes part of the extremely limited distribution of the olm (*Proteus anguinus*) – Europe's only species of cave-dwelling Proteidae.

A useful resource for identifying the reptiles and amphibians of Europe is www.herp.it. For species of snake found in Croatia, see http://www.zh.zadweb.biz.hr/index.htm.

Birds
With its abundant forests, coastline, islands, wetlands and mountains, and its position on the Central European Migration Route or Adriatic Flyway, Croatia is extremely rich in birdlife, with around 380 species having been recorded, many of them threatened on a European level, some on a global level.

Raptors include the Griffon vul-ture (*Gyps fulvus*), a huge, unmistak-able bird with a wingspan of some 2.5m. It once nested among the crags of Velika and Mala Paklenica, but the last surviving pair there were poisoned a couple of decades ago, and the species now only survives in Croatia in the Kvarner region, mainly on the sea cliffs at Beli on the island of Cres. The golden eagle (*Aquilla chrysaetos*) can be seen on Velebit

and in Krka National Park, and lan-ner falcon (*Falco biarmicus*) nest on Mosor. Croatia is the only breeding area in southeast Europe for Eleanor's falcon (*Falco eleonorae*). Other birds of prey include the peregrine falcon (*Falco peregrinus*), kestrel (*Falco tin-nunculus*), short-toed eagle (*Circaetus gallicus*) and common buzzard (*Buteo buteo*).

Among mountain habitats you have a chance of seeing rock par-tridge (*Alectoris graeca*), listed as near-threatened on the IUCN Red List; alpine chough (*Pyrrhocorax graculus*); horned lark (*Eremophila alpestris*), which nests on Dinara; rock bunt-ing (*Emberiza cia*); and Alpine swift (*Alpus melba*) – the fastest bird in Europe, which rockets past high peaks at a phenomenal speed. The caper-caillie (*Tetrao urogallus*) is found fairly widely including on Velebit (and is the symbol of Northern Velebit National Park).

Wetland areas and lakes are home to grey heron (*Ardea cinerea*), purple heron (*Ardea purpurea*), great crested grebe (*Podiceps cristatus*), bittern (*Botaurus stellaris*) and ferrugi-nous duck (*Aythya nyroca*). Lonjsko polje is a particularly good place to see white stork (*Ciconia ciconia*), spoonbill (*Platalea leucorodia*) and, less commonly, black stork (*Ciconia nigra*).

There are numerous seabirds – including a significant popula-tion of the rare Audouin's gull (*Ichthyaetus audouinii*) on the islands

White stork (Ciconia ciconia), Lonjsko polje nature park

of the Lastovo archipelago, Cory's shearwater (*Calonectris borealis*), black-headed and yellow-legged gull, Eurasian black tern, cormorant (*Phalacrocorax carbo*) and pygmy cormorant (*Phalacrocorax pygmeus*).

Other species to look out for include eagle owl (*Bubo bubo*), Europe's largest species of owl, recognisable by its size and its prominent ear tufts; scops owl (*Otus scops*); bee-eater (*Merops apiaster*); black-eared wheateater (*Oenanthe hispanica*), Eurasian Hoopoe (*Upupa epops*); the rare white-backed woodpecker (*Dendrocopos leucotos*); and several species of warbler.

A good online resource for birding in Croatia, including a checklist of species, is http://croatiabirding.hr.

Invertebrates

Croatia has a vast number of invertebrates – over 15,000 land-dwelling invertebrates have been recorded, plus another 1800 or so freshwater invertebrates and more than 5600 seawater invertebrates. More than 600 of them are endemic, with underground karst habitats being particularly rich in endemic species. Invertebrates are also the least studied group of Croatian animals, and several new species have been discovered in recent years – which suggests that there may still be many species that are as yet undiscovered.

Croatia has a spectacular number of butterflies – over 180 species (to put that figure in context there are just 56 butterfly species in the

35

*High Brown Fritillary (*Argynnis adippe*), near the Velebit Channel and Southern Velebit mountains; Southern Comma (*Polygonia egea*), near Zadar*

UK), with 84 species recorded in Paklenica National Park alone. Larger species include the scarce swallowtail (*Iphiclides podaliriu*), which is easily recognisable by the distinctive, very long protruding 'tail' at the back of each wing; the southern swallowtail (*Papilio alexanor*, with shorter 'tails'); two-tailed pasha (*Charaxes jasius*); and Apollo (*Parnassius apollo*). There are several rare and exotic species including blue argus (*Ultraaricia anteros*); anomalous blue (*Agrodiaetus admetus*); Dalmatian ringlet (*Proterebia afra*); bright-eyed ringlet (*Erebia oeme*); large copper (*Lycaena dispar*); Balkan marbled white (*Melanargia larissa*); and southern white admiral (*Limenitis reducta*).

There are also some 71 species of dragonfly and damselfly in Croatia (compared with 38 species of dragonfly in the UK). Krka National Park is a particularly good spot for dragonflies, with 34 species recorded.

For more information on butterflies, including photos for identifying different species, refer to www.eurobutterflies.com and www.leps.it.

Plants

Croatia's mountain plantlife ranges from mixed coniferous and deciduous forests to sub-alpine scrub and stony grasslands. The Dinaric Alps are more heavily forested in the north, on Velebit and especially Gorski kotar.

Mountain and sub-alpine forest is dominated by beech (*Fagus silvatica*) and Aleppo pine (*Pinus halepensis*). Other typical species include black pine (*Pinus nigra*), Dalmatian black pine (*Pinus nigra dalmatica*), holly or holm oak (*Quercus ilex*), kermes oak (*Quercus coccifera*), downy oak (*Quercus pubescens*), oriental hornbeam (*Carpinus orientalis*), hop hornbeam (*Ostrya carpinifolia*), mountain pine (*Pinus mugus*), juniper, sycamore maple (*Acer pseudoplatanus*), silver

*Alpine sea holly (Eryngium alpinum),
Northern Velebit National Park (Route
16); Clustered bellflower (Campanula
glomerata), Snježnica (Route 26)*

fir (*Abies alba*), cypress (*Cumpressus sempervirens*) and laurel (*Laurus nobilis*).

Much of the vegetation typically consists of hardy, low shrubs or maquis, characterised by strawberry tree (*Arbutus unedo*), myrtle (*Myrtis communis*), mastic tree (*Pistacia lentiscus*), turpentine tree (*Pistacia terebinthus*), wild olive (*Olea europaea*), rosemary (*Rosemarinus officinalis*), thyme (*Thymus capitatus*) and rose (*Rosa sempervirens*). In the mountains you will find dense thickets of dwarf mountain pine and juniper (known locally as *planinski bor* and *klekovina*).

Other plant varieties include alpine sea holly (*Eryngium alpinum*), alpine clementis (*Clementis alpina*), and numerous species of orchid.

Numerous endemic plant species are to be found (some 485 in Croatia as a whole), particularly on Velebit, where 78 have been identified. These include *Degenia velebitica, Dianthus velebiticus, Saxifraga prenia, Gentiana lutea, Arbrieta croatica* and *Sibirea croatica*. Endemic species in Biokovo include *Edraianthus pumilo* and *Centaurea cuspidate*.

Conservation initiatives
The website of the State Institute for Nature Protection (www.dzzp.hr) has information on protected areas and species. The LIFE 'Conservation and Management of Wolves in Croatia' Project has several offices in Croatia (Bogovićeva 1a, 10000 Zagreb; tel: +385 (0)1 487 4744). See its website, www.life-vuk.hr, for more information on wolves in Croatia. And refer to the website of the Large Carnivore Initiative for Europe (www.lcie.org) for further details on the status of brown bear, grey wolf and lynx in Europe, along with links to project brochures.

Refugium Ursorum Kuterevo (Velebitsko utočište za mlade medvjede Kuterevo, www.kuterevo-medvjedi.org, tel: +385 (0) 53 799 222) is a sanctuary for orphaned brown bear cubs, in the village of Kuterevo on northern Velebit.

CLIMATE

Croatia experiences two contrasting climatic types: continental inland and in the mountains, and Mediterranean along the coast and on the islands.

The Adriatic coast experiences hot, dry summers and relatively mild, but frequently rainy winters, being protected from the harsher inland climate by the mountain barrier of the coastal ranges.

On Velebit, daytime temperatures during the summer usually hover around 20–25°C; at night they can drop to almost freezing. On balance, summer remains the most pleasant time to visit both Velebit and Gorski kotar, although southern Velebit tends to be rather hot. Summers can be extremely hot on the central and southern coastal ranges (Mosor and Biokovo), and the best times to visit these are therefore spring and autumn. Forest fires pose a major threat both on the lower mountain slopes and on the islands during the summer – a fact clearly illustrated by some great blackened tracts of land in several mountain areas.

Nevertheless, the position of the Dinaric Alps so close to the coast ensures that they get considerable precipitation throughout the year (although all water rapidly disappears underground), and heavy rain and storms can unleash themselves upon the unsuspecting walker at any time. The author has been lost in the clouds on Vaganski vrh in August and lashed by hailstorms on Rožanski kukovi in July.

The Dinaric Alps experience bitterly cold winters, when they are inundated with snow and frequently swept by blizzards. Gorski kotar and Velebit in particular receive abundant snowfall during the winter months, and become largely snowbound. They are, for all that, extremely beautiful at this time of year and remain far more accessible to the winter walker than the mountains in neighbouring Slovenia. Snow usually lies on Velebit for around 132 days per year, and winters with well over 2m of snow are not unheard of. While this snow generally provides an acceptable base for walking, if you lose the path it's not so unusual to disappear suddenly up to your waist in submerged juniper thicket.

Microclimates also occur in the deep karst dells of the Dinaric Alps in the form of temperature inversions, which are reflected in local vegetation patterns.

Slavonia is somewhat more humid in the summer months, and considerably colder during the winter, with heavy snowfalls. Zagreb generally lies under a few inches of snow over the winter months, but during the summer can become stiflingly hot, prompting most residents to escape to the coast.

A number of winds buffet Croatia from different directions – all of them bearing their own names, and all of them well known and discussed by locals. The most important of these from a hiking point of view is the *bura*. A cold northeasterly, the *bura* is the result of cold air accumulating behind Velebit in the Lika basin, where it is effectively trapped until it escapes through the cols and high passes of Velebit to descend in powerful gusts upon the Adriatic. These gusts frequently reach gale force, and the Venetian traveller Alberto Abbé Fortis, writing in the 18th century, even claimed that on occasions the *bura* would pick up young children and dash them against the walls of houses, and throw down horses loaded with salt. There is a saying in Croatia that the *bura* is born in Lika, lives on Velebit and dies on the sea; and a frequently heard observation in the villages beyond the Velebit

Channel is *puše bura* ('the bura is blowing'). When the *bura* is blowing, you can also expect possible disruption to ferry and catamaran services, possible closures of bridges to traffic (including buses) on the main coastal highway, and choppy (and cooler) seas.

The *jugo*, as its name implies (*jug* means 'south'), is a moderate southerly that typically brings cloud and rain to the coastal mountains – and is traditionally associated with bad temper and ill health. (Under the Republic of Dubrovnik, crimes committed when the *jugo* was blowing generally earned a more lenient sentence for their perpetrator, following the belief that the wind had, at least partially, driven them to commit the crime or induced their fit of rage.)

View from the trail to Anića kuk, above Velika Paklenica (Route 17), Paklenica National Park

Croatia climate data

	Jan	Feb	Mar	Apr
Zagreb				
Abs max temp (°C)	19.4	22.2	26	29.4
Abs min temp (°C)	-24.3	-27.3	-18.3	-4.4
Mean average temp (°C)	-0.1	2	6.2	10.6
Total precipitation (mm)	47	40.6	52.2	63.7
Max snow cover (cm)	49	51	63	16
Split				
Abs max temp (°C)	17.4	22.3	23.2	27.1
Abs min temp (°C)	-9	-8.1	-6.6	0.3
Mean average temp (°C)	7.9	8.2	10.6	14.
Total precipitation (mm)	77.3	62.8	63.4	62.
Max snow cover (cm)	21	6	7	0
Zavižan (Northern Velebit)				
Abs max temp (°C)	12.5	13.7	16.5	17.
Abs min temp (°C)	-24.5	-28.6	-22.6	-14.
Mean average temp (°C)	-4	-4.2	-1.9	1.4
Total precipitation (mm)	146.8	146.2	155.9	175
Max snow cover (cm)	240	287	320	29

Source: www.klima.hr

There is also the *maestral*, a brisk sea breeze that tends to blow from the morning to the early afternoon, and the *široko*, a warm, dry southeasterly from north Africa, roughly equivalent to the sirocco in other parts of the Mediterranean.

GETTING TO CROATIA

By plane

Several airlines operate flights from the UK (and other European cities including Paris, Brussels and Frankfurt) to Croatia:

- Croatia Airlines (www.croatia airlines.com) has flights from the UK to Zagreb and all major Croatian cities including Split, Dubrovnik, Zadar and Rijeka.

May	Jun	Jul	Aug	Sep	Oct	Nov	Dec
33.7	37.6	40.4	39.8	33.5	28.3	25.4	22.5
-1.8	2.5	5.4	3.7	-0.6	-5.6	-13.5	-19.8
15.7	19.1	20.8	20	16	10.8	5.7	1.3
76.4	96.7	81.6	89.3	85.9	74.2	81.8	64.2
0	0	0	0	0	0	50	56
33.2	38.1	38.6	38.1	34.2	27.4	25.8	18.1
4.8	9.1	13	11.2	8.8	3.8	-4.5	-6.3
19	23	25.8	25.5	21.4	17.1	12.4	9.2
55.4	49.7	26.1	42.7	71	76.5	112.9	103.5
0	0	0	0	0	0	0	14
22.1	24.4	27.6	27.2	27.2	20.6	19.2	14.6
-9.8	-3.1	0.2	-2	-3.8	-11.5	-16.8	-24.2
6.5	10.1	12.5	12.4	8.9	5.2	0.4	-2.7
51.8	139.3	90.1	131.2	167.1	196.6	229.5	197.2
272	106	3	5	22	87	142	212

- British Airways (www.british airways.com) flies to Zagreb, Pula, Split and Dubrovnik.
- Easyjet (www.easyjet.com) flies to Pula, Zadar, Split and Dubrovnik.
- Ryanair (www.ryanair.com) flies to Zadar, Pula and Rijeka.
- Wizz Air (www.wizzair.com) flies to Split.
- Flybe (www.flybe.com) has routes to Zagreb, Zadar and Dubrovnik.

Flights get heavily booked in the summer – book as far in advance as possible.

Easyjet has the most generous cabin bag allowance of all of the budget airlines flying from the UK to Croatia (large enough that you don't need a checked-in bag, except that hiking poles can't go in cabin baggage); Ryanair has the least generous allowance by far, meaning that you need to add more extras to the fares.

Croatia Airlines flights include a snack and a drink.

By rail
Getting to Zagreb from the UK by rail is a far more straightforward proposal than many people realise. It's also possible to get there for a similar fare to a flight, providing you book well in advance (see below), and once you factor in the extra cost of a checked-in rucksack to an airfare, rail travel is not necessarily more expensive than flying, contrary to popular opinion.

The fastest route from London to Zagreb is around 18 hours, including a comfortable overnight sleeper berth for part of the journey. The best way to book is through Deutsche Bahn (www.bahn.com). Online bookings can be made three months in advance, however phone bookings can be made six months in advance through their UK call centre, and ideally you should aim at using the latter to get the lowest possible fares. The route taken for the lower fares tends to be via Brussels – so for example, London to Paris or Brussels via Eurostar, Paris or Brussels to Munich on a high speed TGV or ICE, then Munich to Zagreb on the direct overnight sleeper, the Lisinski. An overnight on the train through Germany on a RailJet sleeper is another good option. Deutsche Bahn also makes it possible to add a stopover (for no extra charge), even when booking online – Cologne, Salzburg and Ljubljana all make delightful places to break your journey.

It's also worth remembering that Eurostar, TGV, Deutsche Bahn and OEBB all adhere to a mutual guarantee, meaning that if any one service of these operators is cancelled/delayed and this causes you to miss your connecting service run by one of the others, your ticket will be changed to the next departure at no charge, a very simple and straightforward process.

The best source of information on rail travel in Europe is the excellent www.seat61.com, including a page on London–Zagreb (click 'Croatia' and then 'London to Zagreb').

By bus
International coach services run from the UK, Germany and other countries in western Europe (see www.eurolines.com) – but it's a long haul and not that cheap, and if you want to take the 'slow route' to Croatia, travelling by rail is by far the best option.

By ferry
There are regular ferry crossings to Zadar, Split, Istria and Dubrovnik, as well as some of the islands, from various ports in Italy (Ancona, Bari, Pescara and Venice).

VISAS
Visas are unnecessary for visitors from most western countries. For example, a UK passport holder can enter the country for up to three months at a time. After this, it is necessary either to cross over the border

into a neighbouring country before returning or to go through the lengthy process of applying for an extended stay permit. Visitors are still officially required to register with the police within 24 hours of arrival, although if you are staying in hotels, private accommodation, mountain huts or official campsites this is automatically done for you when you hand your passport over to the agency, reception or hut warden.

GETTING AROUND

Croatia is a fairly small country, and getting around on local transport is generally a simple affair. Buses run between most cities; rail services connect Zagreb with Split (6hr, via Knin), Rijeka (3hr 40min, via Delnice) and towns in Slavonia; and a comprehensive ferry service runs between the coastal cities and the islands.

Of these various options, the train (www.hzpp.hr/en) remains the most reasonably priced. Return fares are generally cheaper than two singles; and two people travelling together can get a cheaper ticket covering both of them (ask for a *karta za dvije osobe, na istoj karti*) – so long as they are travelling together, since it's just one ticket covering both passengers. A seat reservation is recommended, but not always essential, on longer journeys, and is mandatory on the overnight or the express train to Split.

Intercity buses cover most towns in Croatia (for services to/from Zagreb, see www.akz.hr; for elsewhere in Croatia, see www.croatia-bus.com). They tend to be slightly

Catamarans moored on the waterfront in Split, with Diocletian's Palace in the background

more expensive than an equivalent train journey, but there are few alternative options along some sections of the coast. Local bus services travel to almost all the villages that lie at the start or finish of the routes in this guide.

The real bargain is the ferries, which provide by far the most pleasant means of getting around the coast. Jadrolinija (www.jadrolinija.hr) is a state-run company, and has services (passenger ferries, car ferries, and fast catamarans) to most towns and islands along the coast. A number of private companies also run catamarans on a limited number of routes.

Croatia Airlines has domestic flights between Zagreb and most major towns in Croatia including Dubrovnik, Split, Pula, Rijeka and Zadar.

For those travelling around by car, Croatia has a good, modern motorway system, which operates a toll system on motorways. Bear in mind that the main road along the coast, known as the Jadranska magistrala, gets extremely busy during the summer months, and accidents are quite frequent. During the winter months Gorski kotar becomes largely snowbound, and travel on the old Rijeka–Zagreb road becomes restricted – in some cases, cars will not be allowed across without chains. The website of the Croatian Automobile Club (www.hak.hr) is the best place to check current traffic conditions and road closures, and can be called in the event

of a breakdown on 987 (from within Croatia only).

Zagreb's tram service covers most parts of the city. Tickets can be bought from newspaper kiosks (cheaper) or straight from the driver, after which tickets must be stamped in the small machines on the tram to be valid. Thereafter you can use them on any combination of services (including buses) for a period of 30–90 minutes from when they are first stamped, depending on the ticket. Day travel cards are also available.

Hitching is an accepted means of transport in the mountains (much less so in cities or on the coast and islands), and in general getting a ride should not pose too much of a problem. However, bear in mind that in Croatia, as elsewhere, hitching can never be recommended as entirely safe, particularly for those travelling alone.

Croatia is great for cycling – with some parts of Croatia promoting cycling more actively than others: Zagreb County Tourist Office produces an excellent series of free cycle route maps (www.tzzz.hr); Istria (see www.istria-bike.com), Lonjsko polje in Slavonia and the Island of Hvar are further places developing a good network of cycle routes. For those who want something a little more challenging, there are long routes over the forest roads of Velebit. However the traffic on Croatia's roads is not always particularly cycle-friendly – in particular, the coast road during summer.

Glavaš fortress, Dinara (Route 20, Stage 1)

ACCOMMODATION

Accommodation in Croatia comes in the form of hotels, private rooms and apartments (*sobe* and *apartmani*), and hostels, and covers a much greater range of budgets that it used to. *Sobe* are roughly equivalent to a B&B in the UK, but typically without the breakfast).

Bear in mind that many private rooms and apartments are booked on a weekly basis; and in some others, a 30% supplement is charged for guests staying fewer than three nights. Still, prices are reasonable for western visitors.

Tarrifs are seasonal, and drop quite considerably outside the high season – although a number of private guesthouses are open only during the summer, or from May to November.

Private rooms are usually booked through an agency. You will pay a commission, but this remains by far the most straightforward way of doing things. Even if you find a place yourself, if it is officially registered with an agency, you still have to pay the same price as you would through the agency, so you may as well let them do the work for you. There are also plenty of unofficial or unregistered rooms and lodgings, the owners of which congregate around local bus and train stations, and who will certainly approach you if they have anything available. In this case, if you go and see the room, this certainly does not bind you to taking if it is not as described. There are fewer private rooms in Zagreb, where accommodation options are centred around hotels and guesthouses (see Appendix B).

Relevant accommodation details are given in the introduction to each walk and in Appendix B. Mountain huts are also plentiful: for details refer to the 'Walking in Croatia' section, below.

FOOD AND DRINK

Croatian cuisine is a blend of influences reflecting its particular geographical position, and is delicious. The menu reader below is far from exhaustive, but should give you an idea of some dishes to track down.

MENU READER

Riba: Fish, of which Croatia (not surprisingly) has plenty. Typically either boiled (*kuhano*), topped with olive oil, garlic and parsley, and served with potatoes and *blitva* (Swiss chard); or grilled (*na žaru*).

Pašticada: Wonderfully opulent Dalmatian speciality, consisting of marinated beef or veal cooked slowly with dried plums. Typically served with home-made gnocchi and parmesan cheese.

Sarma: Slavonian speciality. Cabbage leaves stuffed with rice and ground beef.

Mlinci: Baked noodles, typically served with *puretina* (turkey).

Brodet: Mixed fish stew, similar to Italian brodetto.

Hobotnica na žaru: Along with *pašticada*, the crème de la crème of Croatian cuisine. Octopus, roasted in the oven in its own juices, with potatoes and onions and olive oil.

Salata od hobotnice: Octopus and potato salad, with parsley, onion, garlic and olive oil.

Lignje: Squid, usually grilled (*lignje na žaru*) or stuffed (*punjene lignje*).

Crni rižoto: 'Black' cuttlefish risotto, cooked in its own ink.

Fiš paprikaš: A spicy stew of carp and peppers – another Slavonian speciality.

Ribice: Sprats fried in breadcrumbs – a favourite café snack.

Ćevapčići: Small grilled meatballs, typically served with *ajvar* (roasted pepper and aubergine puree). Not quite as good as those you might find in Sarajevo, perhaps, but still excellent.

Pogača: Pastry filled with anchovies and capers – a speciality of the island of Vis, similar to Italian calzone.

Grah: A hearty bean stew, sometimes made with *kobasice* (sausages).

Juha: Soup. *Juha od povrča* (vegetable soup) and *riblja juha* (fish soup).

Paški sir: Croatia's most celebrated cheese, from the island of Pag.

Pršut: Prosciutto (the best is from central Istria, though Dalmatians might claim otherwise).

Kulen: Slavonian cured sausage, flavoured with paprika.

Palačinke: Pancakes – a favourite Croatian desert.

Sladoled: Ice cream.

Kremšnite: A custard dessert, especially good in Samobor.

Croatia also produces a fair amount of wine (*vino*). The main grape-growing regions are Istria (especially good for Malvazija), the Dalmatian coast and islands (producing predominantly medium to full-bodied reds, and one or two whites) and a number of areas in Slavonia (producing mainly whites). As a general rule, those wines designated *vrhunsko* (from *vrh*, 'top') tend to be much better than those designated *kvalitetno* ('quality'). Dingač and Postup are two small grape-growing regions on the Pelješac peninsula, and are generally considered to produce Croatia's finest red wines, Dingač and Postup. Vugava viška and smokvica are white wines from the islands of Vis and Hvar respectively.

Rajnski rizling, traminac and graševina are all produced extensively in Slavonia, with some of the best coming from Ilok and Kutjevo. Prošek is a sweet dessert wine from the coast.

A number of spirits are also produced, the best-known being *rakija*. This comes in a number of guises, all extremely potent – *loza* is the most common (similar to Italian grappa); *šljivovica* is made from plums; *travarica* is made with herbs.

The two main local breweries are Ožujsko and Karlovačko, although the best is Pivovara Medvedgrad in Zagreb, and Velebitsko pivo, brewed in Gospić, is also good.

Fruit juices are widely available, and the coffee (*kava*) is excellent.

Mosor (Route 23) viewed across Split

LANGUAGE

The Croatian language poses a number of grammatical rules that may be new to the native English speaker, although anyone who has studied a language such as German or Russian should find no more difficulty with Croatian than with these languages.

Croatian is a phonetic language – that is, every letter in a word is pronounced, and the pronunciation of a given letter is always the same, making it far more consistent than English or French. Consonant clusters may prove something of a tongue twister to the uninitiated (try *vrt* 'garden'; *trg* 'square'; *krv* 'blood'), but are easy to get used to.

Croatian belongs to the south Slavonic branch of the Indo-European family of languages and is closely related to, but not the same as, Serbian and Bosnian. The relationship between Croatian and Serbian is variously seen as similar to that between British and American English, or as that between two wholly separate and distinct languages, depending on one's point of view. The standardisation of the language during Croatia's inclusion in the Federal Republic of Yugoslavia (1945–91) resulted in the amalgamation of Croatian and Serbian (as the two dominant languages within the Federation), known as Serbo-Croatian or Croato-Serbian. This was written in the Latinised Croatian alphabet in Croatia, and in Cyrillic in Serbia.

Within Croatia, there are also a number of regional variations, or 'dialects', which typify the language spoken in Zagreb, certain parts of Dalmatia, Slavonia and Zagorje.

Trail to the source of the River Kupa (Izvor Kupe) (Route 8), Risnjak national park

KEY WORDS FOR WALKERS

brdo: hill
kuk: crag, bare limestone peak
planina: mountain
planinari: hikers
planinarski dom: mountain hut
planinarska kuća: mountain hut (open by arrangement)
planinarska staza: mountain path, trail
put: route
sklonište: shelter
vrh: peak, summit

Common abbreviations
GSS (Gorska služba spašavanja, also written HGSS): Mountain Rescue Service
HPD (Hrvatsko planinarsko društvo): Croatian Mountaineering Association
HPS (Hrvatski planinarski savez): Croatian Mountaineering Committee
KT (*kontrolna točka*): hiking checkpoint/register
NP (*nacionalni park*): national park
PD (*planinarski dom*): mountain hut
PDS (*planinarsko društvo sveučališta*): hiking club
PP (*park prirode*): nature park

However, these effectively only differ from one another in a few words and in their accent, and are of little concern to the visitor.

Pronunciation is especially important if you are to be understood, particularly in view of the fact that a number of letters occurring in English are pronounced completely differently in Croatian, most notably 'c' (pronounced 'ts') and 'j' (pronounced 'y'). Refer to Appendix D for further information.

English is widely spoken in Croatia, particularly in Zagreb and major tourist centres, and German and Italian are also common, particularly on the coast. In mountain huts you will frequently find someone who speaks some English, either the warden or local hikers staying there. However, in smaller towns and villages off the main tourist trail you will have to be somewhat more self-reliant.

Appendix D provides an English–Croatian glossary, and a few key words and abbreviations are given above.

MONEY

The Croatian unit of currency is the kuna (abbreviated Kn or HRK), 1 kuna being comprised of 100 lipa. The kuna comes in small coin denominations (currently 1, 2 and 5) and larger notes (currently 5 up to 1000). When changing money, try to get a decent supply of smaller notes (20Kn, 50Kn and 100Kn), as the larger notes can be hard to change in smaller shops and supermarkets. The value of the kuna has remained relatively stable for a number of years, and at the time of writing £1=8.28Kn, 1Euro = 7.44Kn. You may find a number of prices (particularly accommodation) quoted in Euros, which will then be converted into kuna according to the daily rate.

Changing money

Changing money in Croatia is very straightforward. ATMs are common in major towns and cities. *Mjenjačnica* (small exchange booths) are dotted all over the larger towns and cities, and generally give the best rates. Those at bus and train stations tend to give poorer rates. Daily rates are usually posted where you can see them. Changing money in banks usually involves queuing for a long, long time, and you are advised to use the exchange offices or ATMs. A commission is sometimes charged at exchange offices and is always charged in banks. Cash is preferable to traveller's cheques, which you will be able to exchange only in major towns or tourist centres, and which will certainly involve more queuing.

POSTAL SERVICES AND TELECOMMUNICATIONS

The international dialling code for Croatia is +385. If calling from overseas, omit the initial zero from the Croatian phone number. Mobile coverage is fine in some but not all mountain areas, but not in areas of heavy forest cover.

Call boxes are found in post offices, and are the cheapest way of calling overseas. Otherwise, phone cards are available from newspaper kiosks for use in the blue public cardphones, although these will not last particularly long on an international call. Note that addresses in Croatia are given with the street name preceding the street number.

EQUIPMENT

The equipment necessary for the routes in this guide is much the same as it would be for most other European mountain ranges of a similar, or slightly higher altitude.

You should be prepared for rain at any time of year, and a waterproof shell (Gore-Tex or similar) is essential.

Boots or hiking shoes need to be tough, and able to cope with terrain which is almost exclusively either jagged limestone or knotted tree

roots. Although summer walks on the islands can be undertaken in trainers, these are not recommended for the mountains. Trekking in sandals is an open invitation to snakebite in the mountains.

A tent is far from essential, but may be useful on some of the longer itineraries. However, bear in mind that camping is prohibited in national park areas, and that water availability is typically restricted to huts.

Even if you plan to spend all your nights in huts and shelters, you should be aware that solid fuel is scarce and has to be carried up to the mountains by someone: it is therefore prudent to carry a small stove. Camping gas cylinders (*kartuše*) are available from outdoor retailers such as Iglu Sport (www.iglusport.hr), which has branches in Zagreb, Split, Rijeka and Starigrad Paklenica; if you're carrying

a refillable multi-fuel stove, you can buy bottles of kerosine (*kerozin*) or petrol (*benzin*) at a petrol station or some outdoor retailers.

Beyond these items, what you take will depend on what time of year you visit Croatia. Blistering summer temperatures dictate adequate sun protection – plenty of sunscreen, sunglasses and a sun hat.

The shortage (or complete absence) of water between huts on a number of routes makes a supply of water flasks (lightweight aluminium or collapsible plastic, or a combination of the two) essential. I carry a Sawyer Mini filter, which weighs almost nothing.

A lightweight summer sleeping bag will be sufficient for spring/summer/autumn use in huts. It's worth carrying a sleeping mat, as most shelters don't have mattresses.

KITLIST

For those in doubt, the following basic checklist may be useful (for multi-day treks in the mountains from spring to autumn):

* rucksack (approximately 50–60 litres capacity)
* walking boots or walking shoes, with Vibram soles (wear them in before your trip!)
* other footwear for the coast or in towns (sturdy rafting or trekking sandals are perfect)
* rainproof, breathable shell
* warm, preferably windproof fleece or mid layer
* thermal base layer
* shorts and long trousers (lightweight, quick-drying material)
* long-sleeved shirt, T-shirts, underwear
* good-quality walking socks (these counter the need to wear two layers of socks or sock-liners)
* warm gloves and hat
* sun hat
* walking poles
* sleeping bag (1–2 season will be fine for all except winter use)
* sleeping mat (closed cell or inflatable)
* water bottles (lightweight aluminium bottles and/or collapsible plastic bladders)
* stove (cartridge or multi-fuel) and compatible fuel bottle(s) – camping gas cylinders (*kartuše*) are available from outdoor retailers such as Iglu Sport (www.iglusport.hr), which has branches in Zagreb, Split, Rijeka and Starigrad Paklenica
* lightweight cooking pot, fork and spoon
* compass and relevant maps (and the knowledge of how to use them)
* torch (headlamps are best)
* sunglasses and sunblock
* biodegradable soap
* small first aid kit
* Swiss army knife
* whistle (for attracting attention in an emergency)
* emergency reflective bag or 'space blanket'matches (keep them dry in a plastic bag!)
* large plastic rucksack liner
* mosquito repellent
* 2-pin adaptor (same as for most of continental Europe)
* adequate food
* tent (if planning to camp)

During the winter you should be prepared for bitterly cold, frequently sub-zero temperatures in the mountains. A three- to four-season sleeping bag, warm hat and gloves, thermal base layer, and warm and ideally windproof mid-layer are all mandatory. Crampons may be helpful in a year of heavy snowfall in the Dinaric Alps.

MAPS

Croatia's major mountain areas are covered by two detailed (1:25,000 or 1:30,000) series of maps, one published by the mountain rescue service, HGSS (www.hgss.hr), and the other by SMAND (www.smand.hr). They give accurate topographical detail (with contour lines drawn to 25m), and mark both paths and huts. The relevant sheet number is given at the beginning of each route in this guide.

These maps are available in the UK from The Map Shop (www.themapshop.co.uk), and can be ordered online. The maps are also readily available from bookshops in Zagreb, and from hiking clubs and huts, and usually retail at about 45–55Kn.

Some of the national parks and nature parks produce their own maps, including Plitvička jezera, Paklenica, Risnjak, Lonjsko polje, Papuk and Medvednica. More general maps include the Freytag & Berndt series covering the coast in a number of sheets (1:100,000), but note that while OK for planning trips around the islands, these are definitely not suitable for hiking. These maps do not accurately locate paths, while the inclusion of huts and springs is frequently highly misleading or inaccurate, because a number of the huts have been closed for a number of years (or require advance booking if you are to find them open at all), and a number of springs dry up over the summer.

Tourist information offices generally do not carry maps suitable for hiking – a notable exception being the map available free from the tourist information centre in Orebić.

Finally, a number of Croatian language hiking guides include fairly detailed maps.

WALKING AND TREKKING IN CROATIA

Trail markings

Almost without exception, paths and trails in Croatia are clearly marked with a uniform system of waymarkings (refer to Trail markings diagram). Known locally as *markacija* (markings), and almost always in red and white paint on trees, rocks and any other conspicuous object, the main ones are shown in the diagram.

The first of these signs with a cross through it usually indicates a wrong turn, or disused path. A cross usually indicates a junction. Blue, green and yellow paint are often used to indicate caves, sinkholes and other related features.

Trail markings on Dinara (Route 20, Stage 2)

Note that the frequent use of forestry markings, typically a number of lines or bands spray-painted on a tree, have absolutely no connection with marked hiking trails and should be comprehensively ignored.

Croatia's mountain areas feature a number of named trails and footpaths. Those covered by the walks in this guide (either in full or in part), in the order in which they occur in the text, are as follows:

- **RT (Riječka transverzala):** A route from the Istrian coast heading inland over Učka (Route 5).
- **MPP (Mrkopaljski planinarski put):** A route through the limestone scenery of Samarske stijene (Route 13).
- **KPP (Kapelski planinarski put):** A route over Velika Kapela, including Samarske stijene and Bijele stijene (Route 13); overlaps with sections of the GPP.
- **Vihoraški put:** The most impressive section of the KPP between Ratkovo sklonište and Planinarska kuća na Bijelim stijenama (Route 13).
- **GPP (Goranski planinarski put):** A circular route stretching from the Slovenian border traversing most areas of Gorski kotar, including Risnjak and Snježnik (Route 9); Bjelolasica, Samarske stijene and Bijele stijene (Route 13); and Klek (Route 14).
- **SPP (Spojni planinarski put):** A route linking Velika Kapela with northern Velebit, running from Bijele stijene to Oltare via Kolovratske stijene (ie linking Routes 9 and 16).

Trail markings

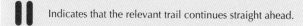

O Simply indicates that you are on a marked trail of some sort. Adjacent signs or names of topographic features (again painted on trees and rocks) let you know exactly which path you are following.

II Indicates that the relevant trail continues straight ahead.

⫻ Indicates a change in direction: not necessarily at a junction.

- **VPP (Velebitski planinarski put – also marked 'v'):** Croatia's finest long-distance footpath, traversing northern, central and southern Velebit, from Oltare in the north to Velika Paklenica in the south (Routes 16 and 19).
- **Premužićeva staza:** The section of the VPP covering northern and central Velebit, from near PD Zavižan to Baške Oštarije. It is (at least at its northern end) the most spectacular route in Croatia (Route 16).
- **BPS (Biokovska planinarska staza):** A route over Biokovo (Route 25).
- **PEP (Poučni ekološki put):** An alternative route over Biokovo (Route 25).

LEAVE NO TRACE

Cicerone guide users will hardly need reminding of the following basic guidelines when travelling in the great outdoors, whether a national park or otherwise.
- Please do not leave any litter – carry it out of the mountains and dispose of it in a town or city.
- Never light any open fires, and be aware of the risks of forest fires.
- Close gates behind you.
- Bury toilet waste.
- Do not pick wildflowers.
- Do not disturb wild animals and birds.
- Camp only at designated areas or well off the main trail.

Forest Fires
Croatia's hot, dry climate makes forest fires a real danger, both in the Dinaric Alps and on the islands, and visitors should be particularly aware of the threat they pose to the environment. There are bush fires somewhere every summer, consuming areas of forest and scrub and in some cases a few mountain huts have also been burnt to the ground. Never light an open fire, and exercise common sense in the use of gas and multi-fuel stoves.

National parks and nature parks
The following areas within Croatia have been designated national parks (*nacionalni park*, usually abbreviated to the prefix NP):

- Brijuni islands
- Kornati islands
- Krka
- Mljet
- Paklenica
- Plitvička jezera
- Risnjak
- Sjeverni Velebit.

An entry fee is payable on entering a national park – either at an entry point (in the case of Plitvička jezera or Paklenica) or at a staffed mountain hut (in the case of Risnjak and Sjeverni Velebit). Tickets are available to cover various periods of time – for example 3, 5 or 7 days – so you can buy one to cover the time you plan to stay within the park. Prices are reasonable for the western visitor (less so for locals); for example, 45Kn for three days in NP Sjeverni Velebit. You should hang on to your ticket to show at subsequent huts. Camping is prohibited in national parks, but in some cases may be allowed next to a hut.

A further 11 areas are designated 'nature parks' (*park prirode*, or PP):

- Biokovo
- Kopački rit
- Lastovo islands
- Lonjsko polje
- Medvednica
- Papuk
- Telašćica
- Učka
- Velebit
- Vransko jezero
- Žumberak–Samoborsko gorje

Unlike national parks, these generally carry no entry fee and in general (but not always) have no restriction on camping, although you should obviously show the same consideration for the environment (see Leave no trace box).

Some areas are UNESCO World Heritage Sites (for example, Plitvička jezera) or UNESCO International Biosphere Reserves (the whole Velebit massif was classified as such in 1978); several are Ramsar Wetlands of International Importance (Kopački rit) and Important Bird and Biodiversity Areas.

Plitvička jezera (Plitvice Lakes) National Park (Route 22)

Mountain huts and camping

Mountain huts in Croatia are excellent and plentiful, and fall into three categories:

- A *planinarski dom* (usually abbreviated to PD) is a staffed hut open to all, regardless of whether you have made any prior booking (and in most cases you will not need to).
- A *planinarska kuća* is usually only open by prior arrangement (either with the relevant hiking club or a private organisation), otherwise you will find it locked.

- A *sklonište* is a small hut or shelter, unmanned and (in most cases) open year round.

A *dom* may be open year round, during the summer months, or only at weekends; the availability of a *kuća* may have similar limitations. In many cases huts have a *sklonište* attached to them, which is opened when the rest of the hut locks up for the winter.

Prices vary from hut to hut, and there is a reduction for members of an HPS-affiliated club; but prices remain extremely reasonable, and it remains unusual for a hut to charge a separate,

---

NOTE

Availability of meals varies from hut to hut (and season to season) and cannot be relied upon.

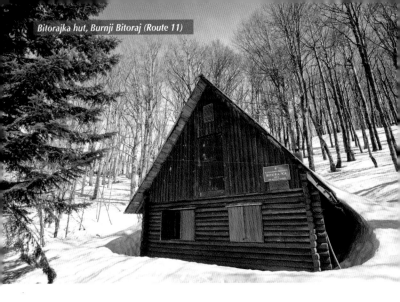

higher tariff for foreign visitors. There is no fee for staying in a *sklonište*. Many huts offer reasonably priced cooked meals, tea and other drinks, or else provide the use of a kitchen. You will need to bring your own sleeping bag and/or liner if you plan to stay at mountain huts or *sklonište*.

Hut staff are in most cases an invaluable source of local information and advice, as are the local walkers and climbers you will doubtless encounter when staying in huts.

Booking huts

It's not usually necessary to book huts, but booking may be advisable for popular huts in peak season (I'm referring to huts designated *planinarski dom* here – those designated *planinarska kuća* always require booking). Staffed mountain huts can be booked through the relevant national park office (see individual national park websites for contact information) or through the hiking club that manages the hut (email first, as the first point of contact at local hiking clubs may or may not speak English). Shelters (*sklonište*) don't require booking.

Camping

Camping is perfectly acceptable in mountain areas, although prohibited within a national park or nature park. Camping on the coast is restricted to large (and usually extremely busy) campsites. Pitching a tent anywhere else on the coast, and particularly on a beach, will almost certainly result in you being asked to move by the police (and potentially fined), and you would do better to find a room, either private accommodation or a hotel.

Water, food and supplies

Cured meats and various cheeses are widely available and, together with dark bread (*alpski kruh* or *crni kruh*), form the staple of most local walkers on shorter hikes. Packet soups and pasta meals are easy to find in any moderate-sized supermarket, as are dried fruits and nuts.

Instant soup and dried meals requiring less than three minutes' cooking time are more difficult to come by, and it is a good idea to bring a supply of such items from home to augment what is available locally. (A more detailed vocabulary for food items is given in Appendix D, and there is further information in the Food and drink section.)

Water is available at most (but not all) huts; springs between these are rare and tend to dry up in the summer. You will therefore need to carry sufficient water for each stage – and, in some cases, for more than one stage (the availability of water is highlighted in the route descriptions).

WHAT TO DO IN AN EMERGENCY

In most cases, your best source of advice will be the nearest staffed mountain hut (refer to the stage introductions). Otherwise, the Croatian Mountain Rescue Service (Hrvatska Gorska služba spašavanja, HGSS or simply GSS) can be contacted as follows:

- Delnice (for Gorski kotar): +385 (0) 91 721 0004

Market stall in Pula

- Gospić (for northern and central Velebit): +385 (0) 91 721 0007
- Makarska (for Biokovo): +385 (0) 91 721 0011
- Split (for Mosor): +385 (0) 91 721 0001
- Zadar (for southern Velebit and Paklenica): +385 (0) 91 721 0010
- Zagreb (for Medvednica): +385 (0) 91 721 0002

These are the full numbers if you are calling from a UK mobile. If calling from a Croatian phone or mobile, omit the +385 and add a zero at the beginning of the number.

The GSS website (www.gss.hr) has contact details of other local offices. Like many such organisations around the world, the GSS provides free mountain rescue but relies on the efforts and bravery of a small group of dedicated volunteers, whose services should not be called upon lightly.

At present, the UK and Croatia have a reciprocal arrangement where emergency state medical treatment is free to citizens of both countries (not including private medical treatment or visits to a GP or dentist). Whether this survives the UK's current (at the time of writing) intention of leaving the EU,

remains to be seen. Missing persons should be reported to the relevant embassy or consulate (see Appendix C).

Snakes

In case of snakebite, immobilise the limb or affected area (but do not apply a tourniquet) and get the victim to a doctor. Anti-venoms are available from hospitals and medical centres; sucking the wound and spitting has been shown to be ineffective and could potentially be dangerous. If possible try to identify the snake in question, but not at the cost getting bitten yourself.

Ticks

Ticks are present in some areas, and tick bites carry a risk of infection with European tick-borne encephalitis and Lyme disease (before that sets off too many alarm bells, the same can be said for several more frequently visited countries in Europe). A tick bite does not necessarily mean that you have become infected – not all ticks carry the bacteria leading to Lyme disease or the virus that causes encephalitis, and not all tick bites lead to infection. However, both are highly unpleasant,

EMERGENCY PHONE NUMBERS

- Police: 92
- Fire: 93
- Ambulance: 94

Emergency services can also be contacted on 112.

debilitating and in some cases, fatal diseases, and it is well worth knowing how to minimise your chances of contracting them.

The best form of protection against ticks is avoidance – wear long trousers when walking through the undergrowth or long grass, or through the forest, along with a hat, particularly in late spring or early summer (when ticks are at their most common). Check your skin and scalp when you finish your walk in the evening (a tick's body is brown and about the size of a pinhead).

In the event that you do find a tick attached to your skin, remove it as soon as possible – the risk of infection becomes higher if the tick remains undetected and is not removed within 24 hours. Ticks should be removed carefully using a special tick-removing tool such as the O'Tom Tick Twister (www.ticktwister.co.uk) or the tick tool made by CarePlus (www.careplus.eu). Do not pull, squeeze or crush the tick's abdomen, or use irritants or cigarettes to encourage it to drop off you – doing so will cause it to regurgitate and therefore increase the risk of infection considerably. Instead, slip the head of the tick-tool under the tick's body, as close to your skin as possible, and twist gently. Once removed, clean the wound with alcohol or iodine, and make a note of the date you were bitten. A rash or fever a few days or more after the bite, or a red area spreading around the bite site, are signs that you may need further medical treatment. For more information about ticks and tick-borne diseases see the website of the British Mountaineering Council (www.thebmc.co.uk/hill-skills-tick-alert) and www.tickalert.org.

LANDMINES

Landmine sign, Kopački rit Nature Park

Certain areas of Croatia remain heavily mined from the 1991–1995 war. These include the area between Karlovac and Knin, the Bosnian border, certain parts of eastern Slavonia, and even the occasional village not far from Zadar. In these areas, stay on sealed roads, and avoid deserted villages and buildings – they are usually deserted for a reason. Similarly, areas of unused farmland should be avoided.

With one exception, none of the routes recommended in this guide passes anywhere near the unsafe areas listed above, and the presence of landmines in these areas should certainly not deter you from visiting the rest of the country. Neither do the above comments on deserted houses and villages apply to those encountered on the routes in this guide, which are typically deserted for economic reasons. The one exception is southern Velebit, certain areas of which are suspected of being mined, and while the paths in this guide are perfectly safe in themselves, adjacent areas are not. The route on Dinara described here is safe; some other areas of the massif such as Troglav are not. Kopački rit in Slavonia lies close to areas with minefields – make sure you keep to roads and marked trails, and follow local warnings. A de-mining programme has been underway for many years, and Croatia aims to be mine-free in a couple of years.

Mine clearance has been hampered by the fact that, in many cases, there are no precise records of mine deployment, making the process particularly hazardous. Furthermore, the high cost of mine clearance operations (roughly US$50,000 to clear an area the size of a football pitch) and the fact that, as one of the wealthier countries requiring landmine clearance, Croatia has to pay the bill itself, have made progress very slow.

Further information on the efforts to clear landmines in Croatia can be found at the Croatian Mine Action Centre (www.hcr.hr), the International Campaign to Ban Landmines (www.icbl.org).

USING THIS GUIDE

Grading and arrangement of routes

A reasonable level of fitness is required for the walks in the Dinaric Alps. None of the routes require any climbing skills or equipment: a number do involve a degree of scrambling, although this can frequently be avoided. Rather than giving each walk a grading, a summary of the terrain and any difficulties is given in the introduction.

The guidebook contains both circular and point-to-point routes, varying in duration from a few hours to several days. In many (but not all) cases there is scope to shorten or extend routes, bypassing more difficult sections or adding more challenging excursions or alternative routes. Such details are given in the introductions to individual routes.

The routes in this guide fall into seven main sections: walks around Zagreb; Istria and the Opatija Riviera; Gorski Kotar; Velebit; the Dalmatian Hinterland; Central Dalmatia; and Southern Dalmatia. Within this format, the arrangement of individual routes does not reflect their technical difficulty, duration or attractiveness.

Walks on the islands are not covered, as these are described in a separate book (see Appendix F). Overall, the more extended, challenging and spectacular routes are those in the Dinaric Alps.

Timings

The timing given in the box preceding the route description refers to an average walking speed, and does not include breaks or stopping time at summits. Excursions not included in the initial route or stage profile are not included in these timings either.

Spelling and local place names

In general, English spelling has been used throughout this guide for the names of Croatian regions and surrounding countries – thus Dalmatia as opposed to Dalmacija, Slavonia

as opposed to Slavonija, Yugoslavia instead of Jugoslavija and so on.

Maps

The routes in this guide are all illustrated by maps at a scale of 1:50,000, except for those such as Routes 6 and 7 which are short and simple enough not to need maps. Map references in the information boxes preceding individual routes or stages refer to the relevant HGSS or SMAND sheet, where available, or reasonable alternative, and you would be well advised to purchase these as they provide more detailed coverage (usually 1:25,000).

Food and lodging

Accommodation is listed in the introduction to each walk or stage. For mountain huts, information regarding their altitude, number of beds, when they are open and whether they serve food/drinks is provided, together with the name of the hiking club or other organisation that manages the hut. Individual contact numbers have not been given as they often change – and an up-to-date list is kept by the HPS. Simply refer to http://www.hps. hr/info/planinarske-kuce/ and click on the relevant hut. You'll find more information on mountain huts in the previous section, which explains the difference between a *planinarski dom*, *planinarska kuća* and *planinarsko sklonište*. Unless stated otherwise in the summary for each hut, you can assume that a *sklonište* is open permanently, is unstaffed and serves

no food or drinks; while a *planinarska kuća* is open for limited days of the weeks/months, or only by prior arrangement (in either case, listed here); and a *planinarski dom* is open for limited days of the weeks/months (listed here) and may or may not serve food (again, listed here). You should assume you need a sleeping mat and sleeping bag for a *sklonište*; and a sleeping bag or liner is sufficient for a *planinarski dom* or *planinarska kuća*.

Water
The availability of drinking water is highlighted in the introduction to a stage or route.

PART 1
WALKS AROUND
ZAGREB

The trail to Grafičar hut, Sljeme (Route 1)

There was a time not so long ago when Zagreb, the Croatian capital, saw relatively few foreign visitors in comparison with the coast and islands. Not any more. While this may still hold true in comparative terms, Zagreb is now most definitely *in*, and attracts far more visitors than it did when the first edition of this guide was published, back in 2004.

In any case, it remains a truly delightful city, with a completely different feel to cities on the coast such as Split or Dubrovnik – very much Central European, as opposed to Mediterranean. With its well-preserved old town centre awash with Secessionist architecture, café-lined streets and squares strewn with flower stalls, elegant parks and gardens, a wonderful Christmas market (voted the best in Europe three years in a row) – not to mention numerous excellent museums and galleries – Zagreb is a beautiful, vibrant and endlessly fascinating place to while away a few days before setting off for the karst wilderness of the Dinaric Alps. It's a city I fell in love with when I first moved there in the late 1990s, an affection which remains undiminished to this day.

Aside from its impeccable cultural credentials, there are some good, easily accessible areas for walking near Zagreb. Medvednica (Routes 1 and 2) is the large, forested massif rising directly from the northern suburbs of Zagreb, crowned by a large TV tower at its highest point, Sljeme (1033m). Medvednica is a nature park (Park prirode Medvednica, www.pp-medvednica.hr) – although any of the bears implied by its name (from *medvjed*, meaning 'bear') were either hunted down or disappeared long ago. Locals flock to Sljeme at the weekends, and during the winter an area just below the summit functions as a small ski slope. Various *gostionica* (small restaurants) serve hearty meals, which you can work up an appetite for on the way up. There are numerous hiking trails on Medvednica, together with a road and a cable car (the latter closed for upgrading since 2009) to the top.

Samoborsko gorje (Route 4) is an area of rolling hills (and vineyards) southwest of Zagreb, beside the bijou Baroque town of Samobor (www.tz-samobor.hr), and forms part of the larger Žumberak area on the border with Slovenia. Like Medvednica, Samoborsko gorje is a nature park (Park prirode Žumberak Samoborsko gorje to give it its full name, www.park-zumberak.hr), and is criss-crossed by well over 300km of marked hiking trails, and dotted with small wooden churches. When in Samobor you should try the obligatory *kremšnite*, a particularly fine custard cream dessert for which the town is famous.

For practical information about Zagreb, including accommodation recommendations, see Appendix B and Zagreb City Tourist Office: www.infozagreb.hr.

ROUTE 1
Grafičar, Sljeme

Start/finish	Šestine
Distance	13km (8.1 miles)
Total ascent/descent	760m (2493ft)
Time	4hr 30min
Terrain	An easy walk on good, clear forest trails; some steps on Poučna staza Miroslavec
Maximum altitude	871m (Grafičar hut)
Maps	SMAND (01) Medvednica (1:25,000); HGSS Medvednica (1:25,000); Park prirode Medvednica (1:30,000), published by the nature park office, is less detailed.
Refreshments	PD Grafičar (food and drinks, closed Mondays); Lugareva kuća (food and drinks, http://lugareva-kuca.com); Šestinski lagvić (food and drinks, www.sestinski-lagvic.hr)
Transport	Take a number 102 bus (either from Britanski trg or Kaptol) to the outlying suburb of Šestine (25min), and get off just before (if you're coming from Britanski trg) or after (if you're coming from Kaptol) the small church with its brightly coloured roof tiles.

The following route starts and finishes in the small village of Šestine, and follows a good, clear forest path to one of the nicest mountain huts on Sljeme, PD Grafičar, which makes a good place to stop for lunch. There's a medieval mine that can be visited near the hut, and a visit to Medvedgrad, a 13th-century fortress on the slopes overlooking Zagreb, is included on the return route. Of the many hiking trails on Sljeme, this is the most enjoyable.

Continue uphill from the **church** in Šestine, passing a cemetery on the left and following the trail markings. After five minutes, you will arrive at a car park and a sign reading 'Park prirode Medvednica' (Medvednica Nature Park), and pass a popular restaurant, Šestinski lagvić,

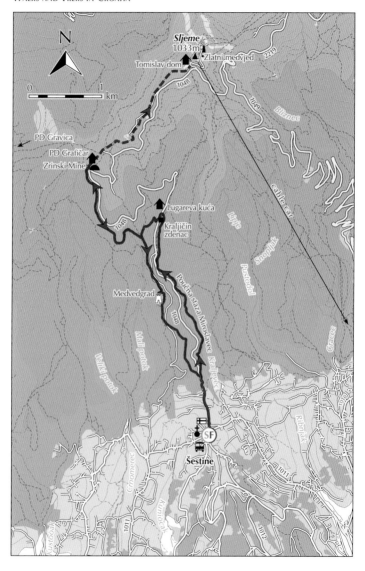

Hiker on the trail to Grafičar hut, Sljeme, above Kraljičin zdenac and Medvedgrad

on your right. When you reach a small wooden shelter on the right, turn right onto a broad gravel path that descends gradually from the road to wind through the shade of tall, ivy-clad oak and beech trees, while a small stream is audible trickling through the gully on the right – all in significant contrast to the harsh and waterless Dinaric peaks that await you along the coast. ▶ The path begins climbing slowly, with wooden footbridges crossing side-streams, to reach a junction 1 hour from Šestine, just above **Kraljičin zdenac**, a small café and picnic area by the road (closed until further notice in 2018).

The trail straight ahead leads to the summit of **Sljeme** (Route 2). Instead of taking this, turn left and descend to the road beside Kraljičin zdenac. ▶ Cross the road and follow the marked path up through fairly open forest, signposted to Grafičar. The path becomes a broad trail and climbs gradually to reach a junction, where you turn right (straight ahead would take you to Medvedgrad, a route which will be followed on the descent). The trail passes a small wooden shelter on the right, and there are some nice views on the left, out to the hills of Žumberak

The path, known as Poučna staza Miroslavec (*poučna staza* means 'educational trail'), is extensively labelled with details of the surrounding trees and rocks.

There's a nice little restaurant, Lugareva kuća, in an old hunting lodge a couple of minutes along the road on your right (uphill).

69

(on the border with Slovenia) and a distant Klek (Route 14) in Gorski kotar.

Where the trail meets the asphalt road, cross straight over and follow the path uphill to reach **PD Grafičar** in five minutes, 2hr 15min from Šestine.

PD Grafičar (food and drinks; closed Mondays) sits at the edge of a grassy clearing, with wooden tables outside, and serves a hearty *grah* (bean stew) and, during the summer, the best *ćevapčići* (grilled meatballs) on Sljeme.

Just to the SW of PD Grafičar you'll find the **Zrinski Mine**, one of a number of medieval mines in the area, where gold, silver and other ores were once extracted. It was in operation from the 16th to the 17th century. The Zrinski Mine was opened to the public in 2004 and has interactive displays. It is open April–October, Sundays and public holidays, 11am–5pm. Tickets cost 23Kn for adults and 18Kn for children. See www.pp-medvednica.hr for more details.

Variations

If you want to connect this route with Route 2, follow a path uphill from PD Grafičar then turn right along an asphalt road, before branching off on a path to the left (but not the trail to Gornja Bistra) to reach vrh Sljeme in 30 minutes. It's also possible to walk to the Veternica Cave and PD Glavica (Route 3) from PD Grafičar, by following a trail W from the hut. Allow 3hr 30min one way.

Descend towards Šestine following the same route in reverse, but at the trail junction above Kraljičin zdenac, turn right. Descend a broad path to reach a cobbled road, then walk up to the entrance of **Medvedgrad**.

Medvedgrad was built in the mid 13th century, but was abandoned in the 16th century following a fire, then restored during the 1990s. There are good views from the restored towers within the ruins, and a grassy terrace makes a good spot for a picnic. The controversial Oltar Domovine (Homeland Altar) is a monument and eternal flame to the memory of Croatian soldiers who died during the Croatian War of Independence, built (at considerable expense) at the order of President Franjo Tuđman. There's a medieval-themed fair held in the fortress during the last week in September. Medvedgrad is open April–September: Tuesday–Sunday 11am–7pm; September–January: Tuesday–Sunday 10am–6pm, January–March: weekends 10am–5pm. Entry costs 15kn (buy tickets at the gate). The ruins of another 13th century fort, Susedgrad, lie on the western slopes of Medvednica.

Return to the main road and turn right, following it for 10 minutes before turning left onto a path marked Šestine. From here, it's another 15 minutes down to the road; continue past Šestinski lagvić and then down to the church in **Šestine**. The bus stop is just beyond the church, by the small newspaper kiosk (for buses towards Britanski trg), or opposite this (for buses towards Kaptol).

Medvedgrad, Sljeme

ROUTE 2
Vrh Sljeme

Start/finish	Šestine
Distance	13km (8.1 miles)
Total ascent/descent	845m (2772ft)
Time	4hr 30min
Terrain	An easy walk on good, clear forest trails; some steps on Poučna staza Miroslavec, and slightly steeper sections of trail between Kraljičin zdenac and vrh Sljeme
Maximum altitude	1033m (Sljeme)
Maps	SMAND (01) Medvednica (1:25,000); HGSS Medvednica (1:25,000); Park prirode Medvednica (1:30,000), published by the nature park office, is less detailed.
Refreshments	Zlatni Medvjed and other restaurants near the summit (many of them are closed on Mondays); Lugareva kuća (slightly off route; food and drinks, http://lugareva-kuca.com); Šestinski lagvić (food and drinks, www.sestinski-lagvic.hr)
Transport	Take a number 102 bus (either from Britanski trg or Kaptol) to the village of Šestine (25min), and get off just before (if you're coming from Britanski trg) or after (if you're coming from Kaptol) the small church with its brightly coloured roof tiles.

Like Route 1, this route starts and finishes in the small village of Šestine, but climbs to the highest point on Medvednica, vrh Sljeme. It's possible to follow a road from vrh Sljeme to just above PD Grafičar, and descend to Šestine following Route 1 in reverse.

Continue uphill from the **church** in Šestine, passing a cemetery on the left and following the trail markings. After five minutes, you will arrive at a car park and a sign reading 'Park prirode Medvednica' (Medvednica Nature Park), and pass a popular restaurant, Šestinski lagvić,

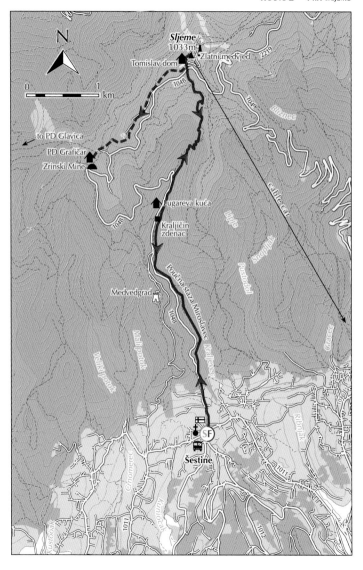

The path, known as Poučna staza Miroslavec (*poučna staza* means 'educational trail'), is extensively labelled with details of the surrounding trees and rocks.

on your right. When you reach a small wooden shelter on the right, turn right onto a broad gravel path that descends gradually from the road to wind through the shade of tall, ivy-clad oak and beech trees, while a small stream is audible trickling through the gully on the right – all in significant contrast to the harsh and waterless Dinaric peaks that await you along the coast. ◄ The path begins climbing slowly, with wooden footbridges crossing side-streams, to reach a junction 1 hour from Šestine, just above **Kraljičin zdenac**, a small café and picnic area by the road (closed until further notice in 2018).

Continue straight ahead at the junction (without turning left as in Route 1, unless you want to stop at Lugareva kuća), following the signs to Tomislavov dom and ignoring tracks to the left, as the path narrows and enters conifers before becoming steeper. After opening out again into a tall stand of beech, the path crosses a side-stream and begins zigzagging up an eroded slope before entering tall conifers once more. The path divides and meets again, with occasional markings, crossing a forest road before veering left and zigzagging up to the main road below Tomislavov dom, 45 minutes beyond Kraljičin

Family hiking on Poučna staza, Sljeme

Sculpture of a bear, Sljeme

zdenac. Turn right onto this before ascending past the cable car station to reach the various cafés and gostionica (many of them are closed on Mondays) and the large TV tower at the top of **Sljeme** (1033m) in a few minutes.

From the viewpoint on top of Sljeme, there's a view down over the scattered houses of Gornja Bistra and the forested spurs of northern Medvednica. **PD Grafičar** (see below) is a more pleasant spot to linger, however if you want to stop here on Sljeme and return by the same route, making a shorter excursion than continuing via PD Grafičar, one of the better places to eat is **Zlatni Medvjed**, near the TV tower.

Descend to Kraljičin zdenac and Šestine following the same route in reverse (allow 2hr). The **bus stop** is just beyond the church, by the small newspaper kiosk (for buses towards Britanski trg), or opposite this (for buses towards Kaptol).

To connect with Route 1
If you want to connect this route with Route 1, turn right just below vrh Sljeme onto a marked trail to PD Grafičar. This joins the asphalt road, passing a trail on the right to Gornja Bistra and a military base on the left. Then, turn left and follow a path down to **PD Grafičar**, around 30 minutes from vrh Sljeme.

ROUTE 3
Veternica Cave

Start/finish	Gornji Stenjevec
Distance	3km (1.9 miles)
Total ascent/descent	190m (623ft)
Time	1hr 30min
Terrain	A short, very easy forest trail
Maximum altitude	360m (Veternica Cave)
Maps	SMAND (01) Medvednica (1:25,000); HGSS Medvednica (1:25,000); Park prirode Medvednica (1:30,000), published by the nature park office, is less detailed.
Refreshments	PD Glavica (420m, 10 minutes from cave; food and drinks, weekends only)
Transport	Take bus 124 from Črnomerec (which is on tram 6 or 11 from Jelačić Square) to Gornji Stenjevec, and get out at the last stop (20min).
Practical information	Medvednica Nature Park www.pp-medvednica.hr; Zagreb City Tourist Office www.infozagreb.hr

A short walk to the Veternica Cave (Špilja Veternica) – Croatia's fourth longest cave, a source of numerous archaeological finds and home to a fairly healthy-sized population of bats – on the SW flanks of Medvednica from Gornji Stenjevec. Veternica can be visited April–October, Saturdays and Sundays, 10am–4pm, with a guide. Tickets (including guide) cost 40Kn for adults and 20Kn for children. Tours of the cave last around 45 minutes. However, the cave is sometimes closed due to bad weather, so it's best to check with the park office (www.pp-medvednica.hr, tel: +385 (0)1 458 6317) before you set off.

Walk north from the end of the road in Gornji Stenjevec, heading into the forest on the path marked špilja veter-nica. It's a 30 minute hike to **Veternica Cave**, climbing gradually.

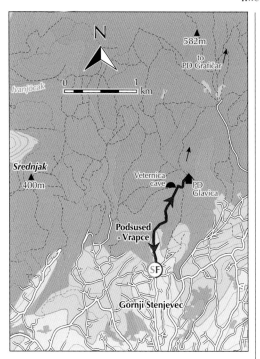

Veternica Cave is some 2,600m long (that's just the main part – with all the other explored passages, the figure is more than 7,100m), of which around 380m are open to the public. Archaeological finds in the form of stone tools and weapons in the cave show that it was used by Neanderthals some 40,000 years ago. The cave was found to contain a large number of animal remains, including bones and skulls of the extinct cave bear (*Ursus spelaeus*). Some 14 species of bat have been recorded in Veternica, including the greater horseshoe bat (*Rhinolophus ferrumequinum*), Mediterranean horseshoe bat (*Rhinolophus euryale*) and Nathusius' pipistrelle (*Pipistrellus nathusii*). The bats hibernate in the cave

*The mouth of
Veternica cave,
Medvednica*

over the winter – one of the reasons it is closed at
that time of year. Although the cave has been protected since 1979, souvenir-hunters had long since
removed most of the stalactites from the initial
sections.

From the cave, you can continue for 10 minutes up
the steep path and steps to reach PD Glavica (420m; food
and drinks; weekends only), which does excellent food.

To connect with Route 1
It is possible to walk to PD Grafičar (Route 1) from PD
Glavica. Continue along the forest road from the hut,
then take a trail on the left marked Grafičar. Allow 3hr
30min one way.

Return to **Gornji Stenjevec** by the same route.

ROUTE 4

Samoborsko gorje

Start/finish	Samobor
Distance	15km (9.3 miles)
Total ascent/descent	750m (2461ft)
Time	4hr 30min
Terrain	Easy paths, with some road walking
Maximum altitude	752m
Maps	SMAND (8) Samoborsko gorje (1:25,000); or Park prirode Žumberak Samoborsko gorje published by the nature park office (1:50,000)
Refreshments	PD Željezničar na Oštrcu. There are restaurants, cafés and hotels in Samobor – cafés on the main square serve *kremšnite* and Hotel Lavica has a good restaurant, www.lavica-hotel.hr.
Transport	Regular buses travel between Črnomerec (at the end of tram routes 6 and 11) and Samobor, leaving from stops 14 and 15. Of the two services available, take the one travelling via Sveta Nedelja (bus 151) rather than the one travelling via Strmec, which takes considerably longer. Local tram and bus tickets are not valid, and you will have to buy a separate ticket. Get off at the bus station in Samobor – the last stop on the bus route (30min).

An easy day trip into the Samobor hills (Samoborsko gorje) from the lovely Baroque town of Samobor, with plenty of scope for extending the route. A visit to Stari grad, the old fortress on the edge of Samobor, is included.

From the bus station in Samobor, walk south into the main square (Trg kralja Tomislava) and turn right. From beyond the square, turn left over the wooden footbridge, walking through the small park with the stream on your right. Follow the left branch of this path up to the ruined fortress or **Stari grad**, built in several phases

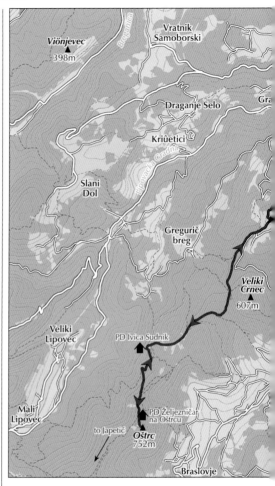

between the 13th and 18th centuries. The walls are
crumbling (don't enter the ruins, and watch out for falling stones), and the interior is overgrown and littered
with broken glass, but the northwest towers are still
impressive. Descend by the same route to the playing

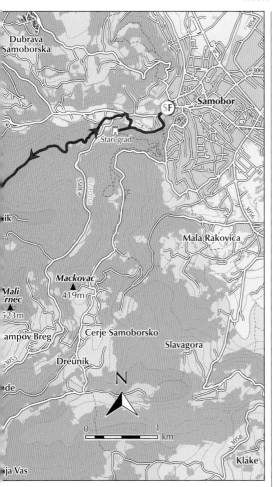

fields, turning left before crossing the stream once more to return to the road. Take the first road on the left (signposted to Rude), following this for a few minutes past a church and over a small bridge, before turning right on a marked trail to Oštrc.

Follow the unsealed road, turning left as indicated and ascending past some houses, with good views of the fortress, before veering right and following the track as it narrows, passing orchards and through intermittent forest cover. Pass under a small and rocky bluff before following a clear and well-marked forest trail up through tall beech and oak to reach a minor road, 40 minutes from the **Rude** turn-off. Turn left onto the road, following it through **Palačnik** (and at one point diverging from it briefly to walk through someone's back garden) before turning off to the right and descending slightly towards Gvozd. Here, turn left and follow the clear trail as it winds its way to PD Ivica Sudnik (530m; weekends only; food and drinks) at Veliki dol. Continue straight ahead past the hut, ignoring the path on the left to Rude, to reach **PD Željezničar na Oštrcu**, approximately 1hr from Palačnik.

> PD Željezničar na Oštrcu (691m; sleeps 37; weekends only; food and drinks; contact HPD Željezničar, Zagreb) sits on a low saddle below Oštrc.

It's an easy stroll up to Oštrc (752m), the low peak just beyond the hut, from where there are pleasant views of Medvednica, and southwest towards Japetić.

Return to **Samobor** by the same route.

To extend the walk
It would be possible to extend this route from Oštrc to Japetić (879m), which has a hut nearby (PD Žitnica; 815m; weekends only; sleeps 21; HPD Jastrebarsko, Jastrebarsko). However buses from Šoićeva kuća (from where there is a trail to Japetić, and which is on local bus route 144 between Mali Lipovec and Samobor) are less frequent than buses between Zagreb and Samobor (timetables at www.samoborcek.hr).

PART 2
ISTRIA AND THE
OPATIJA RIVIERA

View across Pazinska jama ('Pazin abyss') to Pazin castle (Route 6)

Named after the Histri, the Illyrian tribe that inhabited the area before the Roman conquest, Istria is the large, wedge-shaped peninsula protruding into the Adriatic between Slovenia to the north and the Kvarner region to the east. The rolling, fertile interior is dotted with small hill towns; the coastline sees more visitors and sports some of the country's most celebrated architectural monuments, including the huge and remarkably well-preserved Roman amphitheatre at Pula, and the Euphrasian Basilica at Poreč (a UNESCO World Heritage Site). Istria is also the gastronomic highlight of Croatia – its hinterland is famed for its truffles, some of Croatia's best wines are produced here (in particular from the native Malvazija and Teran grape varieties), along with the country's finest olive oils.

The northeast coast of the peninsula (including Rijeka and Opatija) form part of the Kvarner region (as does Gorski Kotar, see Part 3). Opatija became extremely popular as a resort during the 19th century, at which time this area of Croatia still formed part of the Hapsburg Empire, and everyone who was anyone in Austrian high society came here, from Gustav Mahler to Emperor Franz Joseph I.

The best area for hiking on the Istrian peninsula is Učka (Route 5), the mountainous area just inland from Opatija, including the adjacent Ćićarija, which together divide the Kvarner region from the Istrian

hinterland. There are also a few short, easy walks dotted around the coast and hinterland, and some excellent cycling routes.

BASES

Rijeka, the third largest city in Croatia and the capital of the Primorje-Gorski Kotar County, is a convenient base for exploring Istria. It has an international airport and excellent transport connections, including rail and bus links with Zagreb and Pula and bus links with the towns and cities along the western seaboard. For practical information, including accommodation recommendations, see Appendix B.

Other options include the historic coastal cities of **Pula** and **Rovinj**, **Opatija** and various smaller towns and villages. Route 6 starts from **Pazin**, a small city located in the centre of the peninsula, famed for its medieval castle and dramatic limestone gorge.

Local cuisine

Given how exceptionally good the food is here, it would be an unforgivable oversight not to recommend a few restaurants, so here goes: Konoba Nono (Petrovija), Konoba Mondo (Motovun), Konoba Doline (Livade), Konoba Batelina (Banjole, near Pula), Laurus (Villa Kapetanović, Volosko). And some winemakers/vineyards to look out for: Benvenuti (Motovun), Cattunar (Brtonigla), Kozlović (Momjan), Roxianich (Nova Vas), Tomaz (Motovun), Trapan (Pula).

ROUTE 5
Vrh Učka

Start/finish	Lovran
Alternative finish	Poklon pass
Distance	15km (9.3 miles) (11km (6.8 miles) to Poklon pass)
Total ascent/descent	1400m (4593ft) (1410m/510m to Poklon pass)
Time	7hr 15min (5hr to Poklon pass)
Terrain	Forest paths and open hillside, mostly clearly marked, with some steep sections
Maximum altitude	1401m (Vojak)
Maps	HGSS (19) Ćićarija (1:25,000) is best, and covers the whole of Učka as well as Ćićarija; Park prirode Učka (1:30,000), published by the nature park office, covers Učka and the southern part of Ćićarija.
Refreshments	Planinarski dom Poklon; plenty of hotels, guesthouses and restaurants in Lovran
Transport	You can reach Lovran easily enough from Rijeka. Jump on a number 32 bus (from the local city bus terminal) and get out at Lovran (30min), where a road ascends to the right (signposted 'Stari grad'). For those following the alternative descent to the Poklon Pass, there's a bus (number 34) between the Poklon pass and Opatija – but it only runs on Sundays (departure times from Poklon dom 10.30am and 3.45pm; timetables at www.autotrolej.hr/att/wp-content/uploads/2017/11/linija-34a-_02_11_2017.pdf, with the Poklon pass marked as Učka). If you miss the bus from Poklon dom and it's too late to hike over Vojak and back down to Lovran, you can walk or hitch down the main road from the pass to Veprinac, around 7km away (from where there are more regular bus services to Opatija, bus 35A).

Učka is the highest part of Istrian peninsula. Its highest peak, Vojak (also called vrh Učka), rises to 1401m, and divides Istria from the Kvarner region. Despite the presence of a large telecommunications tower near the summit, and a sealed road leading almost to the summit from the Poklon pass, it remains an impressive spot, with breathtaking views over the Istrian hinterland and the Kvarner islands. In any case, the road and antenna are obscured by the summit until the last moment, when approaching from Lovran via Suhi vrh, as described here (not so when approaching from the Poklon pass).

The following, straightforward itinerary starts and finishes at just above sea level in the small town of Lovran, and climbs to the summit of Učka (called Vojak), the highest point on the Istrian peninsula. It's possible to follow an alternative descent as far as the Poklon Pass (922m), where there's a mountain hut (Poklon dom), open at weekends, and a bus down to Opatija. From the Pokon Pass it is possible to extend the route by continuing over Ćićarija.

If you're planning to return to Rijeka from the Poklon pass, note that the bus service only runs on Sundays (see above); on other days, it's better to finish the route at Vojak, without continuing to Poklon dom, and simply descend to Lovran following your upward route in reverse, as described here.

Lungomare, *waterside promenade between Volosko and Lovran, below Učka*

As an enjoyable alternative to the number 32 bus, you can also walk to Lovran, or return from it, along the coastal promenade which stretches along the waterfront between Lovran and Volosko. This promenade, or *lungomare*, is often included in local tourist office literature as a hiking route, but is so straightforward that it really needs no further detail other than the outline given here. It's an easy and very pleasant 3km from Volosko to Opatija, 7km from Opatija to Lovran, passing small coves and beaches, sculptures, and rocks where cormorants perch to spread their wings to dry.

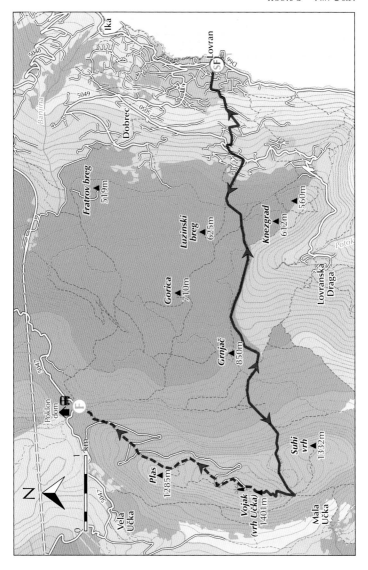

Učka is a nature park, Park prirode Učka (www. pp-ucka.hr). Its particularly rich **flora** includes several rare or endangered species, among them the yellow gentian (*Gentiana lutea*) and cross gentian (*Gentiana cruciata*), endemic species such as the Učka bellflower (*Campanula tommasiniana*), and around 30 species of orchid.

Leave the main road in Lovran at the Stari grad sign, ascending and passing through the small but grandly named Trg slobode ('freedom square') – from which you can turn left to have a look at the old part of town before continuing – to reach a T-junction in a few minutes, where the red-and-white trail markings begin. Turn right, towards Villa Slavija, continuing straight ahead and passing a small votive shrine on the right before following the road round to the left. Here, a sign to Učka leads up the first of many flights of steep, walled steps, crossing minor roads a number of times and passing through the pretty houses and gardens of Liganj, with the sections in between becoming increasingly forested, to reach a junction 1 hour from Lovran.

The trail on the right provides a more direct route to the Poklon Pass but it is considerably less clear and is mostly through forest so you lose out on the views.

◀ Continue straight ahead, following a rocky path (marked 'RT'), which ascends through low trees. On meeting the sealed road one last time, follow this briefly before turning off onto a path marked Vojak and Grnjac, opposite a small crucifix. Continue past some walled gardens, ascending on a rocky, winding trail to a forest road. Turn right onto this, then left on a path which leads up and over a ridge, 20 minutes from the junction.

Grnjač (850m) can be reached in around 20 minutes, following the trail on the right. You can then continue SW and rejoin the main trail just before the forest road.

The path ascends gradually, contouring the side of the valley, with lovely views out over the steep pine slopes to the sea from occasional clearings and rock outcrops. Continue straight ahead, following the RT signs and passing a trail to the small peak of **Grnjač**. ◀

After passing below scree slopes, the path follows a rocky streambed and passes another side-trail, this time signposted to the village of Mala Učka. Continue ascending, following the trail marked Vojak and contouring stone walls; pass a trail to Lovranska Draga, which joins from the left. A few more minutes brings you to a forest road, just after meeting a second path from Grnjač on the right.

Continue straight over the forest road to reach a clearing with low trees, wild roses and nettles. From here you get a brief view of the red-and-white antenna on Vojak before re-entering the trees. Almost immediately, you emerge into a second clearing, with a small cottage or hunting lodge on the left. Continue straight across the clearing, re-enter forest cover and ascend to a third clearing, where another route to the village of **Mala Učka** joins the main trail from the left. Veer right, into the trees, before starting up a relentlessly steep set of switchbacks, at the top of which you pass a trail to **Suhi vrh** ('dry peak') on the left. ▶

Continue straight ahead, through tall beech trees and another clearing choked with nettles and brambles, crossing the forest road twice to emerge on an open saddle between Vojak and Suhi vrh, with a path to the latter leading off on your left, and the imposing white limestone bulk of Vojak towering on your right. Continue up to Vojak, ascending steeply, with any trace of roads, car parks and telecommunications towers well hidden until

Suhi vrh (1332m) offers another possible detour – however the trail from here is steep and less well used: there's another, clearer trail from the saddle between Vojak and Suhi vrh.

View from the summit of Vojak (vrh Učka)

the last moment, when you gain the summit of **Vojak** with its stone lookout tower and the carloads of visitors who have driven up from the coast.

> The view from **Vojak** (1401m) is as huge as it is unexpected. Suhi vrh lies behind you, beyond the open saddle and the forested trail down to Lovran. The land falls away suddenly to the west, where the plains and forests of Istria sprawl below before fading into the distance. Ćićarija extends to the north, while Gorski kotar stretches away to the northeast, and Velebit towers in the distance. Opatija and Rijeka are clearly visible on the coast, as are the islands of Cres, Lošinj and Krk to the southeast.

Retrace your steps from Vojak down to **Lovran** (allow 3hr).

To continue from Vojak to the Poklon pass

Alternatively, if you're planning to descend to the Poklon pass – either to stay at the hut there, Poklon dom (weekends only), or to take the bus back down to Opatija (Sundays only, see transport details at the start of the walk) – continue as follows (allowing 50 minutes from Vojak to the Poklon pass).

Continue N down to the car park and the road, passing the huge **telecommunications tower** on the left and following the road for 5 minutes before branching off to the left on a clearly marked path. Descend alongside a ridge, to reach a tiny trickle of a spring (marked Pitka voda, meaning 'drinking water') in 20 minutes. Continue descending, crossing a broad forest track and the main road a number of times, following the occasional RT or Poklon sign and zigzagging down through mixed beech and pine. A flight of steps brings you round behind the Pansion Učka restaurant (which many people don't recommend – there is no menu or prices, and the latter tend to be quite high) to a forest road, where you turn left to reach the main road at the Poklon pass, 30 minutes below the spring.

Planinarski dom Poklon (Poklon dom; 922m; sleeps 14; weekends only; PD Opatija, Opatija) is just around the corner, about 50m away on the main road leading towards Istria.

Reversing the route

For those starting from the Poklon pass (the Sundays-only bus service to the Poklon pass leaves Opatija at 09.40 and 14.10), the trail to Vojak starts from a little way along the forest road running S from the pass, turning right behind Pansion Učka, to gain the RT trail (marked 'vrh Učka, Vojak'). This zigzags up through tall beech (and later mixed beech and pine), crossing the main road a number of times, to reach a tiny spring (marked 'Pitka voda', 'drinking water'), 50 minutes from Poklon. Continue ascending alongside the crest of a ridge, to reach the road again in 15 minutes, where the large telecommunications tower comes into view. Follow the road to the right, passing the antenna and its fenced enclosure in 10 minutes. Continue straight ahead up a rocky track from the car park to the circular stone lookout tower on the summit of **Vojak**, with the path down to **Lovran** continuing on the other side.

Further possibilities around Učka
Ćićarija

Ćićarija is the large, forested area northwest of Učka, and contains a number of trails. If starting from Poklon dom, one possible route leads across Veliki Planik (1272m), Bončić, Griža (1144m), Šija (1234m), Lisina (1185m) and Crni vrh (1031m) before descending either via Zvončev vrh (975m) and Budišin vrh (903m) to Veprinac, or via Beljač (784m) and Orljak (706m) to Bregi and Opatija. Allow two days from Poklon dom. HGSS publishes a sheet covering both Ćićarija and Učka (Ćićarija, sheet 19).

ROUTE 6
Pazinska jama

Start/finish	Pazin castle
Distance	2km (1.2 miles)
Total ascent/descent	130m (427ft)
Time	40 min
Terrain	Easy forest path, steep in places and subject to flooding
Maximum altitude	360m
Maps	None
Refreshments	Hotel Lovac
Transport	Pazin lies on the railway line between Pula and Ljubljana (75min from Pula; for timetables, see www.hzpp.hr) and there are buses to Pazin from Pula (45min), Rijeka (1hr), Rovinj (45min) and Zagreb (3hr, www.autotrans.hr).

On the edge of Pazin in central Istria, below the town's stout-looking castle, is a deep gorge known as Pazinska jama (Pazin abyss). This is a short and very easy walk down into the forested gorge. A permit is required to enter the cave itself, and you have to go with a guide – but this can be arranged through at the tourist information office in Pazin. After heavy rain, the gorge may become flooded – in which case the route will be closed and should not be attempted.

Both **Pazin castle** and **Pazinska jama gorge** are the setting for part of Jules Verne's 1885 novel *Mathius Sandorf* – the hero of the novel, having been imprisoned in the castle and sentenced to death, escapes through a window and climbs down the cliff face into the gorge below, before entering the cave and escaping along an underground river. Dante is known to have visited Pazin, and it is thought the gorge here may have provided inspiration for the entrance to Hell in his *Inferno*. More recently, a zip line has been added across the gorge.

Pazin castle

From the entrance to Pazin Castle, walk down the street towards the Vršić Bridge, and turn left onto the marked trail leading down into the gorge. The path descends steeply to the Pazinčica, which it crosses by a small footbridge, then ascends on the other side of the gorge. ▶ The path ends at a level grassy area by Hotel Lovac and its restaurant, the terrace of which makes a good spot for lunch with views stretching to Učka.

Follow the road to the Vršić Bridge and Pazin Castle.

From the cave entrance, the cliff down which the hero descends into the gorge in Jules Verne's novel *Mathius Sandorf* is clearly visible.

PART 3
GORSKI KOTAR

Winter on Risnjak (Route 7), Gorski kotar

Gorski kotar is the great crescent-shaped range of mountains stretching down from Slovenia in the north, encompassing Risnjak National Park, together with Bjelolasica, Bijele stijene and Samarske stijene further south (the latter three make up an area collectively known as Velika Kapela), and forming the backbone of the Kvarner region.

Risnjak National Park (http://np-risnjak.hr) was established in 1953, and today covers an area of 6350ha, the boundaries having been extended in 1997. It's a beautiful landscape of rolling, forested mountains riddled with limestone dells, and bald, rocky peaks. The core of the national park is the area around vrh Risnjak, its highest point at 1528m (Routes 7 and 9), while at its lowest point it drops to 290m near the source of the River Kupa (Route 8). Entry tickets to Risnjak National Park cost 45Kn and are valid for two days within the park.

The flora of Risnjak National Park is exceptionally rich, with 1148 plant species and subspecies having been recorded here. As the most heavily forested part of Croatia, Gorski kotar is also the area where you are most likely to see brown bear tracks, although you are very unlikely to see the animal itself. The extensive beech and mountain pine also provide a natural habitat for wild pig, roe and red deer, along with (in very small numbers) the grey wolf. The lynx (whence the park's name – *ris* means lynx in Croatian) was hunted to extinction in Risnjak during the 19th century, but has returned in small numbers since the 1970s, after migrating from Slovenia. Birdlife is equally rich, with 114 species recorded within the national park. One of Croatia's oldest and most popular mountain huts lies within the national park, PD Risnjak or Schlosserov dom, named after the botanist Josip Schlosser who explored the area extensively in the 19th century.

The National Park Office is located at Bela Vodica, near the village of Crni Lug (around 12km NW of Delnice), from where you can set off on day walks or multi-day trails. There's a bus service from Delnice to Crni Lug (weekdays only, timetables at www.autotrans.hr); otherwise buses between Delnice and Gornje Jelenje pass the beginning of a 4X4 road, which can be used as a (less scenic) alternative start to Risnjak, if the departure times are more convenient.

South of Delnice, a road branches east to the village of Mrkopalj, the start-point for walks on Bjelolasica, Bijele stijene and Samarske stijene (Route 13). The karst formations on Bijele stijene and Samarske stijene are particularly impressive; and Kula, on Bjelolasica, is the highest point in Gorski kotar, being a smidgen higher than Risnjak at 1534m.

Klek (Route 14) is a lone, rocky tooth of a hill some 50km southeast of Delnice, which technically speaking lies just across the administrative boundary from the Kvarner region in

Karlovac County. The usual start point is Ogulin, but it can also be climbed from Bjelsko near the end of Route 13.

Several of the walks in Gorski kotar can be combined into a grand loop, known as the Goranski planinarski put or GPP (around 90km); and some have been incorporated into the Via Dinarica (including part of Route 12).

BASES

The gateway to Gorski kotar is the town of **Delnice**, which is easily reached from either Zagreb or Rijeka by train or bus (for timetables, see www.hzpp.hr and www.buscroatia.com, respectively). The bus station, for services to the trailheads for Risnjak and Bjelolasica, is on the main road, opposite the long flight of steps descending from the railway station. There are a few shops in Delnice where you can get a few supplies – there's a small supermarket just left of and opposite the bottom of the steps from the railway station; or turn right from the steps then left along Supilova ulica – but you would do better not to rely completely on these and to stock up in Zagreb or on the coast. Delnice was a major centre of Partisan resistance during World War 2, an episode of history reflected in such local landmarks as Matić poljana on the route to Bjelolasica (Route 13).

Around 12km east of Delnice, beyond the national park boundary,

the small town of **Skrad** is the starting point for two very nice walks – through Vražji prolaz (a dramatic canyon), and to a picturesque waterfall, Zeleni vir, both of which can be combined into an excellent circular route (Route 10). Apartmani Hisa na Loki (www.apartman-gorski-kotar.com/slike-gorski-kotar.htm) is a nice, spacious apartment in the centre of Skrad. The Skrad Tourist Office (www.tz-skrad.hr/en/index.php) is located in the centre of town, by the car park above the main road.

Fužine is a small town around 15km southwest of Delnice, on the edge of a large reservoir (Bajersko jezero, which you'll cross on a viaduct if you're travelling along the motorway between Zagreb and Rijeka). Fužine provides a base for hikes to nearby Burnji Bitoraj (Route 11). Less energetically, there's a path around the lake, and the nearby Vrelo Cave is one of the most impressive show caves in Croatia (Route 12). Hotel Bitoraj (www.bitoraj.hr) offers the best accommodation and also has an excellent restaurant. The Fužine Tourist Office (www.tz-fuzine.hr) is opposite Hotel Bitoraj.

Skrad and Fužine are also on the main Zagreb–Rijeka railway line, although the railway station in Fužine is some distance from the town and less convenient than the centrally-placed bus station. Buses between Zagreb and Rijeka stop in Fužine (3hr 30min).

ROUTE 7
Vrh Risnjak

Start/finish	Risnjak National Park Office, Bela Vodica
Distance	18km (11.2 miles)
Total ascent/descent	860m (2822ft)
Time	6hr 30min
Terrain	Excellent, clearly marked forest trails, with a very short section on asphalt at the start
Maximum altitude	1528m (vrh Risnjak)
Maps	Nacionalni park Risnjak (1:23,000), published by the national park office and available in Bela Vodica; SMAND (14) Gorski kotar IV (1:30,000)
Refreshments	PD Risnjak; restaurant and guesthouse in Bela Vodica (Risnak National Park Guesthouse)
Transport	There are three buses a day between Delnice and Crni Lug (15min, www.autotrans.hr).
Note	Entry tickets to Risnjak National Park (45Kn, valid for two days within the park) can be bought at the National Park Office.

This is one of the best routes in Risnjak National Park, and easily the nicest way to get to Risnjak and the hut just below it. The trail follows part of an educational path (*poučna staza*), then a beautiful trail up into the mountains, known as Šumićeva staza, via a prominent cleft in the rocks called Medvjeđa vrata, which translates as 'gateway of the bears'.

From the car park and information board beside the **National Park Office** in Bela Vodica, walk W on a marked path signposted Poučna staza, which joins a road briefly before branching off on the right, to follow a clearly marked trail through the forest. ▶

Around 40 minutes from Bela Vodica, by an information board about brown bear in the national park and just after a small wooden footbridge, leave **Poučna staza** and

A series of information boards, in Croatian and English, give details of the surrounding geological features, flora and fauna.

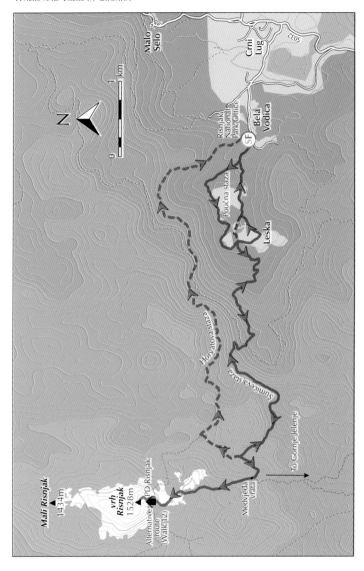

Šumićeva staza in early spring, Risnjak National Park

turn right on a 4X4 forest road (marked Risnjak) and then left where this forks. Follow the forest road for around 20 minutes then turn left onto a path (marked Risnjak) which climbs uphill through the forest. The path becomes a broad, well-engineered forest trail, which climbs steadily and crosses a 4X4 road, then skirts a couple of deep dells, to reach a junction. Turn left here (the path on the right is an unmarked route which links up with another trail from Bela Vodica to Risnjak, called Horvatova staza), to reach another trail junction at the distinctive **Medvjeđa vrata** ('gateway of the bears').

The path straight ahead (W) leads to a rough 4X4 road, which in turn leads to the main road above Gornje Jelenje – a shorter but much less scenic approach to Risnjak.

◀ Turn right through Medvjeđa vrata, contouring the slopes of more dells and ascending gradually, with the hut coming into view after about 20 minutes, as you round a final, rocky bluff. The path descends briefly on the far side of the rocks, to reach **PD Risnjak** itself in another 5 minutes.

PD Risnjak (1418m; also known as Schlosserov dom; staffed May–October; 43 beds; food and drinks; JU NP Risnjak, Crni Lug; unstaffed shelter open all year) was originally known as Schlosserov dom after the botanist Josip Schlosser (1808–1882). It sits perched on a grassy saddle, below the dwarf mountain pine- and juniper-clad peak of Risnjak itself, with forested slopes dropping away on either side. There is a well behind the hut, and a sklonište (just inside the main door) is open through the winter, when the hut itself is closed.

Follow the path behind the hut, ascending steeply through dwarf mountain pine and scrambling over rock, with views back down over the hut and saddle, and

On the trail to PD Risnjak, Risnjak national park

passing a sinkhole on the right, to reach the summit, **vrh Risnjak** (1528m), in 15 minutes. ▶

Descend to the hut (which makes a good stopping place for lunch), then return to the national park office at **Bela Vodica** by the same route.

Alternative descent via Horvatova staza

You can vary your return by following Horvatova staza, a path to the N of Šumićeva staza. Descend as far as the trail junction 15 minutes below Medvjeđa vrata. Instead of turning right here, turn left and follow an unmarked trail that winds alongside dells for 30 minutes. Turn right onto **Horvatova staza**, following the marked path then continuing along an asphalt road to **Bela Vodica**. Allow an additional 30 minutes to return by this route.

The views from vrh Risnjak are fantastic, with Snježnik clearly visible to the northwest, and the sea beyond.

101

ROUTE 8

River Kupa source

Start/finish	Razloge
Distance	4km (2.5 miles)
Total ascent/descent	235m (771ft)
Time	1hr
Terrain	Clearly marked forest trails
Maximum altitude	556m (Razloge)
Maps	Nacionalni park Risnjak (1:23,000), published by the national park office and available in Bela Vodica; SMAND (14) Gorski kotar IV (1:30,000)
Refreshments	Restaurant and guesthouse in Bela Vodica (Risnak National Park Guesthouse)
Transport	There is no public transport to the village of Razloge, 12km north of Crni Lug, so this walk is better suited to those with a bike (cycle hire is possible in Crni Lug) or car. There are three buses a day between Delnice and Crni Lug (15min, www.autotrans.hr). The bus to Crni Lug continues to Gerovski Kraj, next to the village of Gerovo, from where a trail leads down to the Kupa valley at Donji Kupari, but it's quite a long way.
Note	Entry tickets to Risnjak National Park (45kn, valid for two days within the park) can be bought at the National Park Office.

This is a short, easy walk to the source of the River Kupa, in a beautiful setting at the lowest point in Risnjak National Park.

From the car park in Razloge follow the road N briefly then turn left and follow a track, which soon becomes a clearly marked path through the forest. The path zigzags down to the valley floor, where you turn right to reach a small emerald-coloured lake at the source of the **River Kupa** (**Izvor Kupe**), hemmed in by cliffs.

Hiker beside the lake at the source of the River Kupa (Izvor Kupe), Risnjak National Park

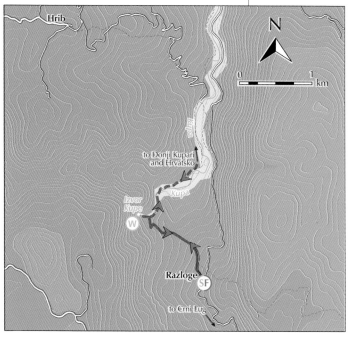

Source of the River Kupa (Izvor Kupe), Risnjak

The **River Kupa** flows N to the village of Hrvatsko, before turning E and running along the border with Slovenia to Brod na Kupi. Later, its course takes it through Karlovac where it is joined by the Dobra and Korana (the latter having flowed from Plitvice Lakes National Park), before flowing into the River Sava at the town of Sisak, near Lonjsko polje.

Optional extensions
It's possible to follow the Kupa as it flows N, first along the right and then the left bank, to Donji Kupari (30min) and Hrvatsko (a further 90min), on the border with Slovenia. Return to **Razloge** by the same route.

ROUTE 9

Risnjak, Snježnik and Hahlić trek

Start	Bela Vodica
Finish	Dražice
Distance	36–38km (22.4–23.6 miles)
Total ascent	1145m (3757ft)
Total descent	1530m (5020ft)
Time	3–4 days
Maps	Nacionalni park Risnjak (1:23,000), published by the national park office and available in Bela Vodica; SMAND (14) Gorski kotar IV (1:30,000)
Refreshments	There is food available at at PD Risnjak and Veliki Planinarski dom Platak
Transport	There are three buses a day between Delnice and Crni Lug (15min, timetable at www.autotrans.hr). At the end of the route, there are buses from Dražice to Rijeka (buses 12 and 16; 30min; for timetables, see www.autotrolej.hr).
Accommodation	Restaurant and guesthouse in Bela Vodica (Risnak National Park Guesthouse); PD Risnjak; PD Hahlić; Veliki Planinarski dom Platak
Note	Entry tickets to Risnjak National Park (45kn, valid for two days within the park) can be bought at the National Park Office.

The following straightforward itinerary takes you via the peaks of Risnjak (1528m) and Snježnik (1506m), and on to Hahlić in the southwest corner of Gorski kotar, an area of low hills known as the Grobnički Alpe, from where the route descends to the village of Dražice, 11km from Rijeka. There's an excellent mountain hut just below Risnjak (PD Risnjak); there used to be a nice hut on Snježnik, but that closed several years ago and has not been rebuilt; and there's a good hut at Hahlić (PD Hahlić). The route also passes accommodation at Platak. Excursions to adjacent peaks are possible from Snježnik

Medvjeđa vrata (Stage 1), Risnjak national park

and Hahlić (Suhi vrh, 1335m; Fratar, 1353m; Obruč, 1376m) and numerous other points along the way. The route has been broken down into three stages, but can be split into four if you want to avoid the longish second stage, and have more time for side trips.

Alternative approach from Gornje Jelenje

While this route is best started from Crni Lug, it's useful to know that there's an alternative, slightly shorter (but much less scenic) approach from Gornje Jelenje – which can also be reached by bus from Delnice – depending on what time you reach Delnice, and onward bus times from there. From Delnice, take a southbound bus to Gornje Jelenje and jump off at the pass (881m), opposite the turn-off to Crikvenica and Krk. (Not all southbound buses follow this road – many take the motorway instead, so check timetables at www.autotrans.hr.) Follow the broad forest road opposite the Crikvenica turn-off, to reach Vilje in 1hr 20 min. Turn right onto a track marked Medvjeđa vrata and Risnjak, taking first one and then another right fork after 10mins. Ascend on a steep, rocky path to reach Medvjeđa vrata and the route described in Stage 1 in a further 20 minutes.

STAGE 1
Bela Vodica – PD Risnjak

Start	Risnjak National Park Office, Bela Vodica
Finish	PD Risnjak
Distance	9.5km (5.9 miles)
Total ascent	860m (2822ft)
Total descent	120m (394ft)
Time	4hr
Terrain	Excellent, clearly marked forest trails, with a very short section on asphalt at the start
Maximum altitude	1528m (vrh Risnjak)
Accommodation	Restaurant and guesthouse in Bela Vodica (Risnak National Park Guesthouse); PD Risnjak

From the car park and information board beside the National Park Office in Bela Vodica, walk W on a marked path signposted Poučna staza, which joins a road briefly before branching off on the right, to follow a clearly marked trail through the forest. ▶

Around 40 minutes from Bela Vodica, by an information board about brown bears in the national park and just after a small wooden footbridge, leave Poučna

A series of information boards, in Croatian and English, give details of the surrounding geological features, flora and fauna.

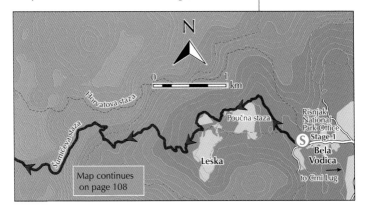

Map continues on page 108

staza and turn right on a 4X4 forest road (marked Risnjak) and then left where this forks. Follow the forest road for around 20 minutes then turn left onto a path (marked Risnjak), which climbs uphill through the forest. The path becomes a broad, well-engineered forest trail, which climbs steadily and crosses a 4X4 road, then skirts a couple of deep dells, to reach a junction. Turn left here (the path on the right is an unmarked route which links up with another trail from Bela Vodica to Risnjak, called Horvatova staza), to reach another trail junction at the distinctive Medvjeđa vrata.

The path straight ahead (W) leads to a rough 4X4 road, which in turn leads to the main road above Gornje Jelenje – a shorter but much less scenic route to Risnjak.

◄ Turn right through Medvjeđa vrata, contouring the slopes of more dells and ascending gradually, with the hut coming into view after about 20 minutes, as you round a final, rocky bluff. The path descends briefly on the far side of the rocks, to reach PD Risnjak itself in another 5 minutes.

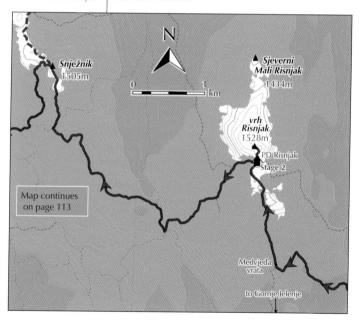

Map continues on page 113

PD Risnjak (1418m; also known as Schlosserov dom; staffed May–October; 43 beds; food and drinks; JU NP Risnjak, Crni Lug; unstaffed shelter open all year) was originally known as Schlosserov dom after the botanist Josip Schlosser (1808–1882). It sits perched on a grassy saddle, below the dwarf mountain pine- and juniper-clad peak of Risnjak itself, with forested slopes dropping away on either side. There is a well behind the hut, and a sklonište (just inside the main door) is open through the winter, when the hut itself is closed.

Follow the path behind the hut, ascending steeply through dwarf mountain pine and scrambling over rock, with views back down over the hut and saddle, and passing a sinkhole on the right, to reach the summit, **vrh Risnjak** (1528m), in 15 minutes. ▶ Descend to the **hut**.

Trail signs, Risnjak national park

The views from vrh Risnjak are fantastic, with Snježnik clearly visible to the northwest, and the sea beyond.

STAGE 2
PD Risnjak – PD Hahlić via Snježnik and Platak

Start	PD Risnjak
Finish	PD Hahlić
Distance	19–21km (11.8–13 miles)
Total ascent	280m (919ft)
Total descent	610m (2001ft)
Time	7hr
Terrain	Forest trails and 4WD roads
Maximum altitude	1506m (vrh Snježnik)
Accommodation	PD Hahlić; Veliki Planinarski dom Platak

Today's route takes us over another beautiful peak, Snježnik, before continuing beyond the boundaries of the national park, through the large clearing at Platak, and along forest roads and trails to Hahlić, on the slopes above the coast.

This is quite a long stage, mainly because the hut on Snježnik (PD Snježnik) – a lovely place, which provided the best spot to stop for the night and break it into two stages – was destroyed several years ago, and has yet to be rebuilt (or even the wreckage of the old hut removed). It's still possible to split the stage into two, with an overnight at the privately run Veliki Planinarski dom Platak, although the location is less spectacular than the old Snježnik hut.

From **PD Risnjak**, follow the Lazac sign and descend NW into the forest on a rocky path to reach a junction in 10 minutes. Continue straight ahead, sign-posted Platak (not right to Lazac), winding through beech trees and over rocks and tree roots to reach the forest road in a further 35 minutes. Turn right onto this, before turning left onto a clearly marked track to Snježnik. Descend through a grassy clearing, then ascend again on a broad forest track, ignoring tracks branching off to the right but turning left as you descend from the crest of a small ridge to reach a T-junction 1 hour from the forest road. Turn right and

follow the signs to Snježnik, before branching off to the left on a rocky path. This brings you out of the trees and up over a grassy knoll, with views east back to Risnjak and southwest to Platak and the sea. Continue along the ridge, following the path and scrambling up over rock to reach **vrh Snježnik** (1506m), 2 hours from PD Risnjak, from where you look directly down onto the ruins of the hut that once stood here.

Trail just below the summit of Snježnik

Variants
A trail leads NW along the ridge from Snježnik, to **Guslica** (1490m), around 45 minutes away; and from there to **Planina** (1425m) and Jelenc (1442m), an additional 2hr walk. These will be too far to reach if you plan to continue all the way to Hahlić as described in one day, and the trail along the ridge is not always clear. However, if you're intending to stay in Platak, Jelenc would make a worthwhile sidetrip, and can be reached from the 4WD road N of Platak in 2hr 45min.

Descend SW from vrh Snježnik, steeply and into the forest, following the signs to Platak to reach a forest track. Take the left fork and you'll arrive at a T-junction, 25 mintes from **vrh Snježnik**. Turn right, then right again

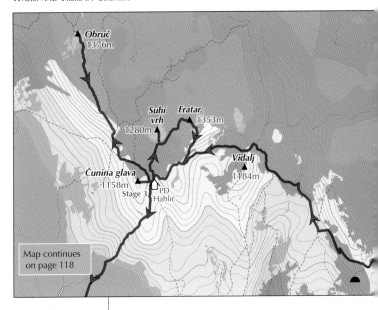

Map continues on page 118

onto a forest road before immediately turning off to the left on another path. Continue down through thick forest, crossing the forest road once more and following the trail markings to reach the road, with **Veliki planinarski dom Platak** beyond, 45 minutes from the hut.

> Veliki Planinarski dom Platak (1100m; 93 beds; food served; www.dom-platak.com) is a large, privately run 'hut', beside the road on the edge of the clearing.

Turn right through the playing fields in front of the hut, keeping parallel to the road and passing a succession of football pitches and ski lifts. You will soon emerge into a second open clearing. Continue straight ahead, then join a broad track entering the forest at the far end of the clearing. This leads to a T-junction in 20 minutes; turn left (there is a small 'H' for Hahlić) before veering

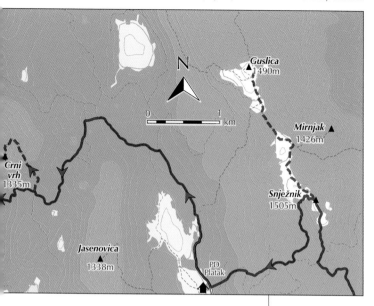

right. Shortly after this, turn onto a path on your left, which soon rejoins the forest road, followed by a path to the right (marked Klek/Hahlić), which again brings you back onto the road. Follow this to the right to reach a crossroads.

To climb Crni vrh

From the crossroads you can make a slight detour, time permitting, to climb **Crni vrh** ('black peak', 1335m) before descending to a small forestry hut, turning left and rejoining the forest road. The approach to Crni vrh is through forest but the summit itself is quite rocky and has good views. Allow an additional 30 minutes.

Continue straight ahead from the crossroads, passing a junction with the other end of the Crni vrh trail in 15 minutes, where you turn left. After a few more minutes, you'll reach a path on the right to Hahlić. Strike out on

113

the Hahlić path, descending through thick undergrowth before emerging into an open, grassy dell. Cut across the side of this, following the now frequent trail markings, to gain the top of a ridge, which is followed to the right. Continue straight ahead, passing a trail on the left to Gogor and a **cave**, and re-entering low forest cover with the sea visible through the trees to the left. After 15 minutes, you will emerge onto an open hill slope, which you should descend, passing two concrete wells with views of the sea and the island of Krk on the left. Turn right at the bottom of the slope, following the signs to Obruč and Hahlić painted on an old concrete trough. Veer left on the lower of two paths and then turn right to gain a broad, leafy forest track. Follow this, turning left after 5 minutes and continuing to a junction, 30 minutes beyond the concrete wells, from where a trail on the right goes to Grleš and Gornik.

The prominent peak ahead of you is Obruč.

Turn left, ignoring the first path on the right but turning onto the second to emerge onto an open, grassy hillside, 15 minutes from the junction. ◄

Here, you have the choice of either continuing straight to the hut in 20 minutes, or ascending over **Fratar** (the peak above you on the right) and **Suhi vrh** beyond, to reach PD Hahlić in roughly 90 minutes. (Those wishing to follow the latter option should ascend on the path to the right to the top of Fratar before following the recommended excursion described below in reverse. Note, however, that both peaks can be reached from the hut without carrying a full pack.)

Continue straight ahead, descending over a rocky saddle into the trees, and veering left on the clear trail to **PD Hahlić**.

PD Hahlić (sleeps 40; weekends only; PD Obruč. Jelenje) sits at the edge of the forest at 1097m. If you find it full, there is some flat ground up on the saddle for a tent. The sound of bells is not goats or cattle, as you might expect, but horses, which come to shelter in the forest at night. The name Hahlić comes from the local dialect for *lokva* (meaning

'puddle'), and refers to the old wells in the vicinity
of the hut.

A quick ascent of Čunina glava

You can get a good preliminary view of the surrounding
terrain by scrambling up **Čunina glava**, the small peak to
the west of the hut, which can be climbed in 5 minutes.
From this surprisingly windy spot there is a full panorama
of the Kvarner Gulf, with Opatija and Učka (1401m,
Route 5) towering beyond (SW); the island of Krk and
the bridge to it from the mainland (SE); Velika Kapela (SE,
Route 13); and closer at hand the hilly Fratar (NE); and
the obvious trail leading up the ridge to **Obruč** (N).

Excursion from PD Hahlić:
Suhi vrh and Fratar

Start/finish	PD Hahlić
Distance	4km (2.5 miles)
Time	2hr 15min
Terrain	Easy–moderate. Some scrambling over boulders
Maximum altitude	1353m (4439ft)

Backtrack through the forest from PD Hahlić (or continue from the base of Čunina glava – the path forms a
loop and brings you back round to the hut). Initially, you
should follow the signs to Obruč before turning off to the
right on a path to Fratar and Suhi vrh. After 15 minutes,
take a track on the left to **Suhi vrh** ('dry peak'). There is
no trail as such, but it is an easy 15 minutes up to the top
(1280m), scrambling over large boulders and loose scree
for good views of Obruč and Fratar.

   Descend by the same route and continue on the main
trail towards **Fratar** ('the friar' or 'the Franciscan'), bearing
right and ascending, to emerge on the open, rocky slopes

beneath the summit. From here, it is 15 minutes to the top, following a clearly marked trail, with little scree.

The summit of **Fratar** (1353m) commands extensive views, which improve slightly from the high ground beyond the summit record box. Snježnik lies almost due east, with Risnjak just visible behind it; Guslica, with the old JNA base on top of it, lies slightly north of these; and the smaller peaks of Klek and Crni vrh are visible in the heavily forested middle ground. Perhaps the most prominent landmark, however, is the large and steep-sided peak a few degrees west of north. This is Snežnik (note the different spelling), much higher at 1797m and actually in Slovenia.

You could extend the excursion by heading north on a trail between Fratar and Suhi vrh to visit the area known as Pakleno ('hell'), with its impressive karst formations, in particular Južno Pakleno (1305m).

Descend and return to PD Hahlić by the same route. Alternatively, descend ESE to rejoin the main path from Snježnik, and continue from there. ◄

Excursion from PD Hahlić: Obruč

Start/finish	PD Hahlić
Distance	5km (3.1 miles)
Time	3hr
Terrain	Easy walking on clear paths
Maximum altitude	1376m (4514ft)

Edelweiss can sometimes be found among the remarkably rich flora of this area.

A clear trail heads north from below Čunina glava, passing an alternative route down to Podkilavac, and following the ridge crest to reach the summit of **Obruč** (1376m) in 90 minutes. There's a marble cross on the summit, and chamois can sometimes be seen wandering on the northern slopes of Obruč. ◄

Descend to PD Hahlić by the same route.

STAGE 3
PD Hahlić – Dražice

Start	PD Hahlić
Finish	PD Dražice
Distance	7.5km (4.7 miles)
Total ascent	5m (16ft)
Total descent	800m (2625ft)
Time	2hr
Terrain	Easy paths on open hillsides and some road walking
Maximum altitude	1097m (PD Hahlić)

Descend over the broad, open slopes below PD Hahlić, following the red-and-white-striped poles and the signs to Dražice and Podkilavac. Take the left fork of this trail (signposted 'Podkilavac preko Čeke'). Enjoy the clear views of Velika Kapela to the southeast. The impressive ridge of exposed rock and forested slopes in the middle ground comprises the peaks Kuk, Hus and Vela Peša. Cross a track before entering sparse, low oak and beech, then join a major track and turn right (again signposted 'Dražice/Podkilavac'). Descend steeply through the forest. Cross a forest road before emerging into a clearing, 90 minutes from the hut, where the path levels.

Following the Podkilavac signs, you should continue on a broad track, veering right and passing the road from Platak (via Mudna dol). Continue past a rubbish dump before veering left and continuing straight ahead through a junction of various tracks. Cross a small, dry streambed to reach the sealed road, where you should turn left. Follow the trail markings, passing some houses and turning left into a shady lane, before turning right again and passing through the small village of **Podkilavac**. Turn left onto a clearly marked path, soon rejoining the road before crossing over the bridge and following the road around the corner to the village of **Dražice**, which you should reach in a few minutes.

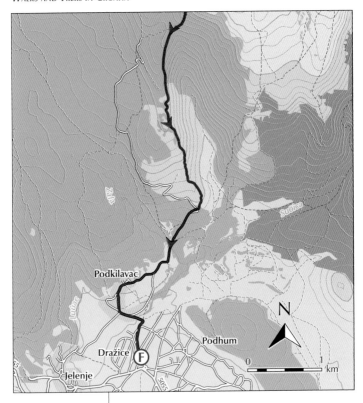

Buses leave for Rijeka (11km away) from the large 'Dražice' sign before the village (buses 14 and 16; for timetables see www.autotrolej.hr).

ROUTE 10

Vražji prolaz ('the devil's throat')
and Zeleni vir

Start/finish	Skrad railway station
Distance	6.5km (4 miles)
Total ascent/descent	405m (1329ft)
Time	2hr 30min
Terrain	Good, clear forest paths; several sections on metal walkways and bridges on the descent, which can be slippery after rain
Maximum altitude	650m (Skrad railway station)
Maps	SMAND covers the area on Gorski kotar III (13)
Refreshments	There's a mountain hut, Planinarski Dom Zeleni vir, at the base of the walk, serving food though opening times vary seasonally.
Transport	Skrad is on the Zagreb–Rijeka railway line (journey time from Zadar 2hr 30min, timetables at www.hzpp.hr/en).

Below the small town of Skrad, around 12km east from Delnice, there's a deep canyon known as Vražji prolaz, meaning 'The Devil's Passage' – it's about 2km long, and in places as little as 2m wide. You can walk down to the canyon entrance from the train station, then descend a steep, spectacular trail (often by way of walkways and metal bridges) to the bottom, where there's a mountain hut and restaurant, and the end of an asphalt road leading up to Skrad. You can then vary your return by following a forest trail up past a beautiful waterfall, called Zeleni vir. Entry to Vražji prolaz costs 7Kn – you can buy a ticket at the Tourist Information Office in Skrad, or when you reach the small ticket office at the end of the route, by the car park.

From the railway station in Skrad, follow the road S alongside the **tracks** a short distance, then turn right and cross the railway tracks, and begin following a trail downhill. Bear right on a 4X4 track (marked 'u prolaz') then left and downhill on a marked trail. This brings you to a

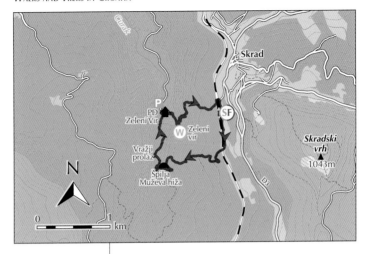

The trail on the left leads to the source of the River Kupa (see Route 8) in 3hr 15min.

junction, 25 minutes from the railway station, where you turn right (marked 'Vražji prolaz'). ◄ Follow the roped path downhill, passing a cave on your right called **Špilja Muževa hiža**.

It is said that once upon a time **Špilja Muževa hiža** was used by locals as a place of refuge from the Ottomans – there's a large chamber inside, around 200m beyond the cave entrance, with a small lake. More recently, speleologists have found the olm (*Proteus anguinus*) in the cave. The name Muževa hiža means 'the husband's house'.

Continue down to a bridge and a small shelter. Beyond this, the trail continues down through the narrow, rocky canyon of **Vražji prolaz** itself via a series of steps, metal walkways and bridges – possibly above a dry streambed, possibly above a roaring vortex of water, depending on the season. The trail then follows the left bank of the streambed, to reach the ticket office, **mountain hut** (Planinarski Dom Zeleni vir) and car park, 1 hour from the railway station.

Planinarski Dom Zeleni vir serves food (**www.jasle. hr/planinarski-dom.php**; grilled meat, some vegetarian dishes, grah, gulaš). Otherwise, there are wooden tables and benches opposite if you want to stop for a picnic.

Follow a trail E from the mountain hut and the hydro-electric power plant (built in 1921, the first in Gorski kotar) above the left bank of the stream, marked *vodapad* and Skrad. The path goes uphill, then descends to a bridge over a weir. Follow the turbine pipe then at the junction bear right to reach **Zeleni vir**, 20 minutes from the car park. ▶

Return to the junction and bear right (marked Skrad) on a trail that zigzags uphill through the forest. Around 40 minutes from Zeleni vir, you'll pass a trail on your right to Jasle. After a further 10 minutes, cross the railway track to reach the railway station in **Skrad**.

Descending through Vražji prolaz

The waterfall plunges down a cliff and in front of the mouth of a large cave, into the green pool from which it gets its name (*zeleni* means green).

ROUTE 11
Burnji Bitoraj

Start/finish	Vrata
Distance	13.5km (8.4 miles)
Total ascent/descent	705m (2313ft)
Time	4hr 30min
Terrain	4x4 tracks and good, clearly marked forest trails
Maximum altitude	1366m (vrh Bitoraj)
Maps	SMAND (12) Gorski kotar II (1:30:000)
Refreshments	A couple of cafés in Vrata (Café Furman is opposite the access road to the railway station)
Transport	Buses between Zagreb and Rijeka stop in Fužine (1hr 45min from Zagreb), and (on request, just after turning off the motorway) in Vrata (timetables for both at www. autotrans.hr). Trains between Zagreb and Rijeka stop at Vrata (www.hzpp.hr/en). The station is tiny, a short platform and not much else; to get to the start of the route, follow the narrow road W from the station to the main road and turn left to where a road on the left crosses the railway tracks.

A well-marked route leads from the village of Vrata on the edge of Fužine, to the summit of Bitoraj, called Burni Bitoraj or vrh Bitoraj. Apart from a small rocky area at the summit, most of the peak is forested (including one side of the summit), so it doesn't quite have the unrestricted views offered by Risnjak and other peaks in Risnjak National Park – however, it's a lovely walk up, and the rocks at the top make a great picnic spot, with a lovely airy view down over Mrkopalj. Unlike Risnjak, Bitoraj is little known outside Croatian hiking circles, so you're unlikely to find the trails crowded.

From the main road S of the railway station in Vrata, follow the minor road E across the **railway tracks** to reach a junction by a prominent forestry sign ('Hrvatske šume šumarija Fužine'), which encouragingly warns you that

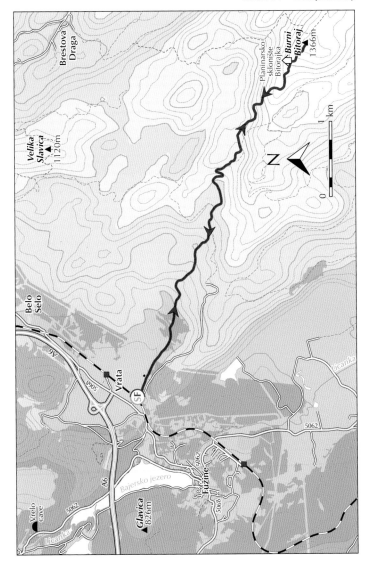

you are entering bear territory ('Oprez! Područje med-vjeda'). Take the left fork, passing an adventure play-ground and paintball centre on your left, then go past a timber yard, after which the 4X4 road continues between open pastures. Keep more or less SE, ignoring any tracks leading off to the left and right, and you will pass a hunt-er's cabin on your left.

Around 35 minutes from the main road in Vrata, go straight ahead off the 4X4 road onto a broad track (the 4X4 road swings left at this point), and follow this uphill. ◄ The track becomes a little rockier and steeper further on, then just over 10 minutes after leaving the 4X4 road, you will reach another 4X4 road, onto which you should turn left. You will reach a junction in another 10 minutes. Here, take the 4X4 road on the right.

After another 30 minutes, leave the 4X4 road and take a marked path on your left. The path ascends through forest, gradually at first then a little more steeply, but it is clearly marked throughout. Around 40 minutes after leaving the 4X4 road, you will reach a shoulder where you should turn left to follow a sometimes faint and a little overgrown path, initially on the far (S) side of the broad, wooded ridge, then along the top of it. Walk for 15 minutes to reach a clearing, with **Planinarsko sklonište Bitorajka**, a small wooden mountain hut at around 1300m, on the far side.

> Planinarsko sklonište Bitorajka (unstaffed) sleeps 10 and is open all year. You'll need your own sleeping bag and food if you wish to stay here. Water can be collected from the cistern next to the hut.

A clearly marked path leads steeply uphill from beside the hut, to reach the summit of **Burni Bitoraj** (vrh Bitoraj, 1366m) in 15 minutes (2hr 30min from Vrata).

> The alternative name of **vrh Bitoraj**, Burni Bitoraj, is a reference to its exposure to blustery winds (*burni* means turbulent). There are good views NE from the summit rocks, to the village of Mrkopalj (Route 13).

In early 2018 there were several fallen trees in this area, following exceptionally bad storms.

A path on the far (SE) side of vrh Bitoraj descends to join the Via Dinarica, which at this point follows the GPP or Goranski planinarski put, and leads NE towards Tuk.

Descend from Burni Bitoraj to **Vrata** by the same route (allow 2hr).

Burnji Bitoraj summit

125

ROUTE 12

Bajersko jezero and
Vrelo cave

Start/finish	Fužine Tourist Office
Distance	6km (3.7 miles)
Total ascent/descent	170m (558ft)
Time	1hr 20min
Terrain	Level concrete track
Maximum altitude	738m
Maps	Not required
Refreshments	Hotel Bitoraj in Fužine

A short and very easy lakeside stroll, following one side of Bajersko jezero, with an opportunity to visit the impressive Vrelo Cave (open daily in the summer, weekends only for the rest of the year, 1–5pm; entry 30Kn; www. tz-fuzine.hr then click Sights, followed by Attractions). The cave is quite cool inside (8°C year round), so take a light fleece.

Turn left from the tourist office in Fužine, then left past the bus station and follow the asphalt road N past the dam and alongside the **lake**. A couple of minutes after the dam, follow some steps down to the lakeside and continue along a broad, concrete path, which contours the E side of the lake.

Bajersko jezero (Lake Bajer) is a man-made lake created in the 1950s when the River Ličanka was dammed. Part of the Vinodol Hydroelectric Power network, it's also a popular fishing spot, well-stocked with trout and pike. A viaduct carries the Zagreb–Rijeka motorway across the lake.

Around 30 minutes from the tourist office, follow a ramp up to the main road, and turn left on this for around

200m to reach the entrance to the **Vrelo Cave** on your right.

Vrelo Cave (Špilja Vrelo) is one of the most impressive caves open to the public in Croatia. Formed between 3.5 and 4 million years ago, it was discovered only quite recently in the 1950s, during the construction of Lake Bajer. A well-lit, level concrete

View from the footpath beside Bajersko jezero, looking towards Fužine

path stretches for around 250m in the interior, passing plenty of stalactites and stalagmites, to a spring at the far end of the cave (the cave often floods after heavy rain).

Return from the cave to Fužine by the same route.

ROUTE 13

Bjelolasica, Bijele stijene and
Samarske stijene trek

Start	PD Tuk
Finish	Jasenak
Distance	28–33km (17.4–20.5 miles)
Total ascent	1070m (3510ft)
Total descent	1360m (4462ft)
Time	4–5 days
Maps	SMAND covers the area in a single sheet: Bjelolasica (11b). The new Samarske Bijele stijene Bjelolasica (11a) sheet is excellent for detailed coverage of the MPP and the route across Bijele stijene, though it does not cover the relevant area of Bjelolasica. These two sheets have now largely replaced the older Gorski kotar I (11) sheet.
Transport	From Delnice, take the local Mrkopalj bus from the main bus station (one bus a day at 2.15pm, 30min, timetables at www.autotrans.hr). Alternatively, take a train from Delnice to Lokve, from where it's another 9km to walk or hitch SE along the road to Mrkopalj. Or take an intercity bus from Delnice towards Lokve or Fužine as far as the turn-off to Mrkopalj, which is on the left (but make sure it's going on the main road and not the motorway, or it won't stop at the Mrkopalj turnoff). If you need to hitch from Delnice, try from just outside town on the main road (SW, uphill). Take the road on the right after the post office (signposted to Tuk and Matić poljana), then the (main) road left to Tuk, which is a further 3km. The large new hut (Planinarski dom Bijele stijene u Tuku, or simply PD Tuk) is on the right. There is no public transport from Jasenak at the end of the route, meaning you'll need to arrange a taxi or hitch.
Accommodation	Planinarski dom Bijele stijene u Tuku; Planinarska kuća Jančarica; Planinarsko sklonište Jakob Mihelčić; Ratkovo sklonište; Planinarska kuća Dragutin Hirc; Planinarsko sklonište Miroslav Hirtz

Note	Mrkopalj is a small village with one or two shops where you can stock up on a few very basic supplies, but it's better to get everything you need in Zagreb/Rijeka or Delnice.

The following itinerary, covering the area of Gorski kotar known as Velika Kapela ('great chapel'), includes the highest peak in the massif (Kula, 1534m, on Bjelolasica) and the spectacular limestone scenery of Bijele stijene and Samarske stijene. The route follows sections of the Mrkopaljski planinarski put (MPP) and Kapelski planinarski put (KPP), including the section of the latter known as Vihoraški put. Generally straightforward, the section of Vihoraški put between Bijele and Samarske stijene known as Ljuska ('shell' or 'eggshell') does, however, involve some more demanding scrambling with the aid of pegs, cables and ladders. Further scrambling is necessary for vrh Bijele stijene (1334m), and sections of the recommended excursion from Ratkovo sklonište (the MPP). Accommodation is provided by some well-placed sklonište and planinarska kuća, and Ratkovo sklonište in particular is one of the nicest (and most popular) in Croatia. The route is divided into four stages, but it could be completed in three.

TRANSPORT

Unfortunately there is no longer any public transport from Jasenak, at the end of this trek, so you may find it easier to retrace your steps from Planinarska kuća Dragutin Hirc to Ratkovo sklonište and then instead of crossing the 4X4 road beyond this towards Planinarsko sklonište Jakob Mihelčić, turn left along the 4X4 and follow it to Planinarski dom Bijele stijene u Tuku. Otherwise, from Jasenak you'll either have to arrange a taxi (which is difficult from here without speaking some Croatian, so I'd advise arranging this in advance through the Ogulin Tourist Office www.tz-grada-ogulina.hr), or you'll need to hitchhike to Ogulin or Bjelsko. You may opt to spend the final night on Klek (Route 14), which can be reached in 1 hour from Bjelsko.

STAGE 1
PD Tuk – Planinarsko sklonište Jakob Mihelčić

Start	PD Tuk
Finish	Planinarsko sklonište Jakob Mihelčić
Distance	8km (5 miles)
Total ascent	680m (2231ft)
Total descent	80m (262ft)
Time	3hr 30min
Terrain	Forest trails and 4WD roads
Maximum altitude	1460m (4790ft)
Accommodation	Planinarski dom Bijele stijene u Tuku; Planinarska kuća Jančarica; Planinarsko sklonište Jakob Mihelčić

This trek begins with an easy stage, some of it along 4X4 tracks, and finishes at a small shelter just below the highest point on Velika kapela

Planinarski dom Bijele stijene u Tuku (875m; sleeps 54; food and drinks; contact Radojka Matijašić +385 (0)99 8401 998) has hot showers and meals. PD Tuk makes a good place to stop if you've arrived late or have already spent several days slogging across Gorski kotar.

Turn right from **PD Tuk**, walking uphill and east on the main road, and then branching right onto a smaller road to rejoin the main road at a bend in 5 minutes. Follow the trail markings on a telegraph pole, which lead up over a grass verge, passing a house on the left. Continue on a clearly marked trail, south-southeast across a grassy slope, to gain a rocky path running along the edge of the trees and then an unsealed road 15 minutes from the hut. Cross this, following the sign to **Matić poljana** and gradually ascending to emerge into the open onto an unsealed road after 10 minutes. Take the left fork of this, signposted to Bjelolasica, Bijele stijene and Samarske stijene.

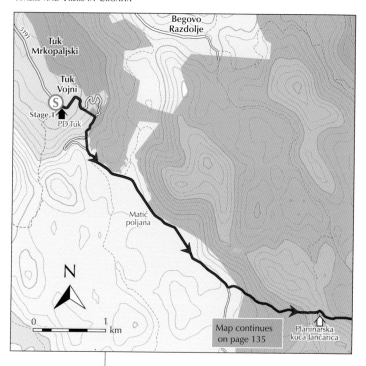

Map continues on page 135

This is Matić poljana ('Matić fields'), where 24 partisans froze to death one night during World War 2 – an event commemorated by the 24 standing stones that appear on the right after around 5 minutes.

Continue past level, grassy fields, surrounded by mixed forest and pine and strewn with flowers. ◄ Continue straight ahead, passing a memorial plaque and a road to Begovo Razdolje on the left. After around 1 hour, turn left onto a track at the end of the fields, signposted to Bjelolasica and Janjčarica, passing a watchtower used for hunting, and continuing straight ahead (not left) on a broad, overgrown track. There are no signs at first, but you will soon see arrows and trail markings on various rocks and stones, when you enter the trees and ascend to rejoin the forest road after 5 minutes.

Turn right onto this, following the signs and ascending gradually, and staying on the road as it switches back to the left. (There is, theoretically, a more direct path up

through the trees, but it was difficult to find on my visit.) **Planinarska kuća Jančarica** is on the right, opposite the (at this end, clearly visible) path coming up through the trees on the left, around 35 minutes from the end of Matić poljana.

Standing stones at Matić poljana

> Planinarska kuća Jančarica (1239m; sleeps 12; open by prior arrangement only; HPD Bijele stijene, Mrkopalj) will be locked unless you've made prior arrangements to stay there. There is also a *sklonište*, but this is rather run-down and best avoided except in emergencies. Still, this makes a fine spot for lunch, with picnic tables and tantalising views almost due east to Bjelolasica from the saddle. There is a well to the left of the *sklonište*.

Descend east following the path at the back of the hut (on the path to Bjelolasica, not the one to Bijele and Samarske stijene), meeting a track joining from the left and continuing on a broad forest road towards the base of Bjelolasica. Pass an open area of rolling grassland and large limestone boulders on the left, veering left and following the KPP signs. Ignore the first, but take the second turn on the right, following the sign to Bjelolasica, 15 minutes from Janjčarica. Follow the trail markings, turning left after 5 minutes onto a broad forest path, then left onto a forest road, and left again onto a rutted track. This narrows and ascends, veering left once more to become a path, before rejoining the forest road. Turn left onto this, then immediately right, again following the sign to Bjelolasica and ascending steeply through the trees. Cross over one more forest track (this one apparently disused) to reach a path on the left to the *vrh* (summit), an hour beyond Janjčarica.

Rather than taking your full pack to the summit, continue (right) past this for another 20 minutes to emerge into a clearing with **Planinarsko sklonište Jakob Mihelčić** nestled below the ridge crest.

> At Planinarsko sklonište Jakob Mihelčić (1460m; sleeps 12; HPD Ina Bjelolasica, Zagreb), you will undoubtedly notice the countless sticks and branches plugging any gaps in the wooden ceiling – this is an attempt to keep out the resident *puh* (dormouse). It usually finds a way in anyway, so hang all food bags well out of reach.

Excursion from Planinarsko Sklonište
Jakob Mihelčić: vrh Bjelolasica

Start/finish	Planinarsko Sklonište Jakob Mihelčić
Distance	1km (0.6 miles)
Time	40min
Terrain	Clear, easy path
Maximum altitude	1534m (Kula)

Leave your full pack at Planinarsko sklonište Jakob Mihelčić, then ascend behind it to the junction and turn left onto the trail marked 'Bjelolasica'. Follow the clear trail markings and scramble along the right (N) side of the ridge. On reaching the first high point, you will be confronted by the unlikely sight of a football pitch with goal

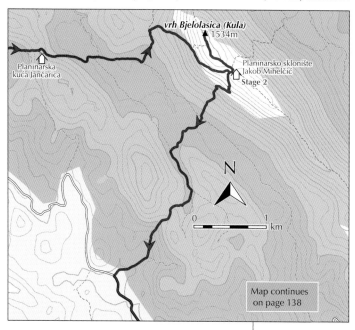

posts in the flat area below you on the right, while Bijele stijene and Samarske stijene are clearly visible to the left. Pass the track coming up from the left (marked 'Tuk') to

Bjelolasica

reach **vrh Bjelolasica** (1534m, also called Kula, meaning 'tower' or 'fortress'), 20 minutes from the *sklonište*.

Vrh Bjelolasica boasts impressive views. The rock tower to the NE is Klek, while to the E the ridge stretches back towards Gomirkovica. Bijele stijene and Samarske stijene are visible to the SE (Samarske stijene, your next destination, is on the right), although the best view of them is from the first high point on the ridge above the improvised football pitch. Janjčarica nestles in a notch in the ridge to the SW, while Snježnik and Risnjak are visible in the distance beyond this.

Continue straight ahead for 5 minutes to see where Croatian climbers trained for an Everest expedition (Staza hrvatskih Himalajaca), over the rocks descending to your right.

Descend to the *sklonište* by the same route. ◄

STAGE 2
Planinarsko sklonište Jakob Mihelčić – Ratkovo sklonište

Start	Planinarsko sklonište Jakob Mihelčić
Finish	Ratkovo sklonište
Distance	9km (5.6 miles)
Total ascent	110m (361ft)
Total descent	490m (1608ft)
Time	3hr 30min
Terrain	Forest trails and 4WD roads
Maximum altitude	1460m (4790ft)
Accommodation	Ratkovo sklonište

It should be pointed out that there is another route (more interesting looking, at least on paper) via Gomirkovica. However, this in reality takes you through a jungle of low mountain pine and juniper, which makes progress impossibly slow and shreds your legs. Unless the path has been cleared, the route described below remains preferable.

Descend from Planinarsko sklonište Jakob Mihelčić, following the clearly marked path at the bottom of the clearing, signposted 'KPP Samarske stijene'. It's 35 minutes down to the forest road, which you should cross onto a rutted track, which is sometimes overgrown but clearly marked and again signposted 'KPP Samarske stijene'. In a further 25 minutes, this leads to another forest road – turn left, as signposted. Turn right after 5 minutes and then descend right on an overgrown path (marked 'Okruglica', if you can find the sign) through a dell. This brings you out into a large, open, grassy clearing, which the road you have just followed skirts to the left. Cross the clearing, and head roughly southwest aiming for the red-and-white marker pole, taking care to avoid the surrounding depressions which disguise sinkholes. The path is faint and ascends at the opposite side of the clearing.

> The surrounding bushes are laden with **blueberries** (*borovnice*) in the summer, making this an attractive destination for the local brown bear population and for hunters (there is another hunting tower at the end of the track beyond the clearing). Locals collect the blueberries to sell.

Ascend southwest from the clearing, passing a small shelter on the left and enter the trees. The winding path is overgrown with brambles, but faint trail markings descend alongside a steep gully, veering slightly left at the bottom of this (not straight ahead) to cut across a streambed and pass through a small clearing. Continue on an open forest track, taking the right fork of this to reach a road 30 minutes beyond the blueberries. The route here is unclear. Do not continue straight ahead as indicated (a signpost reads 'Ratkovo sklonište and Samarske stijene', but there is no path). Instead, turn left and follow the road for 20 minutes, turning right at the nature reserve sign and following the signpost to Ratkovo sklonište and Samarske stijene.

Turn left off this after 5 minutes (marked 'KPP', as opposed to the route ahead marked 'MPP': these

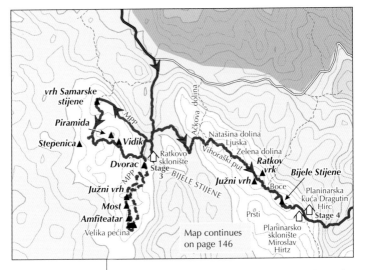

Map continues on page 146

abbreviations, sometimes used interchangeably on the same route, can be a little confusing at first). Ascend, sometimes steeply, through the forest, passing a request to carry up some firewood if you're arriving in the winter. Around 20 minutes from the road, pass a path to the left, marked 'Vihoraški put' and 'Ljuska', which marks the onward route from Ratkovo sklonište.

Continue straight ahead past this, passing some outcrops of rock and descending briefly as you pass tracks on the right marked 'MPP' and 'Samarske stijene'. Re-ascend over rocky ground, coming round a large rock outcrop to find **Ratkovo sklonište** nestled in a large cave below, 30 minutes from the road.

Ratkovo sklonište (1174m; sleeps 12; PDS Velebit, Zagreb) is a small but extremely popular mountain shelter, in a beautiful setting, which many Croatian hikers describe as their favourite mountain hut. Named after Ratko Čapek, a climber from PDS Velebit who was killed in the Alps, Ratkovo sklonište was built in 1982, after the original (built

The extremely popular Ratkovo sklonište

in 1952) burnt down in a fire. Due to the number of visitors it attracts (especially at weekends, when it has not been unknown for a whole busload of people to turn up), there is now a small charge for staying here at weekends. It had to be closed for renovation in 2008/9, having been left in an appalling condition by a succession of unscrupulous hikers.

There is a water pump below the balcony and a remarkably fearless local *lisica* (fox), usually game enough to try stealing your food while you eat it. You would be advised to keep the door of the hut closed to keep the fox out.

Excursion from Ratkovo sklonište:
vrh Samarske stijene

Start/finish	Ratkovo sklonište
Distance	4km (2.5 miles)
Time	3hr
Terrain	Moderate to difficult – a clear but convoluted path through the forest with some scrambling (some of the latter can be avoided, making it just a moderate rating)
Maximum altitude	1302m (4272ft)

Although this circular route could be completed before continuing to Bijele stijene (see Stage 3) on the same day, most people will find this a pleasant enough trip to occupy the rest of the day (particularly if the route is extended), and will want to spend another night at Ratkovo sklonište.

See map on page 138

Bijele stijene is visible to the east, while more of the area's limestone towers crowd the slopes to the southeast, surrounded by pine.

From Ratkovo sklonište retrace your steps as far as the turn-off (now on the left) to Samarske stijene. Follow this path, continuing straight ahead on the route marked 'vrh' (KPP) and passing a track on the left (marked 'MPP') by which you will return. The path ascends steadily, squeezing up through a cleft between two rock outcrops and passing the words '*Još malo!*' ('a bit further!') painted on a rock. Scramble straight ahead up the rock beyond this (passing a path on the right marked 'MPP Ratkovo sklonište') to reach the summit, **vrh Samarske stijene** (1302m), 40 minutes from the hut. ◄

Return to the MPP trail, now on the left, a few minutes below the summit. This descends steeply before veering left, where signs mark the route to Ratkovo sklonište. In 15 minutes, you'll reach a path is reached, which ascends to the right to **Stepenica** (1280m). The route up this appropriately named peak (*stepenica* means 'staircase') spirals clockwise, via a single peg, to a summit register in 5 minutes, before the final scramble to the *kapa* ('cap'), which perches, beret-like, atop a limestone tower. This final section to the kapa is technically more difficult than anything else on this route, and most walkers may want to content themselves with getting to the summit register.

Descend to the main trail, turn right and continue, following the sign towards Piramida. The path ascends, winding around limestone stacks and towers, to reach **Piramida** (1270m) in 15 minutes. Technically easier than Stepenica, it has good views back over the terrain you have covered.

Return to the main track, continuing along this and descending into a dell before re-ascending to the right of a large rock outcrop. Descend and re-ascend once more, scrambling to a junction 20 minutes beyond Piramida, with clear views back to vrh Samarske stijene. A path to the left leads to the top of Vidik in 5 minutes, climbing anticlockwise for good views from the peak. A further 10 minutes along the main path (signposted *kuća*), you will come to the first of two possible onward routes. The path leading off to the right, marked *teže* ('more difficult'), goes through Veliki kanjon ('great canyon'), while that path straight ahead, marked *lakše* ('easier'), bypasses this.

The canyon is definitely worth seeing; and the more difficult section is confined to its lower reaches. If you find it too much of a hurdle (it is something of a scramble), return to the main path and continue for 5 minutes to a second path on the right (marked 'Veliki kanjon', and from where you will emerge if you have climbed up from the bottom). This will take you into the top of the canyon. From here, you can clamber down for a look, before returning to the main path.

After a further 5 minutes, you will reach another junction.

To extend the route

By turning right you could extend this itinerary to include a number of other limestone features. This extended version of the MPP goes via **Dvorac**, **Južni vrh**, **Most**, **Amfiteatar**, **Velika pećina** and Medvjeđa dolina before bringing you back to the junction with the main route back to Ratkovo sklonište. It would require an additional 3–4 hours.

Continue straight ahead past the junction, descend through a precariously balanced stone arch and rejoin the track up from Bjelolasica, to reach **Ratkovo sklonište** in 10 minutes.

STAGE 3

Ratkovo sklonište – Planinarska kuća
Dragutin Hirc, via vrh Bijele stijene

Start	Ratkovo sklonište
Finish	Planinarska kuća Dragutin Hirc
Distance	4km (2.5 miles)
Total ascent	270m (886ft)
Total descent	160m (525ft)
Time	4hr
Terrain	A moderately difficult route in places, with good forest trails and some more demanding scrambling with the aid of pegs, cables and ladders
Maximum altitude	1334m (4377m) (vrh Bijele Stijene)
Accommodation	Planinarska kuća Dragutin Hirc; Planinarsko sklonište Miroslav Hirtz

This is a beautiful walk, though slightly more challenging in places, through lush forest with outbursts of spectacular limestone scenery. There are two huts at the end of the route – a *kuća* (open at weekends) and a *sklonište* (open all year), less than 50m apart.

See map on page 138

This section of the KPP is known as Vihoraški put, from vihor, meaning 'strong wind' or 'gale'.

From Ratkovo sklonište, backtrack for 10 minutes along the main path from the road and Bjelolasica, turning right at the turn-off marked **Vihoraški put** and Ljuska onto the **KPP**. ◄ The path winds through the trees, over rocks and round a cliff, roughly NE and veering left where the route becomes less clear. Some 25 minutes from the turn-off, you will pass a track on yout left marked 'Bijele stijene' and 'Ačkova dolina'. Continue straight ahead past this on a route marked 'Natašina dolina' and 'Bijele stijene', descending into a limestone dell after 10 minutes and continuing straight up the other side of this (not left, as signposted, where the old path is blocked by rock-fall). The path is steep as you scramble towards limestone tops and wriggle through a narrow cleft in the rock (a tight fit with a full pack) to reach a junction and pass below impressive blades of rock, 35 minutes from the last turn-off. ▶

Continue straight over the pass, following the trail marked 'Ljuska', descending slightly into **Natašina dolina** before veering right on the lakši put ('easier route') and entering the area known as **Ljuska**. (The 'difficult' route is somewhere off to the left, and should not be considered: in fact, the 'easy' route becomes quite challenging, as you will soon discover.) Steel cables lead round the edge of a steep-sided pit, beyond which you descend a loose, or unbolted, ladder. Ascend a long steel ladder (loose-looking, but bolted at the top) to impressive views of limestone spires. Descend with the aid of steel pegs, keeping right and close to the cliff. Scramble steeply upwards (possibly slippery), ascend over rocks and then descend into forest cover again to reach a clearing 55 minutes beyond the pass. ▶

Continue up over rocks to reach a trail ascending on the right, marked *vrh*, 15 minutes from the clearing. This is not vrh Bijele stijene, but another peak, known as **Južni vrh** (1300m, not to be confused with the Južni vrh on Samarske stijene), which can be reached after some steep and at times rather awkward scrambling.

Continue on the main trail, following the KPP and *kuća* ('house') signs, and passing a trail down towards Jasenak (marked 'Begova staza') after 10 minutes. Walk straight past this, scrambling again and squeezing through another narrow cleft in the rock, and gaining your first view of the impressive limestone spires known as **Prsti** (literally, 'fingers'), 15 minutes beyond the Jasenak trail. This is followed by a trail, descending on the right, marked *kapelica* (chapel) and an alternative route to the summit, also on the right, marked *vrh*. After a few more minutes, you will arrive at the main summit trail on the right, marked *na vrh*.

Dump your pack here and ascend steeply, with the aid of steel cables and pegs, for 5 minutes to vrh Bijele Stijene (1334m). ▶ Another trail descends from the summit to link up with the alternative summit route.

The track to the left is that via Ačkova dolina, which would have added at least half an hour to your itinerary.

Here, the rocks on the left greet you with the following words: *Kako je lijepa moja zelena dolina* or, more familiarly, 'How beautiful is my green valley'.

The views are extensive, with limestone crags to the northwest and, in the distance, Bjelolasica and Klek (NE, Route 14).

View from vrh
Bjele stijene

Descend to the main trail and continue, as indicated, to the hut. The path descends, branching left to arrive, with the aid of more steel cables, at **Planinarska kuća Dragutin Hirc** in 10 minutes.

Planinarska kuća Dragutin Hirc (1280m; sleeps 15; open weekends 15 May–15 Oct; HPD Kapela, Zagreb) stands on the edge of a large clearing. It has picnic tables and a well (beyond which is an alternative route to the summit). Planinarsko sklonište Miroslav Hirtz (1280m; sleeps 30; HPD Kapela, Zagreb) stands on the other side of the clearing, with plenty of beds, and its own fox.

STAGE 4
Planinarska kuća Dragutin Hirc – Jasenak

Start	Planinarska kuća Dragutin Hirc
Finish	Jasenak
Distance	7km (4.3 miles)
Total ascent	10m (33ft)
Total descent	630m (2067ft)
Time	2hr 15min
Terrain	An easy, downhill stage, on 4WD tracks and forest trails
Maximum altitude	1280m (4199ft) (Planinarska kuća Dragutin Hirc)

Unfortunately none of the various ways to descend from Bijele stijene are as convenient or impressive as the route which you have followed from Samarske stijene. The one described here is simply the most straightforward, and also the shortest. The alternative is to return to Tuk as described in the introduction to this walk, or follow the SPP to the coast as described in the following paragraph.

It is possible to continue from Planinarska kuća Dragutin Hirc via Velika Javornica and Kolovratske stijene before descending to the coast just south of Novi Vinodolski, or even continue all the way south to Velebit (Routes 15 and 16), on a route known as the Spojni planinarski put (SPP). While this may sound attractive, it should be added that much of the walking is on roads, and that altogether more spectacular routes await you further south. Furthermore you will doubtless need to get in supplies before an extended walk on Velebit, so would have to head for the coast first anyhow.

From Planinarska kuća Dragutin Hirc take the Jasenak path, passing **Planinarsko sklonište Miroslav Hirtz** and descending through forest, and then the left fork of this (marked 'Klek, Jasenak') to reach the road and car park in 30 minutes. Turn left onto the road, descending for 5 minutes to a bus stop and turn right onto a broad, rutted track. Turn left off this, descending into a gully and follow this downhill (northeast). The trail is poorly marked at first, and the gully choked with felled trees, but the

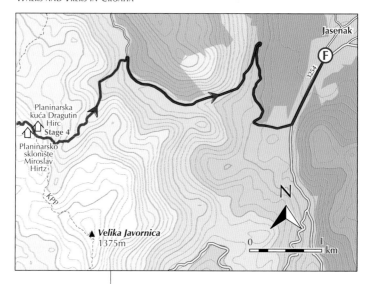

path soon broadens and brings you back onto the road. Follow the road down to the right, ignoring turn-offs to the left. Take one more (poorly marked) shortcut on the right, if you can find it (if not, keep following the road down), to arrive at the main road 2 hours from the hut. Turn left onto this, to reach the largely depopulated village of **Jasenak** in 15 minutes.

Unfortunately there are no longer any buses between Jasenak and Ogulin, so you will need to either call a taxi (arrange this in advance through the Ogulin Tourist Office www.tz-grada-ogulina.hr) to take you to Ogulin (23km) or Bjelsko (12km), or hitch (and there's not much traffic). Contact the Ogulin Tourist Office for more information. (Alternatively, turn right if you intend to try and hitch down towards the coast.) From Bjelsko, you can walk up to Klek in around 1 hour; otherwise, the train from Ogulin will take you back to Delnice and on to Rijeka or back to Zagreb.

ROUTE 14
Klek

Start/finish	Ogulin
Distance	21km (13 miles)
Total ascent/descent	865m (2838ft)
Time	7hr
Terrain	Clearly marked forest trails
Maximum altitude	1182m (3878ft)
Maps	Klek is included on the reverse of SMAND (11b) Bjelolasica (1:25,000)
Transport	Trains between Zagreb and Rijeka stop at Ogulin (2hr from Zagreb, www.hzpp.hr/en); some (but not all) buses running between Zagreb and Rijeka/Istria stop at Ogulin (www.akz.hr). There is no public transport from Ogulin to Bjelsko – if you're coming from Jasenak (Route 13) you'll need to arrange a taxi, or hitch, to Bjelsko (12km).
Accommodation	PD Klek (1000m; sleeps 42; open at weekends; HPD Klek, Ogulin). Due to its popularity, not to mention its relative proximity to Zagreb and ease of access, PD Klek can get quite crowded at weekends, and you might want to phone and book accommodation in advance. There are restaurants and a hotel (www.hotel-frankopan.hr) in Ogulin
Note	If you're following the alternative approach from Bjelsko, there's only one small shop there, which you should rely on only for the most very basic of supplies. Shops in Ogulin are better stocked. Refer to www.tz-grada-ogulina.hr.

Klek, the easternmost peak of Velika kapela, dominates the skyline as you approach Gorski kotar from the north. An impressive tower of limestone protruding above forested slopes, with the two smaller peaks of Klečice ('little Kleks') below, it is one of the most popular destinations for Croatian climbers, and its southwest face has been described as the 'school' of Croatian alpinists. It is the distinctive form of Klek that decorates the logo of the Croatian Mountaineering Association.

This is an easy and straightforward hike from the railway station in Ogulin to the hut (1000m) and summit (1182m) of Klek, following a well-established trail known as Ferdina staza (Ferdo's trail), which can either be walked as a daytrip or spread over two short days with a night in the hut if preferred. The much shorter approach from Bjelsko (included here as an alternative route) is well placed for those heading towards Ogulin from Jasenak at the end of Walk 13, or those with a car to get to Bjelsko.

Ogulin has a particularly strong association with witches and fairy tales – there is an annual witches' festival in June, and Croatia's most celebrated writer of fairy tales, Ivana Brlić Mažuranić, lived here.

From the railway station in **Ogulin**, head roughly SW following the trail markings to Klek (Ulica Augusta Šenoe, then Ulica bana Josipa Jelačića, then left onto the main road, Ulica Vladimira Nazora). Turn right off the main road by a café just N of a roundabout, onto a road (Šetalište Krlenac) which follows the S side of the River Dobra, to the suburb of Vučić selo. Bear right where the road forks, then 20 minutes from the main road, turn left onto a partly wooded trail, which marks the beginning of **Ferdina staza**.

Around 25 minutes after leaving the asphalt road, after ascending gradually and passing a sinkhole (in which the bodies of a number of Ustaša were apparently buried during the World War 2), you will reach a small **lookout point** (*vidikovac*) with views back over Ogulin and the River Dobra. Continue past the lookout point, then bear left onto a dusty track, then left on a broad forest track. Ignore a succession of tracks off to the left and right, and continue across a large, level, grassy clearing, with a wooden hut on the right. Go past the large outdoor recreation centre known as Kneja, then bear left on a path that brings you to the main road from Ogulin after 30 minutes.

Turn left along the main road, following signs painted on the tarmac, then after 5 minutes turn right onto a path, which skirts the edge of a quarry. Bear left again and go through a small clearing, then along

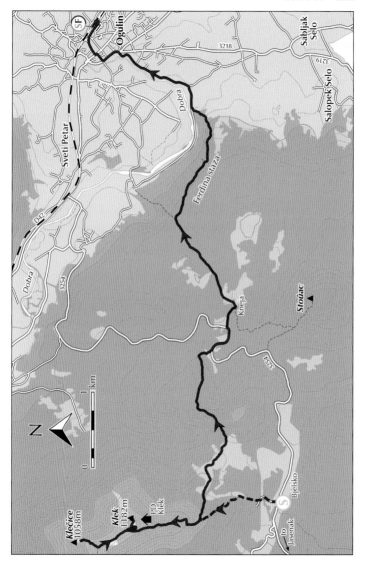

a broad, leafy track. Walk past a quarried area, then roughly W over grassy slopes with good views ahead towards the summit of Klek. Go uphill on a steep path (muddy after rain), then turn right, passing the occasional well-placed wooden bench, and notices requesting that visitors carry some firewood up with them in the winter, to gain a ridge. Here, a banner greets you with the words *Dobro došli u carstvo klečkih vještica* ('welcome to the empire of the witches of Klek'). Klek has long been associated with witches, who according to local legend like to gather on the summit. **PD Klek** lies a few minutes beyond, around 90 minutes from the main Ogulin road.

PD Klek is a two-story stone hut with a dining area downstairs, and sits in a sloping, grassy clearing at 1000m, on the shoulder of Klek, with views to the nearby summit.

It's a further 30 minutes from the hut to the summit of Klek. Continue on the trail past PD Klek, ascending gradually and following the occasional sign to Klek and passing a cave on the right. After 10 minutes, the trail arrives at a junction, from where the path continues straight ahead to **Klečice** (an additional 35 minutes, for those interested), and from where the trail up to the summit of Klek branches off to the right. Follow the path up below the rock face, ascending more steeply with the occasional scramble (aided in places by black electrical cable, rather than the more orthodox steel cables). There are good views of Klečice from just below the summit, followed by a concrete helicopter landing pad. Continue along the ridge, passing a rather precarious-looking, roped shortcut, which is best avoided, to gain the airy summit of **Klek** (1182m), with sheer drops beyond and fine views west to Velika kapela.

Descend by the same route to Ogulin (allow 3 hours).

Alternative approach to PD Klek from Bjelsko

This alternative route to PD Klek is 2.5km (1.6 miles) with 375m (1230ft) of ascent: allow an hour. The route is on good, clear forest paths, though steep in places.

A broad, clear track (marked 'Klek') ascends from opposite the old bus stop on the main road in **Bjelsko**, a few metres from the only store. Follow this straight up before branching off to the left on a marked path, which crosses one track and then merges with another from the left. Some 30 minutes of forest walking brings you to a junction with the trail up from Ogulin on the right. Continue straight ahead to reach the hut, **PD Klek**, in a further 15 minutes. To reach the summit of Klek, continue as described in the main route description.

Return to Bjelsko by the same route or follow the main route description to descend to Ogulin.

View towards the summit of Klek from Ferdina staza

PART 4
VELEBIT

Hiker on Premužićeva staza, near Crikvena (Route 16, Stage 3)

Velebit is Croatia's most extensive massif, containing some of its highest peaks and its most spectacular scenery, and no hiking trip to Croatia is complete without at least a few days here. In fact, it is possible to spend quite some time on Velebit: a full north–south traverse requires at least 10–12 days, if it includes only some of the various possible excursions.

Boasting domed peaks and jagged crags, brilliantly engineered tracks through some magnificent limestone scenery, brown bears and botanical gardens, sinkholes plummeting almost 1400m (that's almost down to sea level) and sheer-sided gorges where until only recently griffon vultures nested above alpine climbing routes, Velebit should have enough to keep most mountain enthusiasts more than busy.

Like its more southerly siblings Mosor and Biokovo, Velebit rises steeply and dramatically from the coast. Perhaps rather appropriately, considering the alarming depth of its sinkholes, the ferocity of its winds (the infamous *bura*), and the peculiarity of its light – the glowing pinks and reds of its limestone buttresses before sunset – the 16th century Croatian writer Petar Zoranić made Paklenica the entrance to hell in his book *Planine* ('The Mountains', 1569). Zoranić describes the *bura* as a harsh wind blowing from *Vražja vrata* ('Hell's gate' – hell in modern Croatian being *pakao*, whence Paklenica), and gives a mythical account of its origin – the sighing of a beautiful woman (named Bura) who was confined to the underworld for her excessive vanity.

The *bura* on Velebit can be particularly strong, and the weather full of surprises, even in the summer – so come prepared. Less stiflingly hot than Mosor and Biokovo during the summer months, winter brings a whole new character to Velebit, with pine trees springing from its snow-bound rocky slopes like something straight out of a painting by Caspar David Friedrich. Despite bitter temperatures, at least one hut remains open throughout the winter (PD Zavižan), when it is possible to look down over the coast and islands from snowbound, icy passes. Those planning a winter trip should note that in a year of heavy snowfall much of the initial section of Premužićeva staza becomes impassable.

The routes described below cover all of the main parts of northern, central and southern Velebit, from the beautiful area around Zavižan in the north to the limestone gorges of Paklenica in the south; when linked, they form an extended trek through Croatia's finest, as well as some of its highest, mountain scenery. There is no opportunity for restocking supplies along the way, so you will need to carry enough to last your whole trip. Those with only enough time for shorter trips should concentrate on the areas around PD Zavižan (in the north) and Velika Paklenica (in the

WARNING

Certain parts of Južni Velebit (southern Velebit) remain unsafe following the 1991–1995 war, and walkers continuing south from Baške Oštarije should read the section on landmines at the end of 'What to do in an emergency' and the beginning of the section 'Južni Velebit (southern Velebit) and Paklenica'.

south), around each of which there are plenty of short day trips.

Northern Velebit, and more specifically the area around PD Zavižan, Rožanski kukovi and Hajdučki kukovi, is a national park (Nacionalni park Sjeverni Velebit, www.np-sjeverni-velebit.hr), as is Paklenica in Southern Velebit (Nacionalni park Paklenica, www.np-paklenica.hr). You'll need to buy entry tickets for each and hang onto them for the duration of your stay in the park. Park entry tickets for Northern Velebit National Park cost 45Kn and are valid for three days; you can buy tickets at PD Zavižan, and should hold on to them for the duration of your stay. Park entry tickets for Paklenica National Park cost 180Kn (Jun–Sep)/120Kn (Mar–May, Oct)/60Kn (Nov–Feb) for a five-day ticket; 120Kn (Jun–Sep)/80Kn (Mar–May, Oct)/40Kn (Nov–Feb) for a three-day ticket; and 60Kn (Jun–Sep)/40Kn (Mar–May, Oct)/20Kn (Nov–Feb) for a one-day ticket, and can be bought from the national park office in the car park in Velika Paklenica. Tickets can also be bought from huts and wardens if you enter from a different route.

BASES

There are various towns and villages along the coast – including **Karlobag** and **Starigrad-Paklenica** – linked by the coastal bus route that connects Rijeka and Zadar. **PD Zavižan** makes an ideal base for exploring Northern Velebit and can be accessed from Gornja Klada (see Route 16), a small village just off the main coast road a little north of Starigrad (not to be confused with Starigrad-Paklenica, which is further south). Starigrad-Paklenica is the gateway to Southern Velebit: the turn-off to the national park entrance at Velika Paklenica is just to the south of the town beyond the Hotel Alan and then it's a further 2–3km up the road.

ROUTE 15

Mali Rajinac, Veliki Zavižan and
Botanički vrt

Start/finish	PD Zavižan
Distance	14.5km (9 miles)
Total ascent/descent	660m (2165ft)
Time	7hr 30min
Terrain	Excellent, clear trails
Maximum altitude	1699m (Mali Rajinac)
Maps	SMAND (16) Sjeverni Velebit
Refreshments	PD Zavižan
Transport	PD Zavižan is best reached on foot from Gornja Klada (see Route 16, Stage 1) or Krasno, but can also be reached by car – it's 17km along a mixed asphalt and unsealed road from Oltare
Note	Park entry tickets for Northern Velebit national park cost 45Kn and are valid for three days; you can buy tickets at PD Zavižan, and should hold on to them for the duration of your stay.

PD Zavižan makes a great base from which to explore Sjeverni Velebit National Park. This longish one-day walk takes in Mali Rajinac (the highest peak in Northern Velebit) as well as another prominent peak, Veliki Zavižan, and passes alongside the nearby botanical garden (*botanički vrt*). It could conveniently be broken into two shorter day walks from PD Zavižan (one to Mali Rajinac, the other to Veliki Zavižan and the *botanički vrt*).

From **PD Zavižan**, follow the path marked Mali Rajinac for a few minutes down to the road, turning left onto this for 5 minutes before reaching a path on the right (marked Mali Rajinac, Otočac and Krasno) and following it into the trees. This brings you out into the open again in 25 minutes, contouring a steep-sided dell to

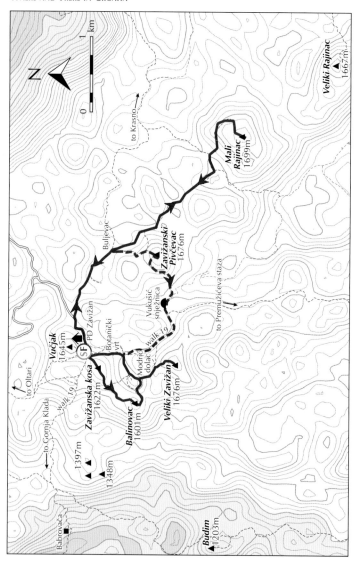

arrive at a signposted trail junction – an area known as **Buljevac**. ▸ Turn right on the path to these peaks, leaving the main trail which continues straight ahead to the village of **Krasno** (meaning 'beautiful'), and then left on the branch to Mali Rajinac, the further of the two peaks. This leads through forest cover before emerging into the open in 10 minutes, with Pivčevac directly behind you.

A further 30 mins of predominantly pine forest, alternating with open, rolling, grassy clearings, leads to another junction, from where it would be possible, by turning right, to continue to Veliki Lubenovac. Instead, take the left (Mali Rajinac, Krasno) branch and after 5 minutes, take a right fork (marked Mali Rajinac). Ascend through forest and then along the final, rocky path to reach the summit of **Mali Rajinac** in 35 minutes.

At 1699m, **Mali Rajinac** is the highest peak in northern Velebit. A grand array of high peaks extends to the SW, with Gromovača (1676m) particularly prominent, almost due SW, surrounded by Rožanski kukovi, the area through which you will continue from Zavižan, following Premužićeva staza. Veliki Zavižan (1676m) is clearly visible to the NW.

Mali Rajinac is visible to the SE, and Zavižanski Pivčevac (from *pivac*, the local dialect for capercaillie – which explains the presence of this bird on the national park logo) to the S (beyond the nearer, wooded peak).

Descend by the same route, returning to the junction at Buljevac in just over 1 hour, before continuing on to reach PD Zavižan in a further 35 minutes.

Optional extension

This route could be extended from the junction at Buljevac by following the trail up to **Zavižanski Pivčevac** (1676m) in 45 minutes. From here, it would also be possible to descend to the road on the other side of Zavižanski Pivčevac before returning along this towards the hut (passing **Vukušić snježnica**, a sinkhole named after the Vukušić family, who used to have a small cottage nearby, where snow remains throughout the year), and then follow the second half of the route in reverse (ie from the botanical garden and Veliki Zavižan to Balinovac and Zavižanska kosa).

From **PD Zavižan** ascend **Zavižanska kosa** from the saddle below the hut, gaining the summit (1622m) in 10 minutes, from where there are views of both Balinovac and Veliki Zavižan ahead, and of the hut nestled below **Vučjak** behind you. Continue beyond the summit on a marked trail, descending steeply to the left for a short distance, before crossing over to the N side of the rocky ridge leading up to **Balinovac**, and finally scrambling up to reach the summit (1601m), 45 minutes from Zavižanska kosa.

Although Veliki Zavižan could be reached along the ridge from Balinovac, the route involves floundering through some particularly hardy dwarf mountain pine and juniper, and it is far more pleasant (and less damaging) to descend to the *botanički vrt* before continuing from there. The path descends into the trees before meeting the main trail above a steep-sided dell (**Modrić dolac**) at the head of the open, grassy meadows of the **botanical garden**.

Velebit's **botanical garden** sits in a sheltered hollow beneath Balinovac, a short distance from the hut and just beyond the small chapel of Sveti Ante. It was established in 1966 by Dr Franjo Kušan, a professor from the University of Zagreb, and contains numerous rare and endemic plant species.

Follow the path around the side of the dell, ascending steeply through the trees from the opposite (S) side before emerging into another grassy clearing below Veliki Zavižan. Cut across the clearing, from where a trail leads up through the trees, around thickets of dwarf mountain pine, and then scramble steeply up to the summit of **Veliki Zavižan** (1676m), 1 hour from the botanical garden.

From the top of **Veliki Zavižan**, there are clear views south along Rožanski kukovi – your onward route from PD Zavižan, if you follow Route 16 – including its highest peak, Gromovača, which is equal to your present altitude. Hajdučki kukovi rises to the SE, with Veliki Kozjak beyond, and Pivčevac and Mali Rajinac are visible to the E.

Descend by the same route to the botanical garden, turning right and contouring the slopes above Modrić dolac to the small wooden shelter before continuing to the chapel, the road and **PD Zavižan**.

*Botanički vrt,
Modrić dolac and
Veliki Zavižan*

ROUTE 16
*Northern Velebit and
Central Velebit trek*

Start	Gornja Klada
Finish	Baške Oštarije
Distance	58.5–75km (36.4–46.6 miles)
Total ascent	2690m (8825ft)
Total descent	2205m (7234ft)
Time	5–7 days
Maps	SMAND covers the area on two sheets: SMAND (16) Sjeverni Velebit and SMAND (17) Srednji Velebit, both 1:30,000. For more detail of central Velebit, there's SMAND (17a) Dabarski kukovi, Srednji Velebit at 1:20,000. For those continuing south of Baške Oštarije there is SMAND (18) Južni Velebit (1:30,000) and SMAND (18a) Južni Velebit II (1:30,000), the latter not necessary if you have SMAND (19) Paklenica (1:30,000) or even better HGSS Paklenica (1:25,000), which has coverage NW as far as Stap.
Transport	To get to Gornja Klada, take a southbound bus from Rijeka (journey time 2hr), either to Starigrad (not to be confused with Starigrad-Paklenica) or Karlobag. Make sure you get a bus travelling via the coast, as a number of buses turn inland at the town of Senj. Travelling south, the road to Gornja Klada is on the left, and is signposted, just before a house advertising private rooms (*sobe* – see below). The village is 5 minutes up the road.
Accommodation	The house on the main road by the turn-off to Gornja Klada has clean, good value rooms (contact Anka Magić, +385 (0)53 625 343); PD Zavižan; Rossijevo sklonište; Planinarska kuća Alan; Planinarsko sklonište Ograđenica; Kugina kuća; Planinarsko sklonište Skorpovac; PD Ravni Dabar; PD Prpa; Planinarska kuća Vila Velebita
Note	Park entry tickets for Northern Velebit National Park cost 45Kn and are valid for three days; you can buy tickets at PD Zavižan, and should hold on to them for the duration of your stay.

The following itinerary leads from the small village of Gornja Klada on the main coastal highway up to the spectacular scenery around PD Zavižan (1594m), which provides an excellent base for exploring the surrounding area, with its numerous peaks between 1600 and 1699m (Route 19). The route south follows the brilliantly engineered Premužićeva staza, from which more peaks and ridges can be reached, varying in difficulty from an easy walk to a challenging and demanding scramble. Caving enthusiasts should note that the deepest sinkhole in Croatia (Lukina jama) lies only a short distance from the main route – although it lies within a protected area and is very much off limits unless you can get a permit. A circular route is possible from PD Zavižan (via Veliki Lubenovac, see extension to Stage 3, below), spread over two or three days and bringing you back to the hut; otherwise the main trail continues south from Rossijevo sklonište for another three days, less spectacularly and largely through forest for the second of these, but ending grandly enough with the very impressive limestone crags of Bačić kuk – making a total of six days if you include all the recommended excursions.

Hiker on Premužićeva staza between PD Zavižan and Rossijevo sklonište

From Baške Oštarije the route can be extended into southern Velebit, to reach Buljma and Struge above Paklenica in a further three stages without descending to the coast (see alternative route to southern Velebit at the end of Stage 5). This unbroken itinerary provides the most rewarding extended mountain trek in Croatia, although once again those continuing south of Baške Oštarije are referred to the warnings in the introduction and at the beginning of the alternative route.

Accommodation south of PD Zavižan is provided by a good selection of huts and *sklonište*, and only at the end of the fourth stage is accommodation inconveniently placed, at which point a tent might make things easier. You'll need to be self-sufficient for most of the route – buy supplies in Zagreb, Rijeka or Split as there's nothing in Gornja Klada.

STAGE 1
Gornja Klada – PD Zavižan

Start	Gornja Klada
Finish	PD Zavižan
Distance	8km (5 miles)
Total ascent	1250m (4101ft)
Total descent	10m (33ft)
Time	4hr 30min
Terrain	Excellent, clearly marked trails on open slopes and through forest
Maximum altitude	1594m (PD Zavižan)
Accommodation	PD Zavižan

This stage climbs from the village of Gornja Klada on the coast, up to PD Zavižan in the heart of Central Velebit National Park.

From **Gornja Klada** follow the trail markings up through the village to gain a clearly marked, stony track, on which you ascend and veer left. The path drops slightly after 15 minutes – pass through a gate and veer right onto a stony plateau. Continue across this, winding your way through rock and scrub as the mountains loom ahead, to gain a well-engineered set of switchbacks in 30 minutes. These lead up, passing a small pool (for watering livestock) on the right and a path joining from the left from below the small peak of Brondinovača (681m) before levelling out again. Ascend gradually, passing through low beech and oak, to gain a second set of switchbacks. These are longer than the previous ones, with a number of shortcuts leading between them. Continue ascending, with views back over the islands of Rab, Goli otok and Pag. The switchbacks become a broad forest track, which leads round a final corner to a gate and the summer cottage of **Babrovača** beyond, 1hr 45min from the village. ▶

Continue past the cottage, passing through another gate. Take the left fork and follow the signs to Zavižan, ascending on a rocky path through pine and then mixed

On the trail from Gornja Klada to Zavižan mountain hut

It is just before this point that you will begin to encounter snow if you arrive in the winter.

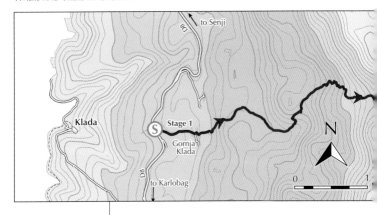

It is possible to ascend from the village of Siča to this point, although the route is far less attractive, being largely along forest tracks with not much of a view, and there is little in the way of transport to get you there.

The snow can be knee-deep here during the winter, burying any sign of a path and slowing progress considerably.

forest cover again, and passing a rock outcrop and a small, flat, grassy area on the right. Walk a further 20 minutes to reach a larger flat area and a rock outcrop with extensive views out over the islands (2hr 30min from the village). There is enough room for a few tents here if you have arrived late and don't have enough time to continue up to Zavižan, but there is no water.

Continue up through forest cover, passing a trail to Alan via Velike Brisnice on your right, followed shortly by a path to Siča on the left. ◀ Ignore these turn-offs and follow the signs straight ahead to Zavižan. Enter a clearing before ascending on a broad, walled track to reach a second clearing 10 minutes beyond the Siča path. Here you will pass two large, man-made ponds (watering pools for livestock) on the left, the second of which has a small and rather murky-looking spring just behind it. Continue, following route markings and wading through clover before re-entering forest cover and ascending a broad, steep, leafy track. Around 25 minutes from the ponds, you will reach a final set of switchbacks, which lead up through the forest and then left along a last, long stretch to gain the pass in another 30 minutes. ◀

The view from the **pass** is breathtaking, particularly if you have arrived in the evening as the sun begins

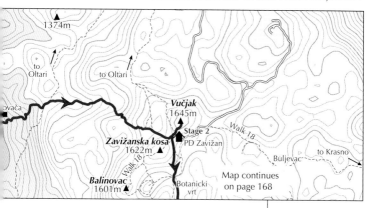

to set across the Adriatic. The islands of Rab, Goli otok and Pag are clearly visible. You may be able to make out the much-touted sandy beach at Lopar on the former. Goli otok (literally 'naked island') once housed a high-security prison, whereas Pag is famous for its cheese (Paški sir). PD Zavižan sits above you on the other side of a deep, bowl-like depression.

Continue for 15 minutes, skirting the side of the large doline and following the trail up to **PD Zavižan**.

Large and well equipped, with numerous beds and the use of a kitchen (for a nominal fee), PD Zavižan (1594m; sleeps 28; open all year; drinks available; HPS, Zagreb, contact +385 (0)53 614 209) makes an unsurpassed base for exploring the surrounding area. There is a lot to see around PD Zavižan, and you could quite easily spend a few days here. Look out for the *poskok* (nose-horned viper) specimen above the door to the sinks and toilets, a good example of what to avoid standing on during your subsequent travels. The hut is actually a meteorological station (which explains why it is open all year round), and it is this which the helpful Ante Vukušić and his family

WALKS AND TREKS IN CROATIA

are officially employed to run, although they effectively end up running the hut as well.

To climb Vučjak

The small peak of Vučjak (1645m), just behind PD Zavižan, is the first place to head for a view of the surrounding area and can be reached in under 10 minutes. The path leads straight up from beside the hut.

From the summit of **Vučjak**, the prominent peak to the NE, crowned by a telecommunications complex, is Plješivica (1654m). More impressive are Veliki Zavižan (1676m) and Balinovac (1601m), SSW above the botanical garden; and Zavižanski Pivčevac (1676m) and Mali Rajinac (1699m) to the SE, the goal of the trip described below. Framed by these two areas of high ground are the cluttered peaks and crags of Rožanski and Hajdučki kukovi.

Descend to PD Zavižan by the same route.

STAGE 2
PD Zavižan – Rossijevo sklonište via Gromovača

Start	PD Zavižan
Finish	Rossijevo sklonište
Distance	7.5km (4.7 miles)
Total ascent	220m (722ft)
Total descent	240m (787ft)
Time	2hr 40min
Terrain	Excellent hiking along a well-engineered packhorse track
Maximum altitude	1676m (Gromovača)
Accommodation	Rossijevo sklonište

The first, and finest, section of Premužićeva staza, a beautifully engineered packhorse track through some of the finest karst scenery in Croatia.

From PD Zavižan follow the road down to the chapel, turning right off this on the path to the botanical garden before rejoining the road in a few minutes. Continue along the road as it veers northeast with views back to the hut, before turning right onto the path marked **Premužićeva staza**, 20 minutes from PD Zavižan.

> **Premužićeva staza** (and more especially this northern section of it) is a particularly well-engineered track built during the early 1930s at the order of Ante Premužić. A local forestry engineer, Premužić

Premužićeva staza

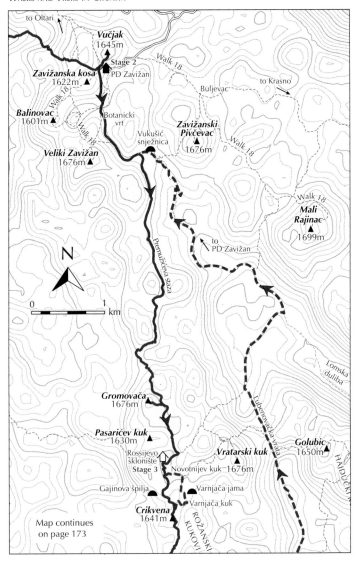

to Oltari

Vučjak
1645m

Stage 2
PD Zavižan

Walk 18

to Krasno

Zavižanska kosa
1622m

Buljevac

Walk 18

Balinovac
1601m

Botanicki
vrt

Vukušić
snježnica

**Zavižanski
Pivčevac**
1676m

Walk 18

Veliki Zavižan
1676m

Walk 18

**Mali
Rajinac**
1699m

N

to
PD Zavižan

0   1
km

Premužićeva staza

Lomska
duliba

Gromovača
1676m

Pasarićev kuk
1630m

Rossijevo
sklonište
Stage 3

Novotnijev kuk 1676m

Vratarski kuk

Golubic
1650m

Lubenovačka vrata

HAJDUČKI

Gajinova špilja

Varnjača jama

Varnjača kuk

Crikvena
1641m

ROŽANSKI
KUKOVI

Map continues
on page 173

168

assigned the building work to local labourers, thus ensuring for them a regular income during this period of economic hardship. Today it provides an outstanding hiking trail. The symbol 'v' is used to mark the course of Premužićeva staza over its entire length.

The path initially passes through trees, but emerges after about 20 minutes to begin winding around cliffs and bluffs, with spectacular views of limestone rock formations and jagged crags, leading up onto the backbone of Rožanski kukovi. 1hr 15min should be enough time for you to to reach a path ascending to the right, which leads to the peak of Gromovača. Turn onto this and scramble up the steep, rocky path, winding your way through dwarf mountain pine to reach the summit of **Gromovača** (1676m) in 10 minutes.

Among those peaks recognisable from the top of **Gromovača** are: Veliki Zavižan (1676m) to the N, Mali Rajinac (1699m) to the NE, Crikvena (1641m) to the S and Rožanski kuk (1638m) to the SW; while the high crags of Rožanski kukovi and Hajdučki kukovi beyond continue to the SE, and the sea and islands are visible to the W.

The etymology of Gromovača (from *grom*, meaning 'thunder') will become evident from your present location if there are storm clouds in the vicinity, with this area attracting them like a magnet. I don't think I have ever seen a darker or more ominously brooding, lowering sky than while clambering over the pass below Crikvena on one of my first visits to the area.

Drop back down to the main trail and continue walking for another 15 minutes, passing a trail on the left to Lomska duliba, Kozjak, Mali Rajinac and Hajdučki kukovi, to reach the turn-off to **Rossijevo sklonište** (also known as Rossijeva koliba), which you will find a few minutes away on the path to the right. ▸

If you require a direct route down to the coast, note that the trail from Rossijevo Sklonište to Velike Brisnice, Modrići and Starigrad, via Plančica is longer than it looks on paper and not particularly interesting.

Rossijevo sklonište and Pasarićev kuk, Sjeverni Velebit National Park

Rossijevo sklonište (sleeps 6; open all year; PD Kailaš, Zagreb) sits in a lovely spot, perched on a ledge at 1580m. Although rather small to rely on during the summer months, it is certainly worth spending some time here if you get the chance. The well beside it is fouled, and you will need to purify water taken from here. Those who are staying may enjoy a moderately difficult scrambling route up to Pasarićev kuk (1630m), directly behind the hut, or the excursion to Varnjača kuk detailed below.

Excursion from
Rossijevo sklonište: Varnjača kuk

Start/finish	Rossijevo sklonište
Distance	1.5km (0.9 miles)
Time	2hr 15min
Terrain	A narrow, rocky ridge walk, mostly unmarked and exposed in places
Maximum altitude	1634m (5361ft)
Maps	SMAND Sjeverni Velebit (16)

The following excursion is a difficult and challenging ridge walk, which (whether or not you choose to stay the night at Rossijevo sklonište) is better undertaken without the burden of a full pack. The route is mostly unmarked and overgrown, and requires some exposed scrambling.

See map on page 168

TAKE CARE

Bear in mind that Varnjača kuk lies in an ecologically sensitive area – both Hajdučki kukovi and Rožanski kukovi are designated as specially protected areas (*Strogi rezervat*). The conservation status of Varnjača kuk remains slightly ambiguous at present, and there has been talk of closing the ridge to hikers. Ask at PD Zavižan or Rossijevo sklonište for the latest information.

Continue S from Rossijevo sklonište on the route to Alan (see Stage 3, below) for a few minutes before picking up the beginning of the faint trail off to the left, marked Rossijev kuk, Novotnijev kuk and Varnjača. ▸ It is 10 minutes to the first of these peaks, from where the route continues via **Novotnijev kuk** (from where it is possible to reach Vratarski kuk) and passes a sinkhole (**Varnjača jama**) in 1 hour.

The Croatian sign at the bottom means: 'Experienced walkers only'.

You can continue by scrambling along **Varnjača kuk**, an airy ridge some 400m long, and in places less than 1m wide, picking your way around its three peaks (Sjeverni, Srednji and Južni vrh) before returning to Premužićeva staza (either from Južni vrh or Sjeverni vrh), making a total excursion of a little over 2 hours. Those not continuing south to Alan should take this opportunity of climbing Crikvena, which is just a little way south along the main trail. Return to Rossijevo sklonište along Premužićeva staza.

STAGE 3
Rossijevo sklonište – Planinarska kuća Alan

Start	Rossijevo sklonište
Finish	PD Alan
Distance	7km (4.3 miles)
Total ascent	120m (394ft)
Total descent	360m (1181ft)
Time	2hr 30min
Terrain	Excellent hiking along a well-engineered packhorse track
Maximum altitude	1641m (Crikvena)
Accommodation	Planinarska kuća Alan

From Rossijevo sklonište, Premužićeva staza continues S though Rožanski kukovi, before crossing Crikvena and heading into the slightly less rocky landscape of Central Velebit.

Continue on the main trail from Rossijevo sklonište, following the signs to Alan and passing a trail to Velike Brisnice (which links up with the route up from Gornja Klada to PD Zavižan, see Stage 1) on the right. Just around the corner a faint trail leads up to the left, which marks the beginning of the Varnjača kuk excursion described above. Continue straight ahead, passing some particularly impressive limestone scenery and the other end of the Varnjača kuk excursion on the left as you head up towards the pass. The path drops down fairly steeply on the other side of this, from which point (leaving full packs) there is an easy scramble up a marked route to **Crikvena** (1641m; from crkva, meaning 'church'). There are good views of the surrounding area from the summit.

Premužićeva staza is somewhat less spectacular beyond this point, and does not regain its grandeur until the section around Bačić kuk, a day and a half beyond Alan. From the base of the pass, continue through forest cover with occasional glimpses out over limestone

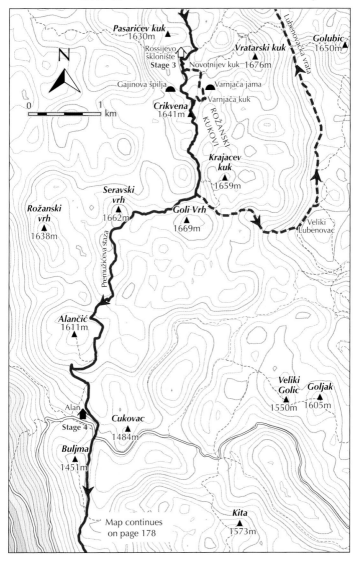

formations, passing one track to the left up to **Krajačev kuk** (1659m), which can be reached in around 30 minutes, and a second, also on the left, to **Veliki Lubenovac**.

Variants from Veliki Lubenovac

Veliki Lubenovac is a level, grassy clearing at 1265m, below Rožanski kukovi, Hajdučki kukovi and Veliki Kozjak. It would be possible, by following this path on the left (see above), to descend to Veliki Lubenovac in 1 hour, from where you could climb **Veliki Kozjak** (1629m). There used to be a *sklonište* at Veliki Lubenovac, but it burned down a few years ago.

To the north of Veliki Lubenovac lies Hajdučki kukovi, an area under special protection. **Lukina jama**, the deepest cave in Croatia (and among the 15 deepest in the world), is on the opposite (NE) side of Hajdučki kukovi, and is usually reached from the road as it passes through Lomska duliba – though it is strictly out of bounds unless you manage to obtain a permit.

Plummeting some 1392m into the bowels of Velebit, **Lukina jama** was discovered only in 1992, and is named after Ozren Lukić, a climbing and caving enthusiast who joined the local volunteer unit (a mountain division) during the 1991–95 war and was killed by a sniper in 1992.

There are a number of other **caves and sinkholes** in the area. In 2003 a Croatian caving team discovered another sinkhole, near Crikvena, which is suspected of being even deeper than Lukina jama. Another sinkhole in Rožanski kukovi, called Slovačka jama, has a depth of 1017m; while Patkov gušt, discovered in 1997, contains a single vertical drop of over 500m.

A marked trail leads back to PD Zavižan from Veliki Lubenovac, heading north between **Hajdučki kukovi** and **Rožanski kukovi** and climbing to a pass (Lubenovačka vrata) below Vratarski kuk, before crossing the road and continuing to meet the trail from PD Zavižan at the base

of Mali Rajinac. This circular route would require a further one or two days to complete, depending on how many daylight hours you have remaining and whether you choose to visit Veliki Kozjak.

Continue straight ahead past the Lubenovac turn-off, and the main trail soon emerges onto open grassland with views behind you back to the high peaks of northern Velebit. A trail on the right up to **Seravski vrh** (1662m), which can be reached in 15 minutes, is followed by another to **Alančić** (1611m, also on the right) 40mins later. Some 10mins beyond this, the sea comes into view on the left before a sudden switchback forces you, rather confusingly, to walk N rather than S. Re-enter the trees, to arrive at a path on the right (marked Alan sklonište) in 5 minutes, which leads down to the **hut** in a further 10 minutes.

Rožanski kukovi, viewed from Premužićeva staza

Planinarska kuća Alan (1340m; sleeps 44; summer only; drinks; food by prior arrangement; PK Sljeme, Zagreb) is open, with use of the kitchen, from June to September. Outside these months, when these facilities remain closed, it is open as a *sklonište*, providing mattresses and shelter. It makes

175

a convenient place to stop for the night, although it is not in quite such an attractive spot as PD Zavižan or Rossijevo sklonište.

To descend to the coast

There is a route leading down to Jablanac from Alan for those who need to descend to the coast; it follows the road in its initial stages but soon diverges from it, emerging onto the coast near the attractive channel, or cove, called Zavratnica. There is a simple hut at Zavratnica, Planinarska kuća Miroslav Hirtz (26m; sleeps 32; open 1 Jun–30 Sep; drinks; HPD MIV, Varaždin).

STAGE 4
Planinarska kuća Alan –
Planinarsko sklonište Skorpovac

Start	Planinarska kuća Alan
Finish	Planinarsko sklonište Skorpovac
Distance	24km (14.9 miles)
Total ascent	590m (1936ft)
Total descent	970m (3182ft)
Time	9hr 30min
Terrain	Excellent hiking along a good, clear trail
Maximum altitude	1624m (Šatorina)
Accommodation	Planinarsko sklonište Ograđenica; Kugina kuća; Planinarsko sklonište Skorpovac

This stage continues along Premužićeva staza, with plenty of views of the sea and islands, and a visit to Šatorina – at 1624m the highest peak in central Velebit. Including Šatorina does make it quite a long day, although there's an option to break it into two stages, or skip Šatorina and proceed directly to Skorpovac, if you prefer.

Of the several choices of accommodation on this section of the route, only the relatively new Planinarsko sklonište Skorpovac is really convenient, being right on the trail and permanently open. Of the other choices:

Ograđenik is close to the main trail, but is very small (sleeps 4) and would make a very short day from Alan – and there's no water, so you'll need to carry enough to last until the following day if you stay here. Kugina kuća is larger and more comfortable, but needs to be booked in advance otherwise you will probably find it locked (as a last resort, there is a small *sklonište* in the woods behind it), and the route from Kugina kuća back to the main trail is far from clear. The old *sklonište* at Radlovac (which was way off the main trail anyway, and fairly run down) is now closed.

From **Planinarska kuća Alan**, follow the path back up through the forest to regain the main trail, turning right onto this to emerge from the trees 15 minutes from the junction. Cross the road (leading up from Alan and on to Štirovača), passing a monument to the Partisans of World War 2 (specifically the Alan Division, formed in 1943) on the opposite side. ▸ Continue straight ahead, following the signs to Kugina kuća and Baške Oštarije. You'll walk through trees at first but soon emerge with a view down across open, rolling grassland to the left, criss-crossed by dry-stone walls (*suhozid – suho* means 'dry', *zid* means 'wall'), before arriving at a junction.

A track just beyond this leads up to Mali Vidik ('little viewpoint'), with not much of a view and some rather ugly pylons.

The trail to the left leads to **Zečjak**, at 1622m the second highest peak in central Velebit, in around 1 hour. The path up to the right goes to **Buljma**, with good views of Rab and Pag – although to be honest the views are just as good further along the main trail.

Continue straight ahead from the junction, walking parallel to the coast with clear views out over the islands, and passing a track on the left to Štokić duliba in 15 minutes. All views are soon lost as the path reenters the forest, continuing a further 90mins to a junction, 3hr 30min from the hut. ▸

The trail straight ahead follows Premužićeva staza to Skorpovac in around 2 hours, without climbing Šatorina.

Turn left and follow the trail as it spirals up around Šatorina (from *šator*, meaning 'tent'). The route takes you up over a saddle below **Ograđenik** (1604m), and Planinarsko sklonište Ograđenica (1400m; sleeps 4; PD Đakovo, Đakovo), around 4 hours from Alan. ▸

The nearest water is at Gornja Korita, back down on Premužićeva staza.

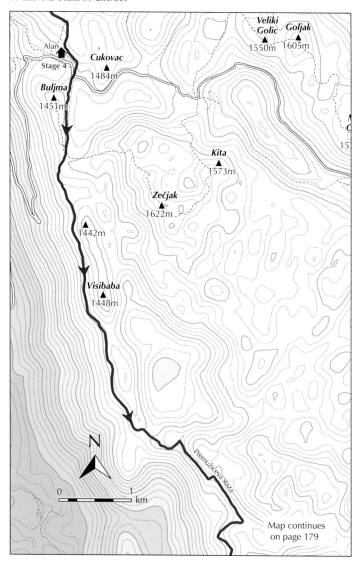

Map continues
on page 179

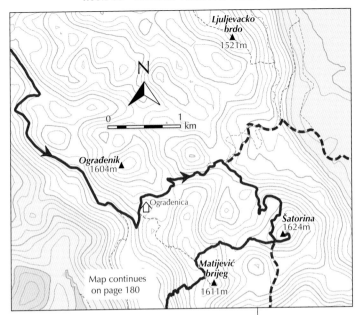

Map continues on page 180

Continue along the main trail from the saddle, passing a turn-off to Štirovača on the left, from where a further 50 minutes brings you to the summit trail, which branches off to the left. It's 10 minutes up this to the top of **Šatorina** (1624m), with clear views north to Veliki Kozjak and south towards Bačić kuk from the summit.

To reach Kugina kuća

For those intending to stay at Kugina kuća (1180m; sleeps 50; open by prior arrangement only; PD Željezničar, Gospić), a not always very clear path leads down from the junction just below the summit of Šatorina to reach this hut in 1hr 30min. Water is available from the well outside, and there's a small *sklonište* behind the hut.

Assuming you intend to continue from Šatorina to Skorpovac, not Kugina kuća: from the base of the

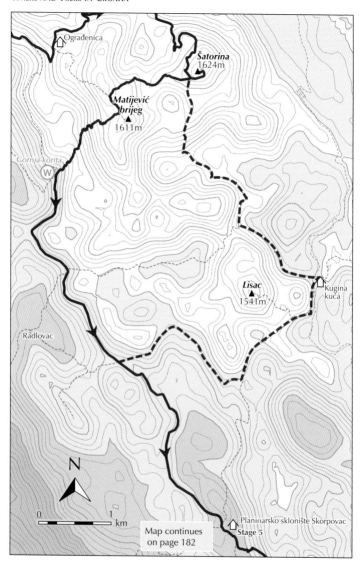

Ogradenica

Šatorina
1624m

Matijević
brijeg
1611m

Gornja korita
W

Lisac
1541m

Kugina
kuća

Radlovac

N

0   1
|_____| km

Map continues
on page 182

Planinarsko sklonište Skorpovac
Stage 5

summit trail a path descends via **Matijević brijeg** (1611m) to rejoin Premužićeva staza at **Gornja korita** in 1 hour. ▶ Continue along Premužićeva staza, passing two trails on the right to **Radlovac** (the old *sklonište* there is now closed) and a faint trail on the left to Kugina kuća marked *težekovac* (a poorly marked and more difficult route). Follow the signs straight ahead to Skorpovac, passing a clearing with a dry-stone wall and a small cottage below on the right. Skirt the rocky hillside to a small, relatively level clearing, where a trail from Kugina kuća joins Premužićeva staza on your left – just over 1 hour beyond the first Radlovac turn-off. Continue along Premužićeva staza, passing a turn-off to Pejakuša on the right, to arrive at Planinarsko sklonište Skorpovac (958m; sleeps 14; HPD Sv. Šimun, Markuševec, Zagreb) and the ruined and deserted village of **Skorpovac** in just under 1 hour, where another path from Kugina kuća joins from the left. ▶

Korita means 'water-trough', and refers to the water-trough downhill a short way from the main trail.

There is a well on the right but the quality of the water is questionable.

STAGE 5
Planinarsko sklonište Skorpovac – PD Prpa

Start	Planinarsko sklonište Skorpovac
Finish	PD Prpa
Distance	12km
Total ascent	510m (1673ft)
Total descent	625m (2051ft)
Time	4.5hr
Terrain	More easy hiking along a well-engineered packhorse track, with some steeper paths around Bačić kuk
Maximum altitude	1317m (Budakovo brdo)
Accommodation	PD Ravni Daba; PD Prpa; Planinarska kuća Vila Velebita

This final section of the route detours off Premužićeva staza and climbs to the spectacular rock formations of Bačić kuk

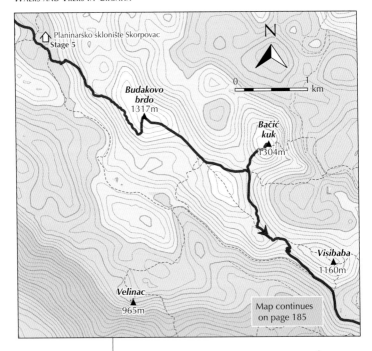

From Planinarsko sklonište Skorpovac, continue along Premužićeva staza, to reach a path on your left for Budakovo brdo and Bačić kuk after 15mins. Turn left onto this, ascending through tall beech forest to emerge into a clearing in under 1hr.

From just above the tree line, follow a path up to the left, which leads to the top of **Budakovo brdo** (1317m) in 10 minutes. From Budakovo brdo, continue southeast along the grassy ridge, with unobstructed and increasingly impressive views of the limestone crags of Bačić kuk, descending slightly before reaching a four-way junction, with the beginning of the trail up to the summit on the left. Follow this to reach **Bačić kuk** (1304m) in 40 minutes, from where there are spectacular views southeast along the spine of Dabarski kukovi.

Low cloud on Bačić kuk

Return to the four-way junction referred to above, and continue straight ahead, re-entering the forest and descending to Premužićeva staza in around 30 minutes. ▸

Alternative route via Ravni Dabar

If you're planning to stay at Ravni Dabar, turn left at the four-way junction and continue over a grassy knoll before descending to the road in 40 minutes, beyond which a saddle is gained, and then descend another 30 minutes to Došen Dabar. From here, the route continues for another 30 minutes, passing between **Čelina** and Rujičin kuk to reach **PD Ravni Dabar** (723m; sleeps 50; weekends only, by arrangement), from where a steep trail climbs back up to Premužićeva staza.

Turn left onto Premužićeva staza, following the signs to Baške Oštarije. You'll pass a trail on your left to Bačić kosa and Visibaba after 50 minutes. Continue straight ahead, passing a spring (marked *voda*, 'water', and known as Kapelica, 'chapel') up over the rocks on the

On the way down you pass a trail on your left to Visibaba (1160m, meaning 'snowdrop'), from where it's possible to descend to Premužićeva staza or continue E to meet the road at Rujičin kuk, above Ravni Dabar.

left in 10 minutes. Beyond this you have fine views to the left of **Dabarski kukovi**; follow the open ridge to reach the road in 25 minutes, just before which you pass a trail descending on the right to Karlobag.

From the road you have a magnificent view down over Ravni Dabar, the hut and Čelina behind it, and of the southern slopes of Bačić kuk. You should be able to pick out the course of the direct route down from Bačić kuk to Ravni Dabar described above, crossing the road on the way down.

From the road overlooking Ravni Dabar, continue along the trail towards Baške Oštarije, passing a trail on the left to **Butinovača** (around 45 minutes away) and re-entering the forest to arrive at a path on the right to Prpa in 20 minutes. Although there are places to stay in Baške Oštarije, the small wooden chalets at Prpa are much nicer. Baške Oštarije, and the extension to Southern Velebit described below, can also be reached by continuing straight ahead. Turn right and ascend through the forest to gain a saddle in 25 minutes. Veer left through a clearing with more dry-stone walls, descending over open slopes towards the houses and a farm track, from which there are good views of Dabarski kukovi to the left. Turn right onto the farm track, passing under the pylons before turning right, ascending and following the wooden telegraph poles towards the pines. Just 5 minutes should be enough to bring you to the Alpine style wooden chalets among the trees at **PD Prpa**.

The chalets at PD Prpa (935m; sleeps 60; drinks; Vlado Prpić +385 (0)98 854 878) come equipped with fridge, stove and toilet. The shower is piping hot, and you can even arrange to have meals provided for you, with a little advance notice.

To descend to Karlobag
For those heading down to Karlobag (about 20km), there are buses from Oštarije – simply continue on the farm track to reach the Oštarije–Karlobag road.

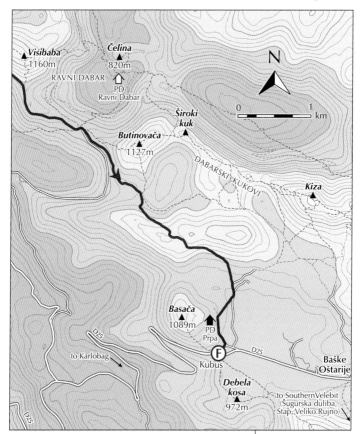

Note the large stone cube (known as Kubus) above the tunnel on the right, which was carved in 1846 when the **Karlobag–Gospić road** was under construction. There was once a Roman road here, too; and the name Oštarije seems to be of Roman origin.

From Karlobag, buses head N and S on the main coastal highway.

Continuing to Southern Velebit via Šugarska Duliba, Stap and Veliko Rujno

Those wishing to continue into southern Velebit on foot, rather than descending to the coast and then climbing all the way back up to Veliki Rujno, can do so from Baške Oštarije. From here it would require a further three stages (with two overnight stops, at Šugarska duliba and Stap, each of which has a *sklonište*) to reach Struge, situated above Paklenica. It is essential that anyone considering this route should carry a decent, post 1991–95 conflict map. SMAND covers the area with a fairly new sheet, Južni Velebit (18); HGSS (18) NP Paklenica has coverage of the route SE from Stap. Park entry tickets for Paklenica National Park vary in price depending on the season (refer to the Part 4 introduction for details). They can be bought from the national park office in the car park in Velika Paklenica or from huts and wardens.

From Baške Oštarije (927m), the route heads south to Sladovača brdo and past Sadikovac to the sklonište at Šugarska duliba (1212m, 6hr). ◄ From here it continues past Mali Stolac (1131m) before veering left to Jelova ruja (not straight ahead to Panos – this small peak (1261m) has an abandoned military installation on it: **do not** approach Panos under any circumstances). The water at Jelova ruja is fouled. The route then turns right (**not** straight ahead – the trail to Visošica east of Jelova ruja leads into an area suspected of landmine deployment: **make sure you turn south after Jelova ruja**) towards Debeli kuk (1269m) and the *sklonište* at Stap (960m), with drinking water available from a cave around 30m from the shelter (5hr). ◄

From Stap, the route continues to Malo and Veliko Rujno, where it links with the Južni Velebit and Paklenica route (see Route 19), and continues to Struge (7hr).

The water from the tank here has been known to run out during summer, and should be purified in any case.

Stap is a flat, grassy area surrounded by limestone crags; the peak itself is around 40 minutes away.

ROUTE 17

Anica kuk

Start/finish	Velika Paklenica car park
Distance	8km (5 miles)
Total ascent/descent	690m (2264ft)
Time	3hr 30min
Terrain	Broad track along the canyon floor, then a clear rocky path up towards Anica kuk
Maximum altitude	712m (Anica kuk)
Maps	HGSS Paklenica (1:25,000); SMAND (19) Nacionalni park Paklenica (1:30,000)
Refreshments	PD Paklenica
Transport	Starigrad-Paklenica is on the main bus route between Rijeka and Zadar (1hr from Zadar). The turn-off to Velika Paklenica is just to the south of the town beyond the Hotel Alan; it's 2–3km up the road to the national park entrance.
Note	Park entry tickets for Paklenica National Park cost 180Kn (Jun–Sep)/120Kn (Mar–May, Oct)/60Kn (Nov–Feb) for a five-day ticket; 120Kn (Jun–Sep)/80Kn (Mar–May, Oct)/40Kn (Nov–Feb) for a three-day ticket; and 60Kn (Jun–Sep)/40Kn (Mar–May, Oct)/20Kn (Nov–Feb) for a one-day ticket. They can be bought from the national park office in the car park in Velika Paklenica.

One of the most popular day walks in Paklenica, this easy hike begins at the car park and national park entry at the end of the asphalt road in Velika Paklenica, and ascends to the top of Anica kuk, the sheer wall of which towers over the southern side of the canyon. This walk can easily be combined with the walk to Manita peć (Route 18) in the same day, or you can continue up the gorge to PD Paklenica.

From the car park and ticket office, follow the broad, clear track up Velika Paklenica, passing a popular

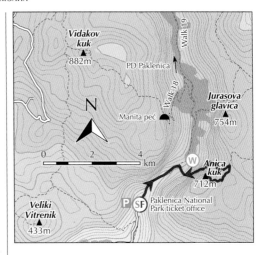

There's a good spring around 5 minutes further along the main trail beyond the Anica kuk turnoff.

On the trail to Anica kuk, Paklenica National Park

climbing area on your left. After around 30 minutes, turn right onto a clearly marked trail to Anica kuk, crossing boulders and then ascending steadily below the shear cliff face. ◄ Around 50 minutes after leaving the main trail along the bottom of the gorge, turn right at a junction, crossing a fairly level area before the last, short ascent to the summit of **Anica kuk** (712m).

Descend to the **car park** by the same route (allow 75 minutes).

ROUTE 18
Manita peć

Start/finish	Velika Paklenica car park
Distance	8km (5 miles)
Total ascent/descent	450m (1476ft)
Time	3hr
Terrain	Good clear rocky trail, minimal shade
Maximum altitude	570m (Manita peć)
Maps	HGSS Paklenica (1:25,000); SMAND (19) Nacionalni park Paklenica (1:30,000)
Refreshments	PD Paklenica
Transport	Starigrad-Paklenica is on the main bus route between Rijeka and Zadar (1hr from Zadar). The turn-off to Velika Paklenica is just to the south of the town beyond the Hotel Alan; it's 2–3km up the road to the national park entrance.
Note	Park entry tickets for Paklenica National Park vary in price depending on the time of year (see Route 17 box for more information). You can buy tickets from the national park office in the car park in Velika Paklenica.

An easy walk to a fascinating cave, with jaw-dropping views. Guided tours of the interior of Manita Peć (included in the price of the entry ticket) last around 30 minutes. The temperature inside the cave remains a constant 9°C, so it's worth carrying a fleece, however roasting the weather might be outside. Opening times: April: Sat 10am–2pm; May/June/October: Mon/Wed/Sat 10am–2pm; July, August and September – daily 10am–2pm.

This walk can easily be combined with Anica kuk (Route 17) in the same day; the trail leading NW from Manita Peć towards Vidakov kuk and Veliko Rujno, although marked on maps, should, however, be avoided. If you want to get to Veliko Rujno from within Velika Paklenica, follow the main trail up the canyon to the hut, then a well-marked trail to Veliko Rujno from there.

From the car park and ticket office, follow the broad, clear track up Velika Paklenica, passing a popular

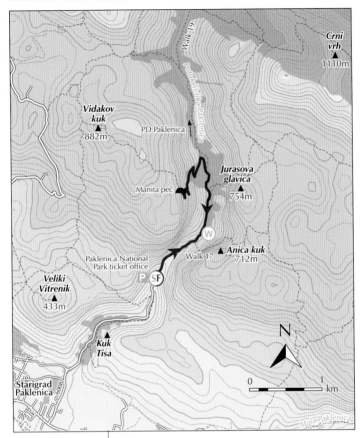

climbing area on your left, and a trail on your right to **Anica kuk** (Route 17). Turn left onto a clear trail to Manita Peć, which ascends the side of the gorge in a series of long, easy switchbacks. There's a small viewing platform just before you reach the entrance to the cave, with stupendous views up and down the canyon, before reaching the entrance to **Manita Peć**.

The interior of **Manita Peć** has plenty of interesting cave formations – stalactites, stalagmites, flowstones – as well as invertebrate cave fauna (two new species were discovered here, a pseudoscorpion *Chthonius radjai* and a small crab *Bogidiella sketi*). The trail to the cave was opened in 1937.

Although there's a trail marked on various maps from Manita Peć to Vidikovac kuk and the 4X4 road leading to Veliko Rujno, this is a route better avoided – in reality it's steep, uncleared and the slope on the initial section has been turned into an open toilet. Really, there are far more pleasant places to hike in the national park!

Descend to the **car park** by the same route.

Hikers taking in the view across Velika Paklenica, from the small viewing platform just below Manita peć, Paklenica National Park

ROUTE 19
Južni Velebit (southern Velebit) and Paklenica trek

Start	Milovci
Finish	Velika Paklenica car park
Distance	39.5–42km (24.5–26.1 miles)
Total ascent	2320m (7612ft)
Total descent	2327m (7635ft)
Time	5–6 days
Maps	HGSS Paklenica (1:25,000); SMAND (19) Nacionalni park Paklenica (1:30,000).
Transport	Starigrad-Paklenica lies on the main coastal highway south from Karlobag (by bus, it's 50min from Karlobag or 1hr from Zadar). The turn-off to Velika Paklenica is just to the south of the town beyond the Hotel Alan; it's 2–3km up the road to the national park entrance.
Accommodation	Accommodation is provided by three *sklonište* – Planinarsko sklonište Struge, Planinarsko sklonište Ivine vodice and Planinarsko sklonište Vlaški grad – at either end of the main ridge, a tiny cave beneath the northern flanks of Bojin kuk, and by a large hut (PD Paklenica) at the head of the gorge below.
Note	Refer to Route 17 information box for details on ticket prices to Paklenica National Park. Tickets can be bought from the national park office in the car park in Velika Paklenica or from huts and wardens. Buy supplies at Starigrad-Paklenica.
Warning	Certain areas of southern Velebit remain heavily mined from the 1991–1995 war. Although the paths followed in this itinerary are perfectly safe, adjacent areas are not always so. In particular, the area beyond Struge, and the eastern side of the main ridge from Struge to Sveto brdo, are suspected of being mined: **do not** proceed east of Struge or descend to the eastern side of the main ridge. **Do not** wander off the main path in this area: if you do not manage to reach a hut and need to bivouac, do so on the path.

Southern Velebit contains some outstanding scenery, not to mention two of Croatia's highest mountains (Vaganski vrh and Sveto brdo) and the limestone gorges of Velika and Mala Paklenica. The following itinerary ascends to Bojinac (1110m) and Veliko Rujno before following the main ridge over Vaganski vrh (1757m) and on to Sveto brdo (1751m), and descending to PD Paklenica. When linked to the route over northern and central Velebit (see Route 16, alternative route to southern Velebit, above), it provides the most rewarding extended mountain trek in Croatia; otherwise, it can be completed in four days.

Although most visitors enter the national park through Velika Paklenica, and begin and end walks at PD Paklenica, it is much more rewarding to start a little further north, and include the twisted limestone crags of Bojinac (1110m). This also allows more of a sense of continuity from the route over northern and central Velebit and joins the southern extension of this (see alternative route to southern Velebit at the end of Route 16, above) at Veliko Rujno.

Velika Paklenica contains numerous climbing routes just beyond the car park and the national park entrance.

Bojinac and Southern Velebit viewed from across the Velebit Channel

STAGE 1
Milovci – Bojinac

Start	Milovci
Finish	Bojinac
Distance	6km (3.7 miles)
Total ascent	1000m (3281ft)
Total descent	30m (98ft)
Time	4hr
Terrain	Clear, rocky track then fainter paths, with one area where trail markings are less obvious
Maximum altitude	1000m (3281ft)
Accommodation	Planinarsko sklonište pećina (small cave)
Note	Although there are two tiny springs on Bojinac, these cannot be relied on and you should bring enough water to last you until Veliko Rujno on Stage 2. The *sklonište* at the end of the stage is just a small cave; you may prefer to carry a tent and continue slightly beyond Bojinac towards Veliko Rujno (outside the national park boundary) and camp.

This stage leads from the village of Milovci near the coast, up to the striking limestone formations at Bojinac, just inside the boundary of Paklenica national park.

From the small car park in **Milovci** follow the signs to Veliko Rujno, before turning left on a path with faint trail markings and the occasional cairn. Cross a plateau, then follow the trail as it zigzags uphill. Continue alongside a dry-stone wall (not over it), following cairns and passing a ruined stone house on your left. Contour the hillside on a well engineered track with views back over the sea, and of a peak on your right. Follow the trail as it zigzags up again, passing alongside another dry-stone wall (which again you don't cross). Pass a trail on your right, and continue straight ahead up the slope, to reach a pass, 1hr 30min from Milovci. ◄

There is a small devotional shrine here, and views back across the Velebit Channel.

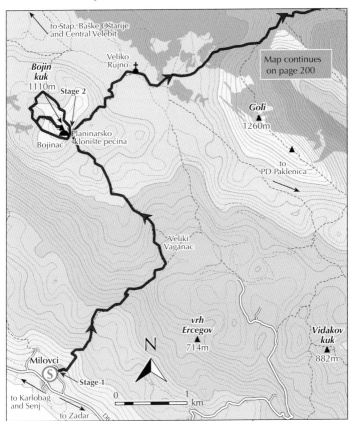

Continue, descending slightly, then ascend again on a rocky path through dry grass and low bushes, to reach a trail on your left to Bojinac in 15 minutes. The path is unclear at first, following a wall before clear trail markings appear, and then climbing steeply with views back towards **vrh Ercegov**. Just after a grassy clearing, you will reach a junction, where a trail on the left leads to a viewpoint in 5 minutes (but the 'view' really isn't worth it – better views lie ahead). Continue straight ahead on the trail marked Bojinac, to gain the edge of a rocky dell in 30 minutes. Descend into this then veer right (look out for cairns), passing a prominent and distinct rock formation which looks like a giant snail (Jagin kuk), with the polished limestone cliffs of **Bojin kuk** beyond. Continue, passing a trail on the left, then scrambling up and turning right then left. Pass a trail to Veliko Rujno on your right, to reach the **sklonište** in a few minutes.

Planinarsko sklonište pećina (also known as Planinarsko sklonište na Bojincu) is nothing more than a small rock cave, which can sleep up to about four people at a squeeze.

If you decide this isn't for you (and it can be rather claustrophobic, and muddy) and you have a tent, continue a short distance along the Veliko Rujno trail (see Stage 2, below), where there are some reasonably level, grassy slopes suitable for camping, just on the edge of the national park boundary. Alternatively, camp at Veliko Rujno itself (Bojin kuk and the dell below it are part of Paklenica National Park, so camping is prohibited

The trail to Bojinac, near Jagin kuk

there). There are two tiny springs in the vicinity (one back in the dell, the other on the excursion detailed below), but (assuming you've brought enough water, as advised) you'd do better to wait until Veliko Rujno.

Excursion from Planinarsko sklonište pećina:
Bojin kuk

Start/finish	Planinarsko sklonište pećina
Distance	2.5km (1.6 miles)
Time	3hr
Terrain	Clear, rocky trail with some scrambling
Maximum altitude	1110m (3642ft)

There are two routes up Bojin kuk – a steep, exposed via ferrata from the S, and a more moderate, rocky scramble up a gully from the W. If you are experienced and properly equipped and want to try the former, ascend that way and descend via the easier route. The following itinerary ascends and descends by the easier route, and continues by making a short circuit of Bojin kuk. You should have plenty of time to complete the excursion and continue to Struge (Stage 2) the same day.

Retrace your steps from the cave/*sklonište*, leaving full packs at the junction with the onward trail to Veliko Rujno, then keep right rather than descending all the way into the dell, and follow the trail marked 'Zliba'. Ascend steeply over limestone formations, to gain a shoulder with fantastic views (the best spot for breakfast). The more difficult and exposed via ferrata route to Bojin kuk starts from just above this. Continue, following the *voda* (water) signs and passing trails on your left, one of which leads to a sinkhole. In 10 minutes, you will come to a tiny, rather dirty spring a little way up the cliff on your right. Pass this

See map on page 195

View across Jagin kuk and other rock formations, Bojinac, Paklenica National Park

to reach a sheltered, grassy clearing, where you turn right on the trail to Bojin kuk. A sign at the bottom reads *Bablji smjer*, which translates, rather mischeviously, as 'granny route' – just so you know you've picked the easier of the two possible ascents. A degree of caution is still advised however: **the trail passes a deep sinkhole** (on your right; nearby rocks are marked *pazi*, danger, and *ponor*, sinkhole), and as you scramble up the rocky gully, watch out for snakes. It's less than 30 minutes to the summit of **Bojin kuk** (1110m), with excellent views. The more difficult routes come up from the other side (not recommended as a descent). Instead, retrace your steps back down to the main trail, and turn right, to gain a small saddle in 20 minutes. Continue beyond this, keeping right and ignoring a trail on the left to Veliko Rujno, to reach the *sklonište* in another 20 minutes. Collect your full packs and continue to **Veliko Rujno** as described in Stage 2.

STAGE 2
Bojinac – Struge

Start	Bojinac
Finish	Struge
Distance	6km (3.7 miles)
Total ascent	520m (1706ft)
Total descent	120m (394ft)
Time	3hr
Terrain	Paths at first then broad, clear trails beyond Veliko Rujno
Maximum altitude	1400m (4593ft) (Struge)
Accommodation	Planinarsko sklonište Struge

From Bojinac, this stage leads through Veliko Rujno before ascending gradually to the shelter at Struge on the main Velebit ridge.

Descend a short distance from the *sklonište*, and turn left on the trail marked Veliko Rujno. Ascend slightly before descending steeply and entering forest. Around 30 minutes from the *sklonište*, you will emerge into a clearing with a water cistern on your left, where a trail marks Stap as three hours distant. Head right then left across the clearing, to reach the main north–south Velebit trail (the VPP) and Veliko Rujno – a large, grassy clearing at 850m.

> The **church** (Gospa od Rujna), where there is a water tank, is a short distance along the path to the left. Numerous people flock to the church on 15 August for Velika Gospa (Assumption Day).

Strike south on the main trail before turning left towards Stražbenica after 10 minutes. ▶ Follow a broad track through pines before veering right and ascending, the pine trees gradually being replaced by beech, to reach a trail to Golić on the right after 35 minutes. Turn right along this before immediately turning off to the left and

The path straight ahead leads down into Velika Paklenica in three hours.

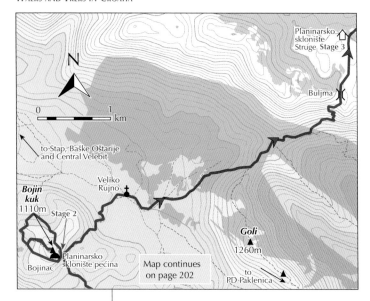

continuing to a small pass with a viewpoint just up to the left (signposted *vidikovac*; from *vidjeti* 'to see'). Descend a few minutes to Stražbenica, a junction near which there is a small spring, and from which a path leads down to PD Paklenica in 90 minutes. Ignore this path and continue straight ahead, ascending at first then temporarily descending, with good views down over Velika Paklenica. You'll pass a small spring on the left and then two more paths down to the hut on the right before ascending the final, steep switchbacks to the **pass** (1394m), which you should reach 35 minutes beyond Stražbenica. ◀

The pass, called Buljma, commands impressive views down over Velika Paklenica, and out over the Velebit Channel and the island of Pag.

Before proceeding any further, read the section on landmines at the beginning of this section and in the introduction (if you haven't already). The paths are perfectly safe, but some of the surrounding areas are not. As a sign on a rock 5 minutes beyond the pass declares, 'Forward you go your own responsibility [sic]'.

Continue to the junction 5 minutes beyond the pass (from where a route leads directly up to the main ridge, joining Bukova staza near Babino jezero). Then, carry on straight ahead for a further 10 minutes to **Planinarsko sklonište Struge**.

Planinarsko sklonište Struge (1400m; sleeps 15; PD Paklenica, Zadar) is a tall, A-frame sklonište. Water is available from the well at Marasovac, 15 minutes away.

STAGE 3
Struge – Planinarsko sklonište Ivine vodice via Vaganski vrh and Sveto brdo

Start	Struge
Finish	Planinarsko sklonište Ivine vodice
Distance	12.5km (7.8 miles)
Total ascent	790m (2952ft)
Total descent	1037m (3402ft)
Time	7hr 30min
Terrain	A long stage, but along good, clear mountain paths for the most part, then along winding forest paths in the latter part. Route finding can become very challenging in poor weather
Maximum altitude	1757m (5764ft) (Vaganski vrh)
Accommodation	Planinarsko sklonište Ivine vodice; Planinarsko sklonište Vlaški grad (closed for reconstruction at the time of writing in 2018)

This is a fairly long day, with some outstanding views – including Vaganski vrh, one of Croatia's highest peaks, and the prominent dome of Sveti Brdo. Start early, as you can't afford to be caught out in the dark on the ridge. Stopping for the night at Vlaški grad would be preferable and shave an hour off this route, but it was closed for reconstruction at the time of writing (2018).

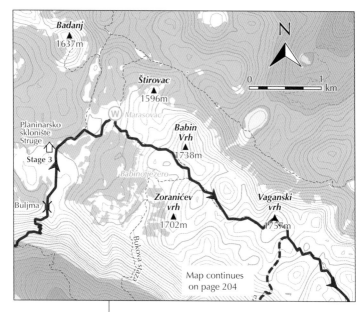

Do not wander off into the forest to the left.

A trail branching off this path before the lake leads up to the top of Zoranićev vrh (1712m), named after the 16th century Croatian writer Petar Zoranić, whose *Planine* ('The Mountains') attempted to imbue the area with mythical history and legend.

Continue from Struge along a clear path. ◄ The path soon veers to the right, around the side of a basin – **do not** follow the path straight ahead beside the trees, and **do not** take a short cut through the basin. Pass a track on the right (leading to the trail from the junction just beyond Buljma, referred to above in Stage 2) to reach the well, known as **Marasovac voda**, 15 minutes from Struge. **Do not** continue N of Marasovac.

From Marasovac, ascend right (roughly S) on the path to Vaganski vrh, passing a small bunker in a group of trees and climbing steadily, to reach a large cairn, with views out over Lika and back towards central Velebit. Continue past the cairn, the path levelling before bringing you to a junction, 45 minutes from Marasovac, from where **Bukova staza** ('beech path') descends to PD Paklenica via Babino jezero on the right. ◄ Continue straight ahead on the main trail, ascending slightly through juniper and dwarf mountain pine, thistles and raspberries, with views

of folded cliffs on your left. The path gradually veers left and then right, ascending to the grassy summit of **Vaganski vrh**, 45 minutes beyond Bukova staza.

The main ridge of Southern Velebit, near Vaganski vrh

> At 1757m, **Vaganski vrh** is the highest peak in Velebit and the third highest in Croatia. It is a far more attractive peak than its slightly loftier sibling on Biokovo, Sveti Jure, which is surmounted by an enormous red-and-white TV antenna and has a road leading to the summit. It offers a lovely view of the surrounding area – providing, of course, that cloud has not brewed up in the east and swallowed the entire ridge, as it is prone to do.

From the summit, descend southeast on a steep and rocky path, over tussock to a junction in 10 minutes.

Shortcut to PD Paklenica

For those short of time, it is possible to descend from here directly to PD Paklenica instead of continuing along the ridge to Sveto brdo and Ivine vodice. This more direct route carries the alluring title **Lipa staza** ('beautiful

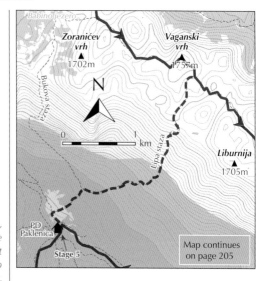

Map continues on page 205

Velika Paklenica, and the main ridge of Southern Velebit ending in Sveto Brdo on the right, viewed from across the Velebit Channel

path'). However, *lipa* it most certainly is not, involving a steep, knee-jarring descent over some horrendous scree

followed by an equally steep and seemingly endless descent through the forest. It is generally accepted that nobody would choose to come up this route.

From the junction below Vaganski vrh, descend a steep path, before ascending to gain a ridge in 20 minutes. From this point, the descent is relentlessly steep over unconsolidated scree, redeemed only by spectacular views before entering forest cover. Continue the steep, rocky descent, passing a path down from Liburnija and Babin kuk on the left before reaching the junction with **Bukova staza**, 1hr 50 min below the ridge. Continue beyond this to a further junction just above a small settlement, where you veer left, descending through mossy forest cover to reach the large PD Paklenica in 40 minutes.

To continue to Sveto brdo and Planinarsko sklonište Ivine vodice, continue straight ahead from the junction, passing a trail to Brundo and **Liburnija** on your right, and

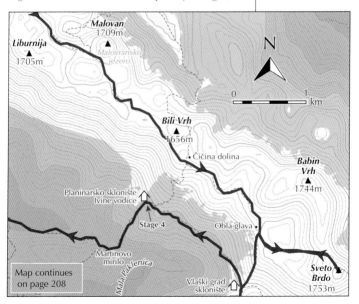

Map continues on page 208

then **Malovan** (1709m) and the small lake, **Malovansko jezero**, both on your left. ◄ Continue, passing a large cairn, and through thick mountain pine, to emerge suddenly on the coastal side of the ridge, with views down over Paklenica and the bridge at the end of the Velebit Channel. ◄ Contour scree slopes, to reach **Čičina dolina**, where a path descends on your right to Ivine vodice (40min) and PD Paklenica (3hr). Instead, continue straight ahead, winding your way over **Obla glava** (1557m) and below **Babin vrh** (1744m) before reaching another trail on your right, to Vlaški grad. Continue past this, and ascend over grassy slopes to reach the summit of **Sveto brdo** (1753m) in 1 hour, with its large metal cross.

> **Sveto brdo** ('Holy Mountain') is the distinctive 'bump' that marks the southern point of the main Velebit ridge, when viewing the range from the coast – and the views, not surprisingly, are spectacular.

Return to the Vlaški grad turn-off on the main trail, turning left and descending to **Vlaški grad sklonište**, just below the peak of the same name, which you should reach in 1hr 15min from Sveto brdo. The *sklonište* here is in a lovely location, however as long as it's closed for reconstruction, you'll need to continue for an hour to the *sklonište* at Ivine vodice instead. ◄

From Vlaški grad sklonište, follow the trail roughly NW through the forest, descending and reascending again before reaching **Planinarsko sklonište Ivine vodice** in just under 1 hour.

> The hut at Planinarsko sklonište Ivine vodice (1250m; sleeps 12; PD Babulj, Bibinje) is in a rather poor state of repair, but the nearby well provides a reliable water source. The flat grassy area here is a helipad.

Climbs on the peak itself are to be strongly discouraged.

Old bunkers are visible on both peaks on your left.

The peak Vlaški grad (1375m) can be climbed – a trail heads up from just above the sklonište.

STAGE 4
*Planinarsko sklonište Ivine vodice –
PD Paklenica*

Start	Planinarsko sklonište Ivine vodice
Finish	PD Paklenica
Distance	6km (3.7 mies)
Total ascent	10m (33ft)
Total descent	780m (2559ft)
Time	2hr 15min
Terrain	Forest paths
Maximum altitude	1250m (4101ft) (Planinarsko sklonište Ivine vodice)
Accommodation	PD Paklenica

This stage is an easy descent through forest to PD Paklenica.

Descend on the main trail for 45 minutes to **Martinovo mirilo** (914m).

> Martinovo mirilo takes its name from the stone **mirilo** of local burial customs. While a body was being carried the considerable distance to the cemetery for burial, the bearers were permitted to stop and rest – and place the body on the ground – at one designated point only, roughly half way. The length of the body would be recorded, and a stone *mirilo* placed here later. It was to this *mirilo*, rather than to the actual grave located in a distant cemetery, that relatives and mourners would come to pay their respects. The custom died out in the 1950s, but the stones are still found here and elsewhere on Velebit, including beside the 4X4 road above Milovci.

Pass two trails on your left to Velika Močila and **Mala Paklenica**, continuing straight ahead and then crossing

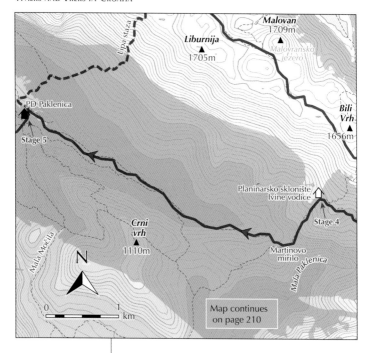

Map continues
on page 210

to the true right bank of the **Velika Paklenica stream**.
Continue through the tiny settlement of Parići, descending between two walled gardens then straight ahead
behind a walled padock, to join the combined Lipa staza
and Bukova staza trails coming down on your right. Turn
left, to arrive at **PD Paklenica** in 5 minutes.

> PD Paklenica (Borisov dom mountain hut; 50 beds;
> open daily June–September, weekends October–
> May) is a large hut at 480m (marked 550m on
> SMAND). Water is available from the tap outside.

STAGE 5
PD Paklenica – Starigrad via Velika Paklenica

Start	PD Paklenica
Finish	Velika Paklenica car park
Distance	9km (5.6 miles)
Total ascent	0m
Total descent	360m (1181ft)
Time	2hr 30min
Terrain	Clear, broad track
Maximum altitude	480m (1575ft) (PD Paklenica)
Maps	HGSS Paklenica (1:25,000); SMAND (19) Nacionalni park Paklenica (1:30,000)
Accommodation	PD Paklenica (Borisov dom mountain hut; 50 beds; open daily June–September, weekends October–May)
Practical information	Paklenica National Park (www.np-paklenica.hr)

From PD Paklenica, cross the bridge and descend, passing the path up to Sveto brdo on the left and following the broad, stone track alongside the river. Pass a track on the left to Mala Močila (see alternative route below), to arrive at a foresters' hut and an old mill, 35 minutes from PD Paklenica. Cross over to the true right bank and continue, passing trails up to Veliko Rujno and to **Manita peć** (Route 18) on the right, and a good spring on the left. After 45 minutes, with increasingly good views of Anića kuk (712m), you reach a track off to Jurasova glavica and Mala Paklenica on the left, and a further 10 minutes brings you to a track on the left to **Anića kuk** itself (Route 17).

> An impressive rock face some 400m in height, **Anića kuk** was first climbed by Dragutin Brahm in 1940. There is a map of climbing routes on the right a little further along the main trail.

Continue, re-crossing the stream and descending, as the route becomes increasingly gorge-like, to the rock

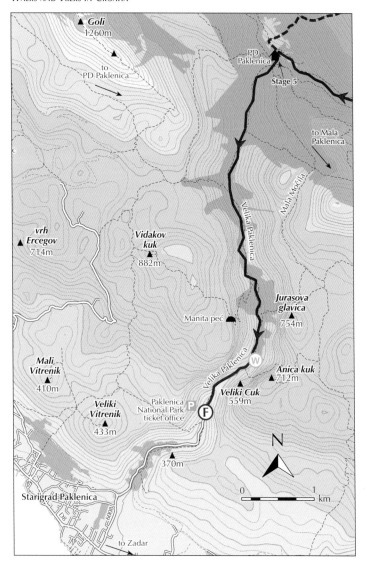

walls and climbing routes and the **car park** beyond. Walk or hitch (or if you're lucky, catch the occasional passing minibus) the last 2–3km down to **Starigrad-Paklenica**.

Alternative route: PD Paklenica–Starigrad via Mala Paklenica

Those who entered the national park through Velika Paklenica may prefer to vary their route out by leaving through Mala Paklenica – but bear in mind that the path crosses the streambed a number of times and may be impassable during the winter, while in the summer you will probably meet quite a few snakes. From PD Paklenica, cross the bridge before taking the path on the left to **Mala Močila** and continuing on the PPP, via Velika Močila, to another Stražbenica, and descending through the gorge of Mala Paklenica to reach the coast road at Seline. Starigrad is around 3km along on the coast road to your right.

Climber in Velika Paklenica, a short way beyond the national park entrance, Paklenica National Park

PART 5
THE DALMATIAN
HINTERLAND

Waterfall at the source of the River Krka, Knin

You wouldn't think you could travel such a short distance inland from the familiar, rocky terrain and olive groves of the Croatian coast for the landscape to change so dramatically and completely.

Dinara, Croatia's highest mountain, forms a magnificent hiking area on the border with Bosnia, sees comparatively few hikers compared with the mountains closer to the coast, and has what is arguably the finest summit panorama of any mountain in Croatia. Two of Croatia's most beautiful rivers, the Krka and Cetinje, emerge in this region, bursting out of karst springs in the foothills of the Dinara massif.

Plitvička jezera (Plitvice Lakes National Park, a UNESCO World Heritage Site) and Krka National Park are two wonderful areas to visit, offering short, easy trails in an unforgettable landscape of rushing water, still and silent lakes and thundering waterfalls.

Culturally, the area is also extremely rich: Knin has a magnificent castle; there are island monasteries on the River Krka; and the town of Sinj has a spectacular three-day tournament in August that stretches back over 300 years – the Alka, in which riders compete to spear a small metal ring from a galloping horse in the narrow streets of the town centre.

BASES

The routes in this chapter are more widely spread than in the other parts. However, they can be reached by bus from **Zadar**, and Routes 20 and 22 have bus connections with **Split**. The city of **Knin** is a good base from which to climb Dinara (Route 20) and the picturesque small town of **Skradin** – a protected cultural monument with narrow paved streets, a Baroque church and an iconic clock tower – is convenient for Krka National Park (Route 21). Hotel Skradinski Buk is a nice little hotel/restaurant in the centre of Skradin (www.skradinskibuk.hr). There are several large hotels at the entrance to Plitvice Lakes National Park. Knin is on the railway line between Zagreb and Split – intercity trains take 4hr 30min from Zagreb (regional trains take longer), 1hr 40mins from Split (timetable at www.hzpp.hr/en). Buses to Knin take 4hr 30min from Zagreb, 2hr from Split and 2hr from Zadar. Skradin can be reached by bus from Zadar (1hr) and other cities. For notes on Zadar and Split, including accommodation recommendations, see Appendix B.

ROUTE 20
Dinara trek

Start/finish	Glavaš
Distance	16km (9.9 miles)
Total ascent/descent	1390m (4560ft)
Time	2 days
Maps	HGSS Dinara (1:25,000) is the best map; or SMAND (40) Dinara (1:30,000). Planinarsko sklonište Drago Grubać was only opened in June 2018 and the trail to it from the spring at 1000m was marked out at the same time, so neither map will show these accurately until they have been updated (at the time of writing, the most up-to-date was HGSS map, dated 2016).
Transport	Buses between Knin and Split stop in Kijevo, around 22km SE of Knin – get out at the far (SE) side of Kijevo (30min from Knin), at a signposted turning on the left to Uništa, which is just before a large double-spired church on a hilltop (Sv Mihovila) – there's a bus stop opposite the turning (say *Za Glavaš i Uništa*). There are no buses to Glavaš, so you have a 7km walk down the asphalt road – the turnoff to the hut and the start of the trail is on the left and clearly marked Glavaš. If you're driving, there's a car park in front of the Glavaš hut.
Accommodation	Planinarsko sklonište Drago Grubać just 1hr below vrh Dinara; Planinarska kuća Glavaš; Planinarsko sklonište Martinova košara

Located SE of Knin on the border with Bosnia, Dinara is the highest mountain in Croatia, a huge, sprawling mass of a mountain, the imposing cliffs of its massive SW face falling some 1,400m to the plains below and stretching in an unbroken wall which completely dominates the surrounding landscape. The whole Dinara massif, which includes Dinara and the two neighbouring mountains of Kamešnica and Troglav (the summit of the latter is over the border in Bosnia), is around 100km long.

Vrh Dinara (also known locally as Sinjal) is 1,831m, which might not sound that much for the roof of Croatia – but the views from the top are absolutely staggering, stretching in an unbroken arc from Biokovo to Velebit and everything in between, including the Kornati islands and on a clear day it is reputedly possible to see mainland Italy. Yet Dinara sees a fraction of the visitors of Velebit, Gorski Kotar and Biokovo, and for much of the time you will have the trails to yourself.

The lush meadows of Dinara are carpeted with wildflowers in the early summer, and together with the rocky karst, cliffs and caves of this mountain they are home to birds and wildlife including stone curlew, golden eagle, peregrine falcon, grey wolf, brown bear, wild boar, the endemic Balkan snow vole, bats including Mediterranean horseshoe bat, and greater- and lesser-mouse-eared bat, masses of butterflies (a recent survey recorded more than 120 species on the Dinara massif), and various reptiles (mostly wall lizards, and notably fewer snakes than in the coastal ranges – in fact I saw no snakes at all on Dinara).

Above the Ošljak cliffs, near Planinarsko sklonište Drago Grubać, Dinara (Stage 1/2)

This area of Croatia once had huge herds of livestock – until the second half of the 20th century, around 150,000 cattle were grazed on and around the Dinara massif.

Much of the Croatian border with Bosnia was mined during the war in the 1990s, and even though hiking trails were soon cleared it was several years before the mountain was more thoroughly de-mined, and Dinara consequently remained off limits to hikers for some time. Now, however, hiking paths and surrounding areas on Dinara have been completely cleared, and hiking here is as safe as other, more frequently visited mountain areas on the Croatian coast. (Note: while Dinara has been de-mined, some surrounding mountains have not – including some parts of Kamešnica and Troglav, on which hikers should keep only to marked hiking paths.)

There are two main access routes for climbing Dinara: one from Suvo polje in the NW, and the other from Glavaš in the SE. The former was the one used most commonly in the past, and there's an old hut there (Planinarska kuća Brezovac, open only by prior arrangement) at Suvo polje – however Suvo polje lies at the end of some 19km of mostly unsealed road (with no public transport), the last part of which (beyond Markov grob) is only passable with a 4X4, leaving another good two hours on foot to the hut. Access from Glavaš in the SE is much better, however – you can get to within 7km of the start of the route by bus, and in 2018 a new hut was installed just 1 hour below the summit. Planinarsko sklonište Drago Grubać is in a specular location above the stupendous cliffs of Ošljak (part of the SW face of Dinara), and open all year. From the summit, an alternative route takes you down towards Glavaš via another, older hut (Planinarsko sklonište Martinova košara), allowing a circular route to be created.

It's possible to climb Dinara in a long, single day from Glavaš – allow 4hr 30min for the ascent and 3hr 30min for the descent. But it's well worth spreading the route over two days as described below, to enjoy the views from above Ošljak in the evening.

While you're in the area, it's also well worth visiting the source of the River Krka, on the outskirts of Knin. The River Krčić, which has carved out a short, 10km canyon across the landscape around Dinara, tumbles over a beautiful waterfall, called Topoljski buk or Topoljski slap, straight into the Krka just a few metres after the latter comes gushing out of the rock. (The Cetinje source is a bit harder to get to without your own wheels – but it's only 5km east of the road leading to Glavaš and Uništa.)

Finally, don't underestimate Dinara. Dense fog and whiteouts can make you lose the trail very easily (even those who know the mountain well treat it with a good deal of respect). The *bura* wind can be extremely strong, and while daytime temperatures can be roasting in the summer, the temperature can plummet during the night – during the author's visit in late June, the temperature at Planinarsko sklonište Drago Grubać dropped to just 1° C during the night, despite being in the high 20s during the day.

STAGE 1
Glavaš –
Planinarsko sklonište Drago Grubać

Start	Glavaš
Finish	Planinarsko sklonište Drago Grubać
Distance	5.5km (3.4 miles)
Total ascent	1,081m (3547ft)
Total descent	15m
Time	3hr
Terrain	Good, clearly marked paths
Maximum altitude	1647m (shoulder above Planinarsko sklonište Drago Grubać)
Accommodation	Planinarsko sklonište Drago Grubać just 1 hour below vrh Dinara; Planinarska kuća Glavaš

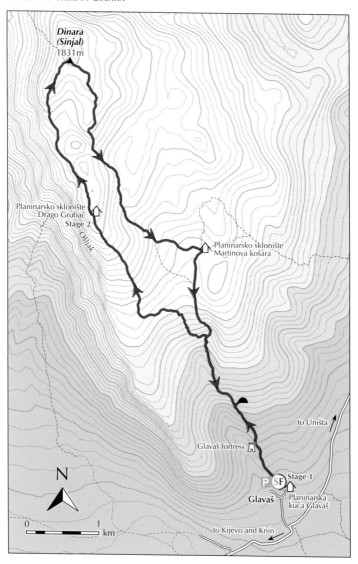

This a fantastic new route, marked out in June 2018 by local mountain rescue teams, leading up to the new hut above Ošljak. There's a good spring around one-third of the way up, at 1000m; a well beside a shepherd's hut further along the trail (needs purifying); and a rainwater tank at Planinarsko sklonište Drago Grubać.

From the car park in front of the blue container-style hut that is Planinarska kuća Glavaš (550m; sleeps 8; open by arrangement, contact HPD Sinjal, Kijevo/Marko Gojević +385 95 5090792), follow the marked path NW and uphill. Within 20 minutes, you will pass the imposing ruins of **Glavaš Fortress** on your left and a stone pond for watering livestock on your right. Around 15 minutes after passing the fortress, there's a cave in a cliff on your right, which is signposted (*pećina*) and is worth going to have a peak at – it's quite deep, fluttering with the occasional bat. The path follows the right-hand side of a ravine, and around 1 hour from Glavaš brings you to a good spring (*izvor*) at 1000m, with some nice square-shaped boulders under the shade of a cluster of young trees nearby.

Glavaš fortress was built in the 15th century as one of a line of defensive fortresses against the Ottomans

The trail on the right leads to the summit via Planinarsko sklonište Martinova košara, and is the route you will descend by in Stage 2.

Just above the spring, the path reaches a junction, where you need to turn left. ◄ Around 30 minutes above the spring is a level meadow that would be suitable for a bivouac. The path now ascends more steeply, following the line of a rocky fault, to reach a stone shepherd's hut 45 minutes above the spring. There's a well here, just past the tree (the water needs purifying). Continue ascending on a clear trail, over a series of shoulders and ignoring a large arrow in orange paint pointing to your right (this was for the benefit of the helicopter when it airlifted the container that forms Planinarsko sklonište Drago Grubać onto the mountain), to reach **Planinarsko sklonište Drago Grubać** on the far side of a small, level meadow, 2 hours from the spring.

Planinarsko sklonište Drago Grubać (open all year, sleeps 10; managed by PU Dinaridi Split; contact Darko Gavrić +385 (0)91 7289963) is constructed from a container with a single dining area below and two sleeping areas above. It was airlifted onto the mountain by helicopter in June 2018, just two weeks before the author stayed (and helped build some of the storage area at the back). Water is available from the rainwater tank by the terrace; the toilet is on the shoulder S of the hut and was built without walls so you can admire the nice view – although this does of course mean any passing hikers can admire the view of you, too.

There's a magnificent panorama from above the Ošljak cliffs – across the rolling plateau of Kamešnica to the SE with Troglav just visible beyond; Svinjal slightly to the right of this, with Peručko jezero, a slender lake near Vrlika, in between, and beyond this the Biokovo massif in the distance; Knin to the SW, and beyond, the Kornati islands and Telašćica; and the prominent bump of Sveto Brdo on Southern Velebit to the NW. In June 2018, the Dinaridi were in the process of fixing a via ferrata route up Ošljak – which, when completed, will be the first extended via ferrata route in Croatia.

STAGE 2

Planinarsko sklonište Drago Grubać
– Glavaš via vrh Dinara

Start	Planinarsko sklonište Drago Grubać
Finish	Glavaš
Distance	10.5km (6.5 miles)
Total ascent	310m (1017ft)
Total descent	1,378m
Time	4hr 15min
Terrain	Good, clearly marked paths; a couple of rocky sections on the descent
Maximum altitude	1,831m (vrh Dinara)
Accommodation	Planinarsko sklonište Martinova košara; Planinarska kuća Glavaš

This stage continues following the cliff tops to the peak of Dinara, before descending along a different trail further E and rejoining with the route you ascended on just above the spring.

From Planinarsko sklonište Drago Grubać, follow the marked trail NW above cliffs and then through wind-blasted tree stumps, keeping to the line of the ridge as

See map on page 218

Dinara summit (Sinjal)

indicated by red-and-white marker poles then bearing right and ascending more steeply, to reach the summit, **vrh Dinara**, in 1 hour.

> The summit of **Dinara** commands spectacular, panoramic views – similar to that from Ošljak, slightly enhanced with altitude, and with the addition of the view NW along the ridge, and E into Bosnia. There's a metal box with a summit register beside the concrete marker pillar.

Take the marked trail SE towards **Planinarsko sklonište Martinova košara**, through thickets of dwarf mountain pine then through flower-filled meadows, and above the edge of a doline on your right. The path descends more steeply, with prominent karst formations on your left, before reaching a junction 75 mins from the summit. Turn left here to reach Planinarsko sklonište Martinova košara (1300m; sleeps 10; very basic, with ancient mattresses; open all year) in 15 minutes. It's a basic stone hut with a few old bunk beds and mattresses, and a well outside (the water needs purifying). (Straight ahead is a slightly more direct path – either way, the two join up again just beyond the hut, and lead down to Glavaš.) ◄

If ascending from the hut, it's 2 hours from here to the summit.

Around 40 minutes from Planinarsko sklonište Martinova košara, you'll reach the trail junction with the route from Stage 1 and then just below it the spring at 1000m. Continue down the left side of the ravine, past the cave and ruined fortress, to reach the car park in **Glavaš**.

ROUTE 21
Krka National Park

Start/finish	Boat departure pier, Skradinski buk
Distance	3.5km (2.2 miles)
Total ascent/descent	150m (492ft)
Time	1hr 30min
Terrain	Clearly marked, easy paths and wooden boardwalks
Maximum altitude	170m
Maps	The national park produces a sheet, Nacionalni park Krka
Refreshments	Cafés in the Skradinski buk area
Transport	There are two main entrances to the park: from the village of Skradin (buses from Zadar take 1hr) and from Lozovac (accessible from the main coastal highway). Boats (included in the entry ticket) run every hour from the waterfront at Skradin, up into the national park near Skradinski buk, from where you can start walking, and back. Shuttle buses run from the ticket office and car park at Lozovac down to a point from which the footpaths and wooden walkways begin.
Note	Entry tickets to the national park cost 200Kn in July/Aug, 110Kn in Apr/May/Jun and Sep/Oct, and 30Kn in Nov–Mar, and include the shuttle boat from Skradin to Skradinski buk. You need to buy a separate ticket for the other boat trips in the national park – it's 100Kn for a 2-hour boat trip from Skradinski buk to Visovac and back, for example. There is a national park office in Skradin.

This is a short, very easy but exceptionally beautiful circuit through the main waterfalls of Krka National Park.

Rising on the outskirts of Knin, at the foot of Dinara, the River Krka carves a spectacular gorge on its way down to sea level, tumbling over seven main groups of waterfalls in its lower course, before flowing into the Adriatic just north of Šibenik. The area was declared a national park in 1985 (www. npkrka.hr).

Aside from the thundering waterfalls (*buk* or *slap* in Croatian), which are hugely impressive – in particular Skradinski buk, Roški slap and Manojlovački slapovi – the biodiversity of the national park is extraordinary. A total of 221 species of bird have been recorded here, 34 species of dragonfly, and 18 species of bat. The otter, wild cat, and golden jackal all inhabit the park, which also forms part of the extremely limited distribution of the olm. There is a Franciscan monastery on Visovac, an island on a lake of the same name, and the ruins of several medieval fortresses are dotted about the park, with Ključica being the most extensive and impressive of these. Trails in the park are well marked, and often along wooden boardwalks above the water – detailed maps are largely unnecessary – and there's plenty of shade from trees.

The Krka Hydro Electric Dam went into operation in 1895, just two days after the one at Niagara Falls in the USA, making it only the second such hydroelectric power station in the world.

From the boat departure pier at Skradinski buk, walk past the cluster of cafés and cross the bridge, with Skradinski buk thundering on your left as people frolic in the water a short distance from it. Follow the path uphill, passing a huge turbine wheel from the hydroelectric power plant that once stood near here. ◄ After the small but informative ethnographic displays and another café, join the asphalt road and follow that for a short distance before turning left and then crossing the water on a series of wooden boardwalks, keeping an eye out for dragonflies. Descend to Skradinski buk on the far side.

Swimmers below Skradinski buk, Krka National Park

ROUTE 22

Plitvice Lakes National Park

Start/finish	Ulaz 2 (Hotel Jezera)
Distance	8km (5 miles)
Total ascent	30m (98ft)
Total descent	170m (558ft)
Time	3hr
Terrain	Very easy walking on clear paths and wooden boardwalks.
Maximum altitude	640m
Maps	The national park office produces a sheet, available from shops and ticket offices in the park: Nacionalni park Plitvička jezera Tourist Map (1:50,000).
Refreshments	Lička kuća is a good (though often fairly busy) restaurant, at Ulaz 1. There is a small shop at Ulaz 1, but aim to buy any food you want before you get here.
Transport	Buses run to the park from Zagreb (2hr 30min), Zadar (2hr 15min), Split (5hr 30min) and other towns. Getting a bus from the park can sometimes be a problem, since they're often full and don't always stop to pick passengers up here (book a ticket online to avoid this). There are shuttle buses (or 'trains') and boats in the park itself, running every 15–20mins.
Accommodation	Should you wish to stay in the area, there are several large – if somewhat characterless– hotels at the entrances to the park. Hotel Jezera, beside Ulaz 2, is the best of the bunch; there's also a campsite at Korana, 8km from Ulaz 1 (you can't camp in the park). Those with their own transport might consider staying in the small village of Rastoke, with its old mills and waterfalls.
Note	There are two entrances, imaginatively named Ulaz 1 and Ulaz 2 (Entrance 1 and Entrance 2). Entry tickets to the national park cost 250Kn in Jul/Aug, 150Kn in Apr/May/June and Sep/Oct, and 55Kn Nov–Mar. Tickets include transport on the boats and small train, which shuttles visitors around different parts of the park.

A short but outstandingly beautiful route around some of the main lakes and waterfalls of Plitvička jezera.

The astonishing series of emerald lakes and travertine falls of Plitvička jezera (Plitvice lakes) were declared a national park (www.np-plitvicka-jezera.hr) – Croatia's first – in 1949 and named a UNESCO World Heritage Site in 1979. It's an incredibly beautiful place, all rushing water set amid lush vegetation and cool, shady beech forest. There are 16 lakes in total. Some of the falls are quite high – Sastavci plunges some 70m into the Korana, and the nearby Veliki slap is 76m high – but it's the ongoing succession of small cascades which are perhaps most memorable and which give the park its character. In winter there's heavy snowfall, and many of the smaller waterfalls freeze, becoming wonderful cascades of ice, festooned with huge icicles. There are bears here – although count yourself special indeed if you actually see one.

The well-marked network of trails and wooden boardwalks makes walking in the national park very easy – but take a map if you plan exploring further afield, in the forests beyond the main circuit of the lakes. Bear in mind that the park gets extremely busy, and you'll be sharing the boardwalks with an awful lot of people – aim to start walking as early as possible (meaning, as soon as it opens and the boats start running), before the park gets too crowded. Spring and autumn are less crowded than July/August – the colours are particularly beautiful in the autumn – and in the winter you'll have whole areas of the park to yourself, although some sections of the park are closed in winter.

Local legend tells that the lakes of **Plitvička jezera** were formed when locals pleaded for rain to the infamous Crna kraljica ('black queen') during an extended period of drought; she replied by unleashing such a deluge that the whole area was flooded and the present lakes formed. In truth, the travertine beds are formed through the precipitation of calcium carbonate onto mosses, leading to the formation of a highly porous sedimentary rock.

The national park also has the unhappy distinction of being the site of the first deaths (both Croat and Serb) during the war in the 1990s, following

the occupation of the park headquarters by Serb militia and the ensuing clash with Croatian police.

From the Ulaz 2 ticket office below Hotel Jezera (marked ST2 on maps), take the electric 'train' up to Labudovac (ST4 on maps). From here, follow a series of paths and wooden boardwalks, passing a succession of picturesque pools, falls and lakes – Okrugljak veliko, Galovac, then Gradinsko. ▶ At the pier (P2), wait for the ferry coming over from the opposite shore, and take this across Kozjak, one of the largest lakes. Walk from the far end (P3) alongside Milanovac, then Kaluđerovac – some of the most impressive sections of boardwalk are in this area, right beside the falls – then pass Sastavci and descend along a path to see Veliki slap, which tumbles down the rock face ahead. Retrace your steps to Sastavci, turn left and ascend a trail towards Ulaz 1 but turn right before reaching this and follow a path above Kaluđerovac and Milanovac to the point where the 'train' picks up for the return to Ulaz 2. Instead of getting the 'train', descend a series of steps through a hole in the rock to Milanovac – there's a fantastic viewpoint over the lakes from the top of the steps

Boardwalks across the edge of Kaluđerovac, one of the lakes in Plitvička jezera National Park

Veliki prštavac is a particularly beautiful waterfall in this area.

Veliki Prštavac waterfall in winter

– then retrace your route taken earlier from Milanovac to P3, and take the ferry back across Kozjak, finishing at the Ulaz 2 ticket office below Hotel Jezero.

Alternative route omitting the train

Obviously, you can just as easily skip the 'train' completely if you prefer – just start out by crossing on the ferry from the ticket office to P2, walk past Gradinsko, Galovac, Okrugljak veliko, then retrace your steps, following the route as described above.

Other walks in the national park

If you want to explore some of the huge area of forest that covers most of the national park, there's a marked forest trail leading NE from Ulaz 2, to Oštri Medveđak, a wooded 889m peak (8km return, allow 90 minutes).

PART 6
CENTRAL DALMATIA

Sveti Ilija from peak near Sedmina, Biokovo (Route 25)

Sculpture of Grgur Ninski (Gregorius of Nin) by Ivan Meštrović, behind the Unesco-listed Diocletian's Palace in Split

The prominent mountain ridges of Biokovo, Mosor and Kozjak in Central Dalmatia – pock-marked with karst formations and covered with only a scattering of hardy, stunted vegetation – are traversed by some spectacular hiking trails, and (with the exception of the area of Biokovo directly above Makarska) see fewer oversees hikers than Velebit and Gorski kotar further north. Access is easy from Split, Trogir and Kašteli (for Mosor and Kozjak), and from Makarska, Bast and Gornja Brela (for Biokovo).

BASES

All of the routes included here can be accessed from the coastal city of **Split**, which has an international airport and good transport links with other resorts along the coast. For practical information, including accommodation recommendations, see Appendix B.

ROUTE 23
Mosor trek

Start	Kućine
Finish	Dubrava
Distance	28.5km (17.7 miles)
Total ascent	2195m (7201ft)
Total descent	1895m (6217ft)
Time	2 days
Maps	At the time of writing, there was no detailed map available covering all of Mosor, although HGSS Kozjak (1:25,000) includes the western part of Mosor including Debelo brdo.
Transport	Bus 32 for Kućine leaves from Split's local bus station (on the corner of Domovinskog rata and Gundulićeva; the same one as for buses to Trogir) every hour or so (timetables at www.promet-split.hr). The journey takes around 20 minutes. Bus 28 runs from Dubrava and Gornje Sitno to Split.
Accommodation	Planinarski dom Umberto Girometta; Planinarska kuća Lugarnica; Planinarsko sklonište Kontejner-Ljuto kame
Note	Unless you visit at the weekend when the Umberto Girometta hut is open, it is essential that you carry enough water for the whole trip. There is no water outside the huts, and there is unlikely to be any water at the *sklonište* either. If you get stuck, you'll need to descend to the village of Gornje Sitno for water before plodding back up.

An impressive ridge stretching from the ancient fortress of Klis in the north to the gorge of the River Cetina in the south, the main blade of Mosor rises like a dorsal fin above Split, reaching its highest point at Veliki Kabal (1339m). It is a harsh and desiccated landscape, having suffered particularly severe deforestation over the course of history, and what limited vegetation there is consists primarily of stunted, thorny maquis. It gets ferociously hot during the summer, and there is little or nothing in

Late evening light on Mosor

the way of surface water, or shade for that matter, so it's best visited in the spring or autumn. But there are plenty of hiking trails, and the main ridge of Mosor has some breathtaking views.

Mosor forms a natural barrier, and due to its geographical isolation an independent republic, known as the Poljička kneževina, had developed around Poljica (the area behind Mosor) by the 11th century. Later, the Glagolitic priests of Poljica, having fled the Ottomans during the 16th century, settled on the island of Brač, where they founded the hermitage at Blaca. Split itself is justifiably famous for its Roman ruins, first and foremost among these being the palace of Diocletian, a UNESCO World Heritage Site, and nearby Trogir also has a beautiful, UNESCO-listed old town centre.

The main entry points for walks on Mosor are Grlo (near Klis), Kućine and Gornje Sitno. The latter is the most convenient for day trips up to the main ridge and Veliki Kabal. However, Kućine (as described here) or Grlo are preferable for a full traverse.

The following flexible itinerary covers the main peaks of the Mosor ridge, including its highest points,

Vickov stup (1325m), vrh Mosor (1329m), Veliki Kabal (1339m) and the more distant Kozik (1319m). The route is spread over two days, with a night at PD Umberto Girometta (or a bivouac on the main ridge). Otherwise, the walk could be spread over three days, with two nights at PD Umberto Girometta and a day trip sandwiched in between. Buy all your supplies in Split/Trogir.

STAGE 1
Kućine – PD Umberto Girometta via
Debelo brdo and Ljubljan

Start	Kućine
Finish	PD Umberto Girometta
Distance	14km (8.7 miles)
Total ascent	1,312m (4304ft)
Total descent	644m (2113ft)
Time	7hr 30min
Terrain	Rocky mountain paths, mostly well marked, with a considerable amount of ascent and little or no shade.
Maximum altitude	1262m (Ljubljan)
Accommodation	Planinarski dom Umberto Girometta; Planinarska kuća Lugarnica; Planinarsko sklonište Kontejner-Ljuto kame

This is the first half of a full traverse of Mosor, taking in Debelo brdo and Ljubljan.

Get off the bus at the last stop in **Kućine** and walk up the road from the small café, following the signs to Lugarnica. Take the marked shortcut on the right, continue up the road, and then turn left just before a small church dated 1871, ascending a steep track between houses towards the pines, with Split sprawled below you.

Ascend diagonally (ENE) on a well-marked trail, through scrub and trees blackened by recent fires,

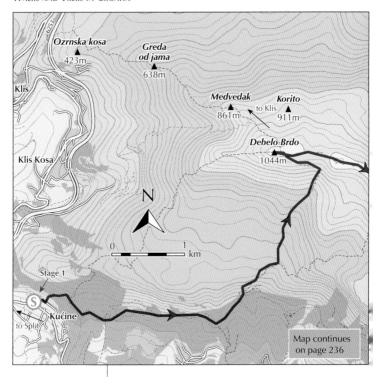

There is nothing in the way of shade, and the heat is intense in the summer.

doing your best to ignore the unsightly quarry to the right. ◄ Walk under the pylons, heading for the obvious notch in the cliffs above, to reach the pass, 45 minutes from the church. Here, you can shelter briefly from the sun under a lone, shady tree – although the stagnant little pond makes this spot less attractive than it might otherwise be.

Continue past the pond, veering right on a rocky path leading towards the main ridge. In 15 minutes, you'll reach a relatively flat area with a small shepherd's hut. Continue over dry grass and scrub, walking parallel to the low cliffs on the left as the sea comes into view on the right. Heading almost due E now, the path goes straight

over a stone wall, with Kozik visible at the far end of the main ridge, before winding through stunted holm oak, where a Lugarnica sign painted on a rock confirms that this is the right track. Zigzag up before scrambling over low cliffs, heading for the small hut visible just below the skyline and taking the left fork (marked 'Lugarnica') to arrive at a junction, just over an hour beyond the pond.

The main Mosor ridge seen from Debelo brdo

Instead of continuing directly to Lugarnica, turn left here and ascend towards the tiny spring (called Živca) and Debelo brdo (literally, 'fat hill'). The path is sometimes unclear but continues straight up to arrive at a further junction in 40 minutes. Turn left here (marked *voda* and Debelo brdo) to arrive at a small spring in 15 minutes. It's little more than a stagnant pool in the rock, which would need purifying but hopefully you won't need to rely on it. Turn left at the next junction, from where it's around 20 minutes to the summit of **Debelo brdo** (1044m), where there are good views out over Split and ESE along the main ridge. ▶

A path beyond the summit descends to Grlo and Klis.

Return to the spring and continue straight ahead, passing the trail by which you came up on the right, together with a faint trail to Ljubljan and a path to Plišivac ((1053m), which it's possible to reach in 30 minutes), both on the left. The path descends slightly, before you

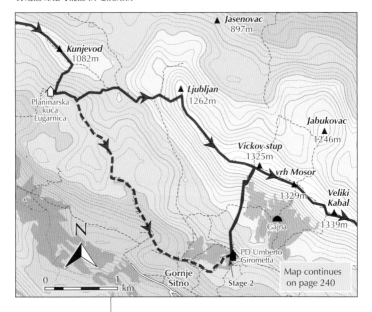

Map continues
on page 240

If you are pushed for time, the path on the right provides a more direct, fairly level route to PD Umberto Girometta and takes around 90 minutes. See Alternative route, below.

take the right fork to Lugarnica, to arrive at a T-junction 25 minutes below Debelo brdo. (Planinarska kuća Lugarnica (872m; weekends only; sleeps 20; contact Velibor Marković +385 (0)91 7925 229 at HPD Mosor, Split) is just a few minutes down the trail on the right; note there is no water outside the **hut**). Turn left on the track marked 'Planinarski dom' and 'S. Gornje' (Gornje Sitno) and continue walking for 10 minutes to a junction, where you turn left. ◄

Ascend on a steep but marked trail, passing a path on the left to Dugo Polje, to reach **Ljubljan** (1262m) in 1hr 30min. Here, you can enjoy more views of the main ridge, Vickov stup and Veliki Kabal. From the summit, the route leads along the ridge, scrambling for much of the time, towards the red shelter on Vickov stup. Just before reaching this, you arrive at a junction, with a route down to Dugo Polje on the left, and the trail descending to PD Umberto Girometta on the right. This is the point to which you will have to return tomorrow to continue the ridge walk. For now, descend steeply to the right on a path that is steep and thorny, and surrounded by rosehip and wild roses. Cross a small valley, passing a trail on your left to **Gajna**, a 170m-deep sinkhole, before climbing slightly to a pass and descending over rocky slopes to **PD Umberto Girometta**.

> PD Umberto Girometta (sleeps 82; food and drinks available; contact Špiro Gruica +385 (0)98 659 442 at HPD Mosor, Split) is a large hut at 868m, open at weekends during the summer but with no water available outside the hut. It is named after Professor Umberto Girometta (1883–1939), considered by many the founding father of alpinism in Dalmatia. There is no *sklonište* as such, although the small stone building beyond the hut will provide emergency shelter if not beds or mattresses; it also has its own resident dormouse. There is a level area below the hut suitable for pitching a tent, which is reached by descending through the trees.
>
> If you arrive mid-week and are low on water, you will have to descend to the village of Gornje Sitno to fill up there. It's an easy 30 minutes straight down the *prilaz* (meaning 'approach') trail; a steep 45 minutes back up to the hut. The path descends through trees before veering right, then roughly follows the course of the telegraph poles. There is a shop with a water tap outside, just round the main bend beyond the café.

Alternative route

To continue directly to the hut without climbing Ljubljan, continue from the junction (see above) on the right-hand (S. Gornje) path for 20 minutes before taking a right fork (marked 'S. Gornje' again) and passing through some ruined stone cottages. A further 20 minutes brings you to another junction where you take the right (unsignposted, but still clearly marked) trail for 5 minutes before continuing straight ahead (marked 'Dom', rather than right, marked 'Sitno'). Continue walking for 20 minutes before taking a right fork (marked 'S. Gornje' again) and passing through some ruined stone cottages. A further 20 minutes brings you to another junction where you take the right (unsignposted, but still clearly marked) trail for 5 minutes before continuing straight ahead (marked 'Dom', rather than right, marked 'Sitno'). Scramble up a rocky path, at times overgrown and only faintly marked, contouring the steep side of the valley and following the dom signs (first right and then veering left and ascending) to arrive at a junction with a large red sign in 30 minutes. The path to the left leads off to join the main trail to Vickov stup, Ljubljan and the main ridge; that to the right joins the main trail down to Gornje Sitno. Continue straight ahead on the trail marked 'dom', heading SE into the pine trees and passing a cave on the left, to arrive at the main trail up from Gornje Sitno (marked 'prilaz', meaning 'approach'). Turn left and you'll reach PD Umberto Girometta in 5 minutes.

STAGE 2

PD Umberto Girometta – Dubrava via Vickov stup, Veliki Kabal and Kozik

Start	PD Umberto Girometta
Finish	Dubrava
Distance	14.5km (9 miles)
Total ascent	884m (2900ft)
Total descent	1252m (4108ft)
Time	6hr 45min
Terrain	Rocky mountain paths, mostly well marked, with little or no shade.
Maximum altitude	1339m (Veliki Kabal)

This is the second part of a full Mosor traverse, taking in the peaks of Vickov stup, Veliki Kabal and Kozik.

Vickov stup, Veliki Kabal, Kozik

Retrace your steps from PD Umberto Girometta, ascending the trail to the main ridge that you descended yesterday – it's 25 minutes to the small pass, and a further 1 hour to the crest of the ridge. Turn right and follow the ridge SE to arrive at the small red shelter on top of **Vickov stup** (1325m) in 10 minutes. ▶ Continue along the airy ridge for another 5 minutes to vrh **Mosor** (with the rather precisely calculated altitude of 1329.63m).

A further 5 minutes brings you to a junction, by way of a few steel cables, from where a technical route on the left (marked 'Planinarska staza') continues to **Jabukovac**. Descend slightly to the right, before continuing along the line of the ridge, passing a trail on the right (which descends to PD Umberto Girometta in 45 minutes, via some rather loose steel cables), and ascending the final section to **Veliki Kabal** (1339m), 30 minutes from Vickov stup.

Continue SE along the ridge from Veliki Kabal, descending and then bearing right to reach the trail from PD Umberto Girometta to Kozik, near Kontejner-Ljuto kame (1055m; open all year; sleeps 10) – a simple *sklonište* made from a container (*kontejner* – remember, 'j' is pronounced 'y' in Croatia). It has a few mattresses and a large plastic water tank (empty on my last visit). Pass a trail on your left, picking your way along an overgrown path, which ascends slightly to the left.

The views from the ridge crest are, as you might expect, expansive, with Kozik particularly impressive further to the SE.

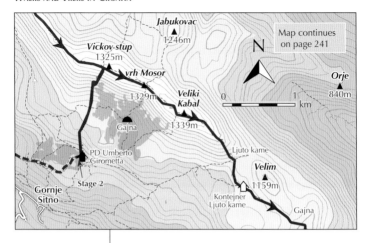

Map continues on page 241

Rather than ascending directly to the high ground to the right as you might expect, the path leads first to a saddle to the left (N) of this, 35 minutes beyond the **sklonište**. From here, ascend right for a further 10 minutes to gain the main ridge, and follow this for 10 minutes to the point where the sea and islands come into view. Kozik is now clearly visible ahead, as you continue along the ridge; then the trail drops down to the left slightly, losing some altitude and the sea view in exchange for a mossy forest trail.

In another 25 minutes the path re-emerges into the open, and leads back onto the ridge top, with impressive views of the ridge beyond Kozik and of Biokovo towering in the distance. In a further 25 minutes the path arrives at a junction, from where the route to Dubrava descends to the right. Continue straight ahead up the final pyramid, scrambling over rock to reach **Kozik** (1319m) in less than 30 minutes.

The views from **Kozik** are breathtaking; and, although slightly lower than Veliki Kabal, it feels a lot higher. The ground falls away in sheer cliffs to the SW, while the full length of the main Mosor ridge extends to the NW – a great blade of rock, with the shelter on Vickov stup reduced to a red dot, and Kozjak beyond. Split sprawls below this, and Biokovo looms up beyond the chasm-like gorge of the River Cetina to the south. Alpine swifts dart and dive about the summit at an incredible speed, and crows flap about the cliffs below. The islands of Brač and Hvar are clearly visible, against the blue of the Adriatic. The stone ruins are those of a small chapel, Sveti Jure. It is possible to continue along the ridge beyond Kozik, initially following the trail marked 'Skočibe', before descending to Gata.

To return to Dubrava, retrace your steps to the junction below the summit pyramid, and descend steeply to a level trail leading to a broad farm track in just under 1 hour. Turn right on this to reach **Dubrava** in a further 20 minutes. From the bus stop just beyond the car park on the main road you can catch a bus back to Split, passing through Gornje Sitno on the way.

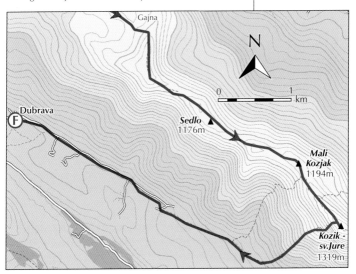

ROUTE 24
Kozjak

Start	Kaštel Stari
Finish	Kaštel Kambelovac
Distance	10.5km (6.5 miles)
Total ascent	650m (2133ft)
Total descent	675m (2215ft)
Time	5hr
Terrain	Rough rocky path, with road walking on asphalt at the start at finish.
Maximum altitude	631m (Sv Ivan)
Maps	HGSS Kozjak (1:25,000)
Refreshments	Planinarska kuća Malačka
Transport	The most convenient starting point is the railway station at Kaštel Stari, on the main railway line from Split (20min). Otherwise, take the Trogir bus (number 37) from Split's local bus station and get out at the stop, by a Kaštel Stari sign, at the point where one of Kaštel's bell towers is just coming into view on the left. Just beyond this and opposite a signpost to Trogir and the airport (Zračna luka), a road turns off to the right with red-and-white trail marking painted on the corner. Following these will bring you to Kaštel Stari station in around 20 minutes.

The long, rocky ridge of Kozjak stretches above Kašteli, the area between Trogir and Split, for about 16km. Although not as high or nearly as spectacular as Mosor, it is equally prominent from Split, and well worth a day trip for those with some extra time in the area. Due to the intense heat, summer is not the best time to visit Kozjak.

The following is a straightforward and fairly flexible day trip, climbing to the ridge from Kaštel Stari before following it SE via the small church at Biranj (631m) then descending past PD pod Koludrom to the coast road at Kaštel Kambelovac. If you plan to continue along the ridge all the way to Klis, a section of trail E of Debelić, known as Pejšin put, involves crossing an exposed rocky shelf with the aid of steel pegs and cables, so it's preferable to drop down from the ridge before reaching Debelić, as described here, then

continue to PD Putalj. There are a number of huts on Kozjak, most of them
only open at weekends or by arrangement, and alternative routes down to
the coast for those who want a shorter or longer route.

From the railway station at **Kaštel Stari** cross the railway
line, veer right, then continue straight ahead (not right to
Sveti Ivan and Sveti Juraj), following the 'dom' signs. Ascend
a broad, rather grubby track, which eventually narrows,
crossing the road twice before contouring the hillside. The
path soon veers to the right, leading up the slope to reach
Planinarska kuća Malačka (477m; sleeps 57; weekends
only; food served; run by HPD Malačka), 50mins from the
railway station. There is no water outside the **hut**. **Orljak**
(522m) is less than 15 minutes away to the left.

Continue along the ridge on the trail marked *izvor*
(spring), crossing the road and then taking the right fork
towards Biranj, passing a number of stone shelters dug
into the ground and another hut, and continuing along
the cliff top. Around 40 minutes from Malačka, the trail
arrives at the small church of **Sveti Ivan Biranj** (631m),
which sits perched on the crest of the ridge, surrounded
by picnic tables and shady trees. ▶

There is a water
tap on the wall
of the small café,
although – as the sign
states – its supply its
limited (*ima malo*
– 'there is little').

Continue past an unsightly rubbish dump on the left
and a ruined stone hut, and descend to the point where
an unsealed road crosses the ridge. Descending to the
right from here will bring you back to the main road
and the railway station; the track to the left descends to
a sinkhole, some 90 minutes away. Otherwise, continue
straight ahead until, shortly before Planinarsko sklonište
Orlovo gnijezdo (598m; open all year; sleeps 10; HPD
Ante Bedalov, Kaštel Kambelovac). Here, the ridge begins
rising up to Debelić. Turn right and follow a path down
to Planinarski dom pod Koludrom (325m; open only for
local hiking club members by arrangement) in another 90
mins, which sits on the slopes below Koludar, the prominent cliff above. From here, a trail leads down to a road,
which you can follow down into **Kaštel Kambelovac**, on
the bus route between Trogir and Split.

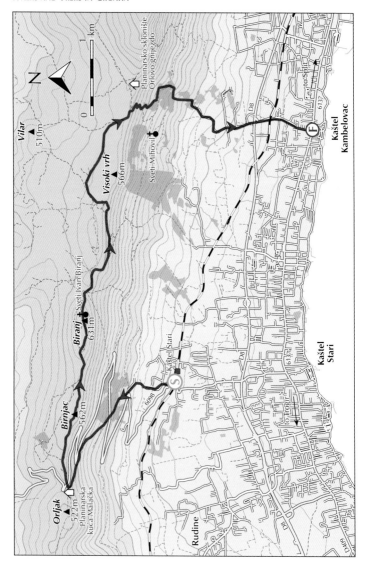

ROUTE 25

Biokovo traverse trek

Start	Bast
Finish	Makarska
Distance	23km (14.2 miles)
Total ascent	1965m (6447ft)
Total descent	2270m (7448ft)
Time	2 days
Maps	HGSS Park prirode Biokovo (1:25,000) is the best; or SMAND (32) Biokovo – Park prirode (1:25,000)
Transport	To reach Bast from the north, take a southbound bus from Split's main bus station (next to the railway station and ferry port) – there are almost hourly services to Makarska. (Avoid taking a bus going to Šestanovac, which would turn inland before Baška Voda, unless you want to start from Gornja Brela.) Ask to be let out just after Baška Voda on the main road (1hr from Split), at the turn-off to Bast on the left, from where red-and-white trail markings begin. It's around 30 minutes up to the village (unless you're lucky enough to hitch a lift), veering right on the main (sealed) branch and ascending towards the church.
Accommodation	For such a big, popular massif, there is a distinct shortage of places to stay on Biokovo, the few huts in the area being privately owned or requiring some prior arrangement with the relevant organisation in Makarska if you are not to find them all locked: Planinarska kuća Slobodan Ravlić; Planinarski dom Toni Roso; Planinarska kuća Pod Sv Jurom. Camping is officially prohibited on Biokovo, since it's a nature park. However, in case you are unable to arrange a stay at one of the huts, you might want to carry a tent anyway.
Note	As on Mosor to the north, there is an acute shortage of reliable water sources on Biokovo, so bring enough to last the whole route. Bring all supplies from Split/Makarska, as there's almost nothing in Bast itself.

Rising almost sheer from the narrow strip of coastal settlements and towering over the picturesque town of

View NW towards
Omiška Dinara,
from below
Motika, Biokovo

Makarska, Biokovo is one of the most imposing mountains on the Croatian coast. The terrain consists primarily of bare karst tops riddled with limestone pits and dells, with scattered low beech and mountain pine. These saucer- or funnel-shaped depressions, or dolina, are known in Croatian as *vrtača* (*vrt* meaning 'garden') – and as the word implies they often have walled gardens at the bottom, where fertile soil has accumulated, and crops such as potatoes are grown despite the tendency of the depressions to become flooded. Together with the larger dells and depressions, they are typically drained by some alarmingly deep and cavernous sinkholes, in a number of which water remains frozen throughout the year. There are a number of endemic plant species in the area, and large numbers of mouflon, or wild mountain sheep (*Ovis aries musimon*), wander freely below the crags. At 1762m, Sveti Jure is Croatia's second highest peak. Unfortunately, it is crowned by a huge TV antenna and has a road (known as Biokovska cesta) leading up to the summit, making it one of the least inspiring peaks in the area to climb.

There are three main points of access: from Gornja Brela to the north; from Makarska itself – the most popular for day trips; and from the village of Bast – arguably the most impressive approach, and the one taken in the following itinerary.

This steep though spectacular route runs from the village of Bast (about 300m) to the pass below Motika (1400m) and the peaks of Sveti Ilija (1642m) and Sveti Jure (1762m), before descending from Vošac (1425m) to the town of Makarska on the coast. Some of the route is shared with the Biokovska planinarska staza (BPS) and the new Via Dinarica. A two-day traverse is recommended if you are to do the area justice, although day trips are quite feasible.

Biokovo sees more call-outs for local mountain rescue teams than anywhere else in Croatia, generally the result of people walking up from Makarska completely unprepared for changes in weather conditions encountered on a karst plateau at 1400m and above.

STAGE 1
Bast – Lokva via Motika and Sveti Ilija

Start	Bast
Finish	Planinarska kuća Slobodan Ravlić, Lokva
Distance	12km (7.5 miles)
Total ascent	1440m (4724ft)
Total descent	275m (902ft)
Time	7hr
Terrain	Rocky mountain paths, only faintly marked in places, and a section of walking on scree near the start
Maximum altitude	1642m (Sveti Ilija)
Accommodation	Planinarska kuća Slobodan Ravlić

This is a spectacular route across the northern part of Biokovo. Planinarska kuća Slobodan Ravlić is only open by prior arrangement (see contact details above), and there's no water outside the hut – make sure you're carrying enough to last for two days. If you are unable to arrange to stay at Lokva, try to arrange to stay at Planinarski dom Toni Roso, which is on Vošac, instead – it's just over 1 hour from Lokva to Vošac, skipping the detour to climb Sveti Jure which you could easily come back for the following morning.

Continue past the church in **Bast** until you arrive at a water fountain on the left and a walled track (leading to a second, smaller church). Follow this walled track behind the fountain (ie not to the church itself), ascending

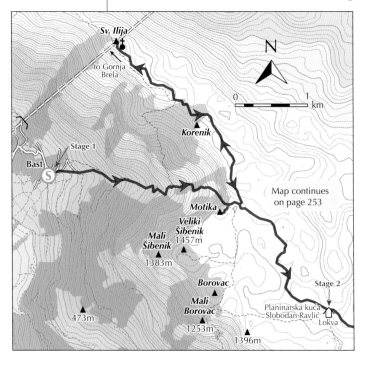

concrete steps to some houses and turning right between these, before veering left up an unmarked walled track, 10 minutes to the bottom of the scree. From this point turn right and continue straight along a level path across the scree, 5 minutes to a junction. Here, you will find a sign to Sveti Ilija on a rock, and have a good view out over Brač. (Alternatively, continue straight past the fountain to the end of the asphalt, ascend left between the last houses by way of some steps, to reach a trail with route markings on rocks and trees, which leads up to the same junction.) From here the route heads up the scree slopes towards that notch in the cliffs far above.

From the junction, ascend over rock and scree, following clear trail markings, to reach a spring (located on the right, a little below the path) just after a small devotional shrine, around 20 minutes from the junction. ▶

Continue ascending, over increasingly steep scree, passing a sign to Motika painted on a rock. The view up the steeply inclined couloir above is stunning. The path zigzags and gradually veers to the right, leading you off the scree and, for the time being, onto more stable ground. (The route can be a bit unclear, but it takes you

Take the opportunity to fill up all available water flasks: this is the last reliable water source until Makarska.

View NW from below Motika, Biokovo

off the scree to the right – don't follow the scree indefinitely, or you'll end up on a faint trail leading up towards Osićine, a small hunting lodge nestled under the cliffs.)

Around an hour from the spring, you'll reach a saddle, from where you ascend, following minimal trail markings and keeping slightly below the crest of the ridge on its other (S) side. Aim for the needle-like point of Motika. A final, narrow gully with steep stone steps leads up to a grassy area at the top of the cliffs, just below **Motika**, a total of 2 hours from the spring. At 1400m this makes a fine spot for lunch, sheltered behind a protruding outcrop of rock, with spectacular views out over the islands and north towards Sveti Ilija, and with Motika (meaning 'hoe') just above at 1473m. ◀

> A small plaque just below the cleft in the rock (from which there is a sheer drop at the far end) reads: *Uvijek gledah na liticu od koje se otcijepih* ('I always looked on the cliff from which I broke away').

There are two trails from here: left to Sveti Ilija and the BPS to Lokva and Sveti Jure; and right to Veliki Šibenik (1467m, not to be confused with the town of the same name) and Borovac (1413m), a route marked 'PPP', which passes a large, walled enclosure followed by a gaping sinkhole on the right. **Veliki Šibenik** is a spectacular viewpoint and is well worth the detour if you have time – allow 90 minutes return.

Take the left (northernmost) path from Motika (avoiding what looks like a partially filled sinkhole between the two trails), contouring the rim of a doline and passing a trail to Sveti Jure (marked 'BPS') on the right, to arrive at a cluster of ruined cottages in less than 5 minutes. If you're short of daylight hours and don't think you'll have time to continue as far as Lokva, this is the last level spot to discreetly pitch a tent, bearing in mind that camping is officially prohibited on Biokovo.

Ascend left over the slope behind the ruins, following the occasional faint trail mark and some cairns, to gain the top of the main ridge. Follow the back of this, bearing roughly NW. The trail is faint, with the occasional cairn, sometimes running along the crest of the ridge itself and sometimes contouring the slopes of *vrtača*, deep funnel-shaped depressions with stonewalled gardens at the bottom. These features, so characteristic of Biokovo and the other karst areas, are particularly impressive in this area. ▸ The trail continues past **Korenik** (1556m), and the trail up from a small hunting lodge, to reach **Sveti Ilija** (1642m), with its small **chapel** and extensive views in all directions, a total of 90 minutes from Motika. A trail continues NW from Sveti Ilija to **Ščirevac** (1619m), and on to Gornja Brela, while one heading E leads down to the village of Dedići on the Šestanovac–Vrgorac road.

Retrace your steps to the ruined cottages, and then continue back slightly further to the trail, now on the left, to Sveti Jure. This immediately ascends, taking you scrambling over a succession of tops and crests, and past the fringes of the occasional stand of low beech and oak. After about 30 minutes the words 'Lokva BPS' painted on the rock confirm that you are on the right trail; and a further 30mins of walking and scrambling should bring you to **Lokva**, with its small hut, **Planinarska kuća Slobodan Ravlić**, a total of 7 hours from Bast.

> Planinarska kuća Slobodan Ravlić (Lokva, 1467m; sleeps 10; by prior arrangement only; contact Darko Erceg +385 (0)98 225 852, HPD Biokovo) sits in a nice location, with views of Sv Jure. It will be locked if you haven't managed to arrange to stay here, and there's no drinking water outside the hut. As an indication of the appalling weather conditions which can unleash themselves upon the unsuspecting hiker in the Dinaric Alps, this hut is named after a local walker, Slobodan Ravlić, who was killed in 1980 during a monstrous hailstorm on Biokovo. There's a small, rather unpleasant-looking pond nearby from which the area derives its name (*lokva* means 'puddle' in Croatian). If you need to continue to Planinarski dom Toni Roso for the night, it's 1 hour further to Vošac, skipping the detour to Sveti Jure as described in Stage 2.

Sveti Jure, crowned with a huge red-and-white antenna, dominates the skyline to the right, appearing much closer than it actually is.

STAGE 2
Lokva – Makarska via Sveti Jure and Vošac

Start	Planinarska kuća Slobodan Ravlić, Lokva
Finish	Makarska
Distance	11km (6.8 miles)
Total ascent	525m
Total descent	1995m
Time	7hr (1722ft)
Terrain	Rocky mountain paths, only faintly marked in places; a long descent but this is on a good, clear path and is not too steep.
Maximum altitude	1762m (Sveti Jure)
Accommodation	Planinarska kuća pod Svetim Jurom; Planinarski dom Toni Roso

This stage continues the traverse of Biokovo, climbing to its highest peak (Sveti Jure, the second highest peak in Croatia after Dinara) and crossing some beautiful karst terrain before the long, steep descent to Makarska.

Leave Lokva on the trail marked 'Vošac and Sveti Jure' from beside the hut. Clearly marked and well maintained, this section has clear views back (N) along the main ridge to Sveti Ilija and (SSE) to Vošac, with its small hut perched on top. After around 15 minutes you pass a particularly deep depression with a massive cave on the left, below **Sedmina** (1563m) and Ćavlenovaća.

A further 5 minutes beyond this, you'll arrive at a junction, with Vošac marked a further 45 minutes straight ahead, and Sveti Jure marked 1 hour to the left. Take this latter (left) fork regardless of whether you intend to climb Sveti Jure itself, as there are some particularly good views on the way. The path leads up through intermittent beech and over limestone tops, with Sveti Jure disappearing for a while before looming back into view above and ahead.

A road leads to the summit, and the trail joins it just beyond Planinarska kuća pod Svetim Jurom (below

Sv Jure, 1584m; sleeps 18; by prior arrangement only; contact Darko Erceg +385 (0)98 225 852, HPD Biokovo). Like the previous hut, this is likely to be locked unless you have made prior arrangements to stay there. It's

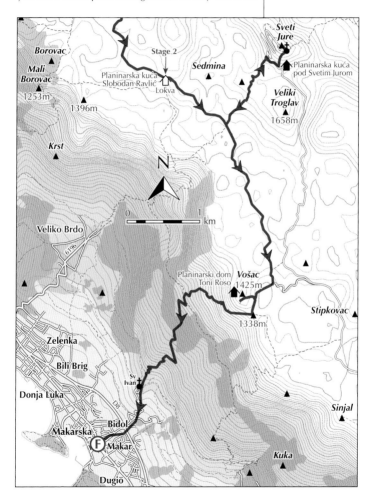

Sveti Ilija, Biokovo

somewhat uninspiring after the more unspoilt trail from Bast. However, at 1762m, Sveti Jure is Croatia's second highest peak, and since you are here you may just as well climb it.

Variant

Before arriving at the road itself, note the series of small peaks off to the left, their tops marked by short red and white poles. Scrambling up to these gives superlative views N to Sveti Ilija and beyond, with Omiška Dinara and Mosor in the distance.

The most direct route up Sveti Jure leads from the hut (**Planinarska kuća pod Svetim Jurom**) and follows steel cables to gain the summit of **Sveti Jure** (1762m) in 30mins.

> With its TV antenna and small chapel of the same name, **Sveti Jure** commands unobstructed and panoramic views. On a particularly clear day, it is reputedly possible to see the Apennines in Italy. The chapel originally stood on the highest point, but was moved to its present location to make way for the TV antenna. A trail to the deepest sinkhole in the area, Amfora jama, 614m deep, begins a little way down the road.

Retrace your steps from Sveti Jure and descend to Planinarska kuća pod Svetim Jurom and from there to the trail junction between Lokva and Vošac. Turn left towards Vošac, passing through the occasional stand of trees and arriving at a further junction, 35 minutes from the Sveti Jure turn-off. Here, turn right towards Planinarski dom pod Voščem (ie turn off what at this point appears to be the main trail straight ahead), and follow clear trail markings and descend to the road. There used to be a large hut just beyond the car park, but this has been closed for many years. A sign marks Makar, the small village above Makarska, as 2hr 30min away.

Follow the Škrbine trail, which drops slightly before ascending in long switchbacks, with a number of shortcuts between these. It is around 20 minutes up to **Vošac** (1425m), passing Škrbine (the lookout point, *pogled*, and the beginning of the descent to Makarska) about half way and off to the left.

> The hut here, Planinarski dom Toni Roso (Vošac, 1422m; by prior arrangement only; contact Vojo Ribičić +385 (0)98 1814 051, SAK Ekstrem, Makarska), is usually open during the summer (but check in advance if you're planning to stay there – see contact details above), sleeps 20, and sells drinks. Regardless of whether it's open, however, the view from here is quite magnificent – the land falling away in great cliffs down to the red-tiled roofs and beaches of Makarska.

Drop back down to Škrbine (1388m), passing a trail to Kotišina on the left and turning right onto the path down to Makarska. The descent is far less gruelling than might be expected, following long and easy switchbacks below the cliffs. ▶ Around 75 minutes should bring you to a small but unreliable well and, in a further 30 minutes, to the upper houses of Makar. Follow the road down, with the occasional shortcut, to **Makarska** itself, crossing a bridge over the main road and continuing straight down past the market to the church of sveti Marko in the main square and to the sea beyond.

Scattered beech gradually give way to pine and cypress, while wild mountain sheep bound over the rocks above.

PART 7
SOUTHERN DALMATIA

Sveti Ilija, Pelješac (Route 27), viewed from the island of Korčula

Croatia becomes progressively narrower as it progresses through Southern Dalmatia to the border with Montenegro, and the mountains south of Biokovo are much lower than those further north – but there are nevertheless a couple of beautiful hikes in this area too.

The best areas for hiking in Southern Dalmatia are Snježnica, SE of Dubrovnik near the border with Montenegro and at 1,234m the highest peak in southern Dalmatia (Route 26); and Sveti Ilija which lies near the tip of the Pelješac peninsula (Route 27). Southern Dalmatia is very hot in the summer and that combined with the lack of shade on these walks means that they are best done in the spring or autumn.

BASES

The main reason for coming to southern Dalmatia for most people is to visit **Dubrovnik** – an incredibly well-preserved walled medieval city, with a fantastically rich history, which is not surprisingly a UNESCO World Heritage Site. Dubrovnik was already bursting at the seams with visitors even before it became famous all over again as the set for King's Landing from *Game of Thrones*. Still, it remains an unforgettable place, at its best when visited well outside the summer months to avoid the crowds. Dubrovnik has an international airport (at Čilipi, towards the Montenegrin border) and good transport links with the other Croatian cities and resorts. For practical information, including accommodation recommendations, see Appendix B.

Both of the routes included here can be reached from Dubrovnik or the pretty town of **Cavtat**, although **Orebić** (www.tz-orebic.hr) at the start of Route 27 lies on the long Pelješac peninsula and is actually much closer to the idyllic island of **Korčula** (www.visitkorcula.eu) than anywhere else (a 10-minute boat ride links Orebić with the island's capital, Korčula, one of the loveliest towns on the Croatian coast and supposed home of a certain Marco Polo).

ROUTE 26
Sniježnica (Ilijin vrh)

Start/finish	Kuna Konavoska
Distance	11km (6.8 miles)
Total ascent/descent	745m (2444ft)
Time	3hr 30min
Terrain	Good path with an initial section along a 4WD track.
Maximum altitude	1234m (Ilijin vrh)
Maps	HGSS Konavle (1:25,000) or HGSS Sniježnica (1:20,000); at the time of writing the Konavle sheet was the most up to date (published 2017).
Transport	Local bus 25 runs from Dubrovnik to Vodovađa and back around three times daily (timetables at www.libertasdubrovnik.hr/suburban-timetable, and click on East), stopping at Mihanići (40min), from where there's a marked path up to Kuna Konavoska. Bus 30 goes to Vodovađa from Cavtat but is less frequent; I suggest taking a taxi to Kuna Konavoska (around 220kn from Cavtat) to give you an earlier start than the 9.30am bus, then on the return walking down to Mihanići and picking up the bus there in the afternoon. I found Pavo Zvirko in Cavtat to be honest and reliable and he knows where the start of the route is, (tel +385 (0)98 549 914). Bus 10 runs between Cavtat and Dubrovnik via Zvekovica, where you could change onto the 25.
Note	Make sure you carry enough water; there's none on the route.

This is a lovely walk up to Ilijin vrh, for most of the way following a well-engineered old Austro-Hungarian packhorse track, with fantastic views from the summit.

Sniježnica rises steeply above the level strip of cultivated land that is Konavle fields, the last mountain in Croatia before the borders with Montenegro and Bosnia-Hercegovina. At 1,234m, the highest peak on the mountain, Ilijin vrh, is the highest mountain in southern Dalmatia. The Austro-Hungarian packhorse track leads up the summit from the village of Kuna Konavoska. Built to transport cannons to the top of the mountain, it now provides a great hiking route. Locals make a pilgrimage to the small 19th century chapel on the summit on Whit Monday, and also on Boxing Day.

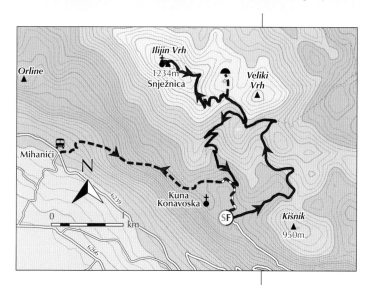

To reach Kuna Konavoska from Mihanići

If you want to walk up to Kuna Konavoska from Mihanići, the marked trail starts from near the bus stop, following a narrow road NE, then a path SE which ascends past the small 16th century church of Sv Nikola, with some interesting medieval tombstones (stećci, a joint UNESCO listing of these along with those in Bosnia-Hercegovina) to Kuna Konavoska (3.5km, allow 90 minutes).

From the asphalt road, turn right (NE) around 300m SE of **Kuna** onto a clear but unmarked 4WD track leading gradually uphill, with open views on your left. After 30 minutes, just before the end of the 4WD, turn right onto an unmarked walled path along the edge of vegetable patches, passing a wooden tower. The path becomes slightly overgrown, but after 5 minutes you turn left onto a

The upper part of the trail to Snježnica

much clearer stone track that climbs gradually uphill, with clear views behind you of the Orjen massif in Montenegro. The track switches right over a shoulder; shortly after this I found the track partly blocked with a bundle of wood but it was easy enough to step over. Around 1 hour after leaving the asphalt road, you'll pass a trail coming up on your left, which is the marked route from Kuna.

> Snježnica forms part of the very limited distribution of the **mandragora** (*Mandragora officinarum*), more commonly known as mandrake. This is a toxic, hallucinogenic plant used in the ancient world as a surgical anaesthetic, but also generally associated with witchcraft and occult practices partly due to the strange, human shape of the root. In any case, it's a protected species in Croatia, and not easy to find. According to local folklore in Konavle, if a man picks mandragora, he and his family will be cursed.

Continue straight ahead, on a marked trail now, which from here on is a well-engineered old Austro-Hungarian packhorse track. Pass a trail on the right that leads to a

sinkhole on the far side of a doline, and a series of crosses at the corner of switchbacks (stations of the cross, at which pilgrims pause at when ascending the trail on Whit Monday). Around 45 minutes beyond the junction with the marked trail brings you to the summit, **Ilijin vrh**.

Ilijin vrh, Snježnica, view of Orjen massif in Montenegro

> **Ilijin vrh** (1,234m) has wonderful views over the surrounding landscape, stretching out across the fields of Konavle to the S, with Dubrovnik's airport clearly visible; out to sea you can see the Elaphite islands and Mljet; and the Orjen massif in Montenegro dominates the view to the E. There's a helicopter pad and a small telecommunications antenna, and on the far (SW) side of the summit area a small 19th century chapel (locked).
>
> The name Snježnica comes from snijeg, meaning **snow** – with the summit often being dusted with snow in the winter months, in stark contrast to the warmer plains below. During its heyday the Republic of Ragusa (Dubrovnik) would arrange for snow and ice to be collected on Snježnica, and stored in caves on the mountain to be used for as

long after the winter as possible, with the ice then being transported down to Cavtat by packhorse at night, and shipped on to Dubrovnik to be sold to its wealthy inhabitants (apparently up to 170kg could be sold in a day).

Descend by the same route as far as the junction then turn right, continuing along the marked route above walled enclosures and descending another series of switchbacks. It's easy enough to take a wrong turn here and leave the marked route accidentally, but either way you'll end up down by a cluster of walled enclosures and a small, stone pond.

There's an information board here on rock bunting, rock partridge and other rare species found in the area, where the trail has been given the name Betsa staza.

This small pond, built to water livestock, is a magnet for wildlife – within seconds of arriving, my footsteps had disturbed a grass snake which slithered off into the water, some kind of leech, several large and very noisy frogs, a Balkan green lizard, and lots of dragonflies. ◄

Continue down the track, passing another information board, to reach the houses of **Kuna** and the asphalt road in 10 minutes. The path emerges onto the road opposite house number 18. For the path down to Mihanići, follow the road to the right for a short distance. If walking the route up to Ilijin vrh here rather than starting along the 4x4 road as described, look for the stone steps opposite house 18. The owners of Stone House Kuna guesthouse plan to renovate the little stone building at the top of the steps, and turn it into a small café.

ROUTE 27
Sveti Ilija (Pelješac)

Start/finish	Orebić
Distance	13.5km (8.4 miles)
Total ascent/descent	1040m (3412ft)
Time	6hr
Terrain	Good paths, clearly marked for most of the route; some road walking at the start.
Maximum altitude	961m (Sveti Ilija)
Maps	HGSS Pelješac – Sveti Ilija (1:20,000). There's also a free local map ('Pješice krajolicima pelješke rivijere', 'Walking through the countryside of the Pelješac Riviera'), with contour lines and text in Croatian, English, German and Italian, available from the tourist information centre in Orebić.
Transport	There are direct buses to Orebić from Dubrovnik via Ston (timetables at www.arriva.com.hr), journey time around 2hr 30min. Alternatively there are regular (hourly, in summer) passenger ferries to Orebić from Korčula, leaving from near the tourist information office (the car ferry is less convenient as it leaves from around 3km outside the town itself); and a fast catamaran service to Korčula from Split (www.krilo.hr), as well as a catamaran and ferry (both Jadrolinija) between Split and the town of Vela Luka, at the other end of the island, from where there are buses to Korčula itself.
Note	Start early in the day – the path is exposed to the sun for much of the route – and make sure you take enough water, as there's none on the trail.

One of the most impressive day trips on the Croatian coast, this is a straightforward circular route over Sveti Ilija (961m), starting and finishing at sea level in the small town of Orebić.

The long, slender Pelješac peninsula runs some 70km from Ston in the south, almost touching the island of Korčula in the north, and is mountainous for much of its length. The northernmost area, just inland from Orebić, is one of the best hiking routes, with fantastic views due both to its height and isolation at the tip of a peninsula, rising up to the high point of Sveti Ilija at 961m (not to be confused with the Sveti Ilija on Biokovo, or Ilijin vrh on Sniježnica).

Illyrian presence on the **Pelješac peninsula** is attested by graves and ruins at Ston, while Greek and Roman settlements existed at Orebić, Viganj and Trpanj. Pelješac came under Byzantine rule before being absorbed by the Republic of Dubrovnik, at which time Orebić was the seat of the local duke. From the 17th century, wealthy merchants and sea captains built numerous villas on the peninsula, many of which survive. The sprawling medieval walls of Ston are impressive (Ston is also known for its oyster beds). Pelješac is also the home of two of Croatia's most celebrated wine-producing areas, Dingač and Postup – which, rather conveniently, are only a few kilometres from Orebić – and the beautiful walled town of Korčula is just across the Pelješac Channel from Orebić.

Turning left onto this road will bring you to the Franciscan monastery (Franjevački samostan) and church (Gospa od Anđela, 'Our Lady of the Archangels').

Head north along the main road from the harbour at **Orebić** until you reach the Hotel Bellvue and its adjacent tennis courts on the left. A forest road opposite these (on your right) has red-and-white trail markings and a sign to Sveti Ilija. Follow this, and almost immediately turn left onto a clearly marked trail, which zigzags up through the trees to reach a minor road in 10 minutes. ◄

Continue N along the road from the monastery, reaching an unsealed road on the right in 15 minutes, which is signposted to Sveti Ilija. Follow this, then continue up a fairly steep marked trail, bearing left. This contours the hillside and ascends gradually, passing a trail coming up from the **small chapel** of Sveti Lovrinac after around 10 minutes and, soon afterwards, a dry well at just over 300m. Around 40 minutes later the path begins to veer right and inland, arriving at a wooden gate in a further 15 minutes. Beyond this the path continues through pine trees, arriving at a junction in 5 minutes.

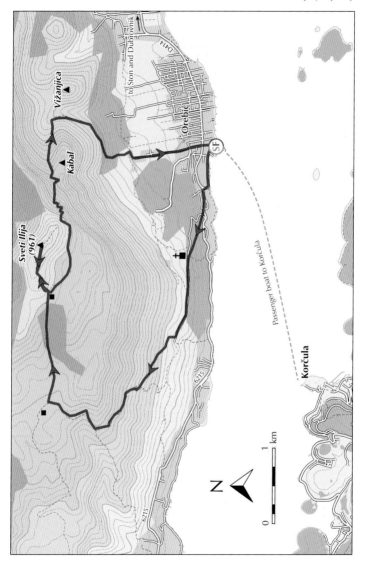

Take the right fork, marked '**Sveti Ilija**' (the left fork leads in 5 minutes to an old hunting lodge, which is locked, and where the water would certainly need purifying). Ascend fairly steeply again for 35 minutes to reach a small hunting lodge (again locked, with no water), from where a trail branches left to the **summit**. It's about 20 minutes up to the top, following a clear trail and scrambling over rocks and boulders. On the way, take the opportunity to have a look at a deep, yawning sinkhole, which is reached from a junction on the left after around 5 minutes, and is a only a couple of minutes from this point.

The view from the summit of **Sveti Ilija** (961m) is spectacular, west over Korčula and south along the ridge towards southern Pelješac. (There's no trail along the rocky ridge – the path just visible at the far end of this ridge comes up from Orebić then descends again on the NE side, rather than following the ridge crest.)

Descend to the hunting lodge and the main trail. The next section of the route is less clear, since forest fires a few years ago removed most of the trail markings and any sign of a path. Follow the Orebić trail down through the trees, but not too far: **avoid veering too far right** or descending all the way to the paddocks, beyond which is a field of particularly jagged rock followed by a sheer drop halfway down to sea level. The trick is to stay roughly on a level, heading for the base of the small cliff below the upper slopes of Sveti Ilija, steering a route through the trees and ascending slightly to a point where the path once more becomes clear. (If you descend too far, skirt the edge of the rock field, ascending left towards the base of the low cliff already mentioned).

The cliffs below Kabal are now visible on the right, falling in sheer crags from the field of jagged rocks, which hopefully you avoided straying into.

Once back on a clear trail, you'll soon regain the view along Pelješac and down over Orebić, crossing scree above steep cliffs and then descending through forest. ◄ The path once more emerges into the open, becoming a well-engineered trail below Vižanjica, just above 300m. Orebić soon comes into view, and the trail narrows to become a thorny track. Around 75 minutes from the summit trail junction, you arrive at the first houses, and a sign back to Sveti Ilija (marked as 2hr 45min). Continue straight ahead down a four-wheel drive track, veering left then right through olive groves and more houses to reach the main road in **Orebić** after a further 15 minutes. Cross over, and continue straight down past the church to the waterfront.

Sveti Ilija and the Pelješac peninsula viewed across the roofs of the medieval town of Korčula

APPENDIX A
Route summary table

Route	Start/finish	Distance – km (miles)	Ascent/descent – m (ft)	Time	Page
Part 1 Walks around Zagreb					**65**
1	Grafičar, Sljeme	Šestine	13 (8.1)	760 (2493)	4hr 30min	67
2	Vrh Sljeme	Šestine	13 (8.1)	845 (2772)	4hr 30min	72
3	Veternica Cave	Gornji Stenjevec	3 (1.9)	190 (623)	1hr 30min	76
4	Samoborsko gorje	Samobor	15 (9.3)	750 (4593)	4hr 30min	79
Part 2 Istria and the Opatija Riviera					**83**
5	Vrh Učka	Lovran	15 (9.3)	1400m (4593)	7hr 15min	85
6	Pazinska jama	Pazin	2 (1.2)	130m (427)	40min	92
Part 3 Gorski kotar					**94**
Risnjak national park					
7	Vrh Risnjak	Bela Vodica	18 (11.2)	860m (2822)	6hr 30min	97
8	River Kupa source	Razloge	4 (2.5)	235m (771)	1hr	102
9	Risnjak, Snježnik and Hahlić trek	Bela Vodica/ Dražice	36–38 (22.4–23.6)	1145 (3757)/1530 (5020)	3–4 days	105
Skrad and Fužine					
10	Vražji prolaz and Zeleni vir	Skrad	6.5 (4)	405m (1329)	2hr 30min	119

Route	Start/finish		Distance – km (miles)	Ascent/descent – m (ft)	Time	Page
11	Burnji Bitoraj	Vrata	13.5 (8.4)	705m (2313)	4hr 30min	122
12	Bajersko jezero and Vrelo cave	Fužine	6 (3.7)	170m (558)	1hr	126
Velika kapela						
13	Bjelolasica, Bijele stijene and Samarske stijene trek	PD Tuk/Jasenak	28–33 (17.4–20.5)	1070 (3510)/1360 (4462)	4–5 days	129
14	Klek	Ogulin	21 (13)	865 (2828)	7hr	147
Part 4 Velebit						**152**
Northern Velebit national park and Central Velebit						
15	Mali Rajinac, Veliki Zavižan and Botanički vrt	PD Zavižan	14.5 (9)	660 (2165)	7hr 30min	155
16	Northern Velebit and Central Velebit trek	Gornja Klada/ Baške Oštarije	58.5–75 (36.4–46.6)	2690 (8825)/2205 (7234)	5–7 days	160
Paklenica national park and Southern Velebit						
17	Anica kuk	Velika Paklenica car park	4 (2.5)	690m (2264)	3hr 30min	187
18	Manita peć	Velika Paklenica car park	5 (8)	450m (1476)	3hr	189
19	Južni Velebit (southern Velebit and Paklenica trek	Milovci/Velika Paklenica car park	39.5–42 (24.5–26.1)	2320 (7612)/2327 (7635)	5–6 days	192

Route	Start/finish		Distance – km (miles)	Ascent/descent – m (ft)	Time	Page
Part 5 The Dalmatian Hinterland						**212**
20	Dinara trek	Glavaš	16 (9.9)	1390m (4560)	2 days	214
21	Krka National Park	Skradinski buk	3.5 (2.2)	150m (492)	1hr 30min	223
22	Plitvice Lakes National Park	Ulaz 2 (Hotel Jezero)	8 (5)	30 (98)/170 (558)	3hr	225
Part 6 Central Dalmatia						**229**
23	Mosor trek	Kućine/Dubrava	28.5 (17.7)	2195m/1895m (7201//6217)	2 days	231
24	Kozjak	Kaštel Stari/ Kaštel Kambelovac	10.5 (6.5)	650m/675m (2133/2215)	5hr	242
25	Biokovo traverse trek	Bast/Makarska	23 (14.2)	1965/2270 (6447/7448)	2 days	245
Part 7 Southern Dalmatia						**256**
26	Sniježnica (Ilijin vrh)	Kuna Konavoska	11 (6.8)	745 (2444)	3hr 30min	258
27	Sveti Ilija (Pelješac)	Orebić	13.5 (8.4)	1040 (3412)	6hr	263

APPENDIX B
Gateway cities – Zagreb, Rijeka, Zadar, Split

Zagreb

Tourist information: Zagreb Tourist Office (info centre at trg Bana Jelačića 11, tel. +385 (0)1 4814 051, www.infozagreb.hr)

Transport: Most international flights arrive at Zagreb airport's new terminal (www.zagreb-airport.hr), which opened in 2017, 10km south of the city (although some international flights still arrive at the older terminal nearby). The main railway station (Glavni kolodvor) is located at the southern end of Trg kralja Tomislava (King Tomislav Square). The main bus station (Ausobusni kolodvor, www.akz.hr) is a 10 minute walk east from the railway station on Avenija Marina Držića (tram #6 goes from Ban Jelačić Square to the railway station and the bus station). Tram tickets are bought from the driver and must be stamped in the small machines at the front of the tram to be valid, after which they're valid on any combination of trams and inner city buses going in the same direction for 30 minutes.

Recommended accommodation: B&B Lobagola (www.lobagola.com – excellent value and very knowledgeable about hiking and cycling), Hotel Jägerhorn (www.hotel-jagerhorn.hr), Zagreb Apartments (www.zagrebapartments.eu)

Recommended restaurants: Zvrno (www.zrnobiobistro.hr – best vegetarian restaurant in Zagreb), Korčula (www.restoran-korcula.hr – best seafood restaurant in Zagreb), Ivica i Marica (https://www.facebook.com/ivicaimarica/), Pivnica Medvedgrad (www.pivovara-medvedgrad.hr – Zagreb's best brewery has several taverns, the best is the one on Ilica)

Rijeka

Tourist information: Rijeka Tourist Board (info centre at Korzo 14, tel. +385 (0)51 335 882, www.tz-rijeka.hr)

Transport: Ferries and catamarans leave from the long jetty near the town centre; the bus station is on Žabica, just west of the Korzo; the train station is a 10 minute walk west from this on Zvonimirova.

Recommended accommodation: Grand Hotel Bonavia (www.plavalaguna.com/en/hotels/bonavia), Hotel Continental (www.jadran-hoteli.hr), youth hostel (www.hfhs.hr)

Recommended restaurants: Pizzerija Bracera (Kružina 12, an alley off the Korzo), Ristorante Spagho (I Zajca 24), Konoba Feral (Matije Gupca 5b)

Zadar

Tourist information: Zadar Tourist Board (Mihovila Klaića 1, tel. +385 (0)23 316 166, www.tzzadar.hr); Zadar County Tourist Board (Sv Leopolda B Mandia 1, tel. +385 (023) 315 316, www.zadar.hr)

Transport: Zadar airport is at Zemunik, east from the city; a shuttle bus runs from Zadar bus station. Zadar's bus station is a 15 minute walk SE from the old town on Ulica Ante Starčevića. Larger ferries depart from Gaženiva, outside the town centre – a bus for Gaženiva leaves from near the ferry ticket office, around 40 minutes before the ferry departure time. Catamarans depart from Liburska obala, on the northeast side of the old town.

Recommended accommodation: Kuća Bajlo (www.bajlo.com – the only vegetarian B&B in Croatia, a lovely place with outstanding food), Hostel Forum (https://hostelforumzadar.com/en – best value accommodation in the old town, with ensuite doubles), Central Apartments Integrated Hotel (www.centralapartments.hr)

Recommended restaurants: Pizzerija Tri Bunara (Trg tri bunari, behind Hotel Bastion), Dva Ribara (Ulica Blaža Jurjeva 1), Providenca (Varoška 6), and some of the best ice cream in Croatia from several ice cream shops along Kalelargo.

Split

Tourist information: Split Tourist Board (info centres on the peristyle, Peristil bb, tel. +385 (0)21 345; and on the Riva, Obala HNP 9, tel. +385 (0)21 360 066 606, www.visitsplit.com)

Transport: Split airport is at Kaštel, about halfway between Split and Trogir – a shuttle bus leaves from the bus station in Split or you can take local bus 37 (from the local bus station on Domovinskog rata northeast of the palace, not the main one on the waterfront) towards Trogir, which goes past the airport but not into the airport car park. Most ferries and catamarans depart from the ferry port by the bus and railway stations, on Obala Kneza Domogoja, under a 10 minute walk from Diocletian's Palace (some of the departure points, specifically those with a higher number, eg 'gat 23', are a 10 minute walk further along the waterfront from the main Jadrolinija office, so allow yourself enough time to get there), with a couple of catamaran services leaving from in front of the palace itself.

Recommended accommodation: Villa Simoni (www.sobesimoni.com), Villa Matejuška (www.villamatejuska.hr), Goli & Bosi Design Hostel (www.gollybossy.com), and best of all Tiramola (www.apartmentstiramola.com – a beautiful and very welcoming place to stay, in nearby Trogir)

Recommended restaurants: Kod Jože (Sredmanuška 4, beyond the park behind the palace), Noštromo (Kraj Sv Marija 10, by the fish market), Šperun (Šperun 3, in the Varoš neighbourhood)

APPENDIX C
Useful contacts

Embassies and consulates in Croatia
British Embassy in Zagreb
Ivana Lučića 4
PO Box 454
10000
Zagreb
tel +385 (0)1 600 9100
www.gov.uk/world/organisations/
british-embassy-zagreb

British Consulate in Split
Obala Hrvatskog narodnog preporoda
10/III
21000
Split
tel +385 (0)21 346 007
https://www.gov.uk/world/organisations/
british-consulate-split

German Embassy in Zagreb
Ulica grada Vukovara 64
10000
Zagreb
tel: +385 (0)1 630 0100
https://zagreb.diplo.de/

French Embassy in Zagreb
Hebrangova 2
10000
Zagreb
tel: +385 (0)1 48 93 600
https://hr.ambafrance.org/

United States Embassy in Zagreb
Ulica Thomasa Jeffersona 2
10010
Zagreb
tel: +385 (0)1 661 2200
https://hr.usembassy.gov/

Canadian Embassy in Zagreb
Prilaz Gjure Deželića 4
10000
Zagreb
tel: +385 (0)1 488 1200
https://www.canadainternational.gc.ca/
croatia-croatie/offices-bureaux/index.
aspx?lang=eng

Embassy of the Netherlands in Zagreb
Trg N.Š. Zrinskog 7-8
10000 Zagreb
tel: +385 (0)1 456 9964
http://nl.mvep.hr/nl

Croatian National Tourist Board
www.croatia.hr

UK Office (London)
tel 020 8563 7979

Croatia (Head Office, Zagreb)
tel +385 (0)1 469 9333

Regional tourist boards
Zagreb County Tourist Board
www.tzzz.hr

Kvarner County Tourist Office
www.kvarner.hr

Split Dalmatia County Tourist Board
www.dalmatia.hr

Zadar County Tourist Board
www.zadar.hr

Šibenik-Knin County Tourist Board
www.sibenik-tourism.hr/en/

Dubrovnik and Neretva County Tourist
Board
www.visitdubrovnik.hr

Transport

Buses
Autotrans
www.autotrans.hr
This is a good place to start for bus times; one of Croatia's largest transport networks, with good coverage of the Kvarner region

Bus Croatia
www.buscroatia.com
This website doesn't provide a definitive list of bus times; searching through the relevant tourist information office, bus company or bus station will usually show more results

Zagreb bus station (with timetables)
www.akz.hr

Trains
Train times
www.hzpp.hr

International rail services
www.bahn.com

Driving
(For information on motorway tolls, road closures and traffic conditions)

HAK (Croatian Automobile Club)
www.hak.hr

Croatian Motorways
www.hac.hr

Cycling (both websites in Croatian)
www.pedala.hr
www.bicikl.hr/bike-bed

Croatian government ministries
State Institute for the Protection of Nature
www.dzzp.hr

Croatian Meteorological Service
www.meteo.hr

Hydrographic Institute of the Republic of Croatia
www.hhi.hr

Croatian Bureau of Statistics
www.dzs.hr

Ministry of Foreign Affairs
www.mvp.hr

Wildlife and conservation
Snakes of Croatia
www.zh.zadweb.biz.hr

Croatia Birding
www.croatiabirding.com

Matt's European Butterflies
www.eurobutterflies.com

Moths and Butterflies of Europe and North Africa
www.leps.it

State Institute for the Protection of Nature
www.dzzp.hr

Blue World Institute of Marine Research and Conservation
www.blue-world.org

Accommodation
Croatian Camping Union
www.camping.hr

Croatian Youth Hostel Association
www.hfhs.hr

Apartmanija
www.apartmanija.hr

Gdje na more?
www.gdjenamore.com

Mountain huts
http://www.hps.hr/info/planinarske-kuce/

Hiking and mountain rescue
Croatian Mountain Rescue Service
(Hrvatska Gorska služba spašavanja,
HGSS or GSS)
www.gss.hr
Delnice (for Gorski kotar): +385 (0) 91
721 0004
Gospić (for northern and central Velebit):
+385 (0) 91 721 0007
Makarska (for Biokovo): +385 (0) 91
721 0011
Split (for Mosor): +385 (0) 91 721 0001
Zadar (for southern Velebit and
Paklenica): +385 (0) 91 721 0010
Zagreb (for Medvednica): +385 (0) 91
721 0002

Croatian Mountaineering Association
(Hrvatski planinarski savez)
www.hps.hr

Maps
HGSS Cartography (hiking maps)
http://www.gss.hr/hgss/kartografija/

SMAND (hiking maps)
www.smand.hr

APPENDIX D
Croatian language notes and glossary

A note on grammar
In the Croatian language, nouns and adjectives are governed by seven cases (common in many other languages, they will be familiar to anyone who has studied German, for example). These cases are: nominative (subject); accusative (direct object, and verbs of motion); dative (indirect object); locative or prepositional (used with positions); genitive (used with possession or amounts); instrumental (used with the word s or sa, meaning 'with'); and vocative (used in some forms of address). Thus the same noun (for example *kava*, a feminine noun meaning 'coffee') may take a number of forms, depending on its function within a sentence: *dobra je kava* ('it's good coffee' – nominative); *daj mi jednu kavu, molim* ('give me a coffee, please' – accusative); *u kavi* ('in the coffee' – locative); *s kavom* ('with coffee' – instrumental). Similarly, taking Zagreb as an example of a masculine noun: *Zagreb je lijep* ('Zagreb is pretty'); *idemo u Zagreb* ('we're going to Zagreb'); *ja sam u Zagrebu* ('I'm in Zagreb'); *on je iz Zagreba* ('he's from Zagreb').

Nouns may be masculine (usually ending with a consonant in the singular, and -i in the plural), feminine (usually ending with -a in the singular, -e in the plural) or neuter (-o or -e singular, -a plural). There are also a number of irregular exceptions to the above rule. Adjectives agree with nouns.

Pronunciation

Pronunciation is very important if you are to be understood clearly. As a number of Croatian letters are not found in the English alphabet, and some familiar letters are pronounced differently in Croatian (in particular j, which sounds like an English 'y'), a list of letters requiring particular attention is given below.

a	pronounced as the 'a' in father
c	pronounced as the 'ts' in cats
č	pronounced as the 'ch' in church
ć	very similar to č, but slightly softer, as the 'tj' sound in picture
đ	pronounced as the 'j' in jam
dž	very similar to the above
e	pronounced as the 'e' in egg
g	pronounced hard, as the 'g' in give
i	pronounced as the 'i' in ill
j	pronounced as the 'y' in yes
lj	pronounced as the 'lli' in million
nj	pronounced as the 'ni' in onion
o	pronounced as the 'o' in hot
r	rolled slightly
š	pronounced as the 'sh' in shake
u	pronounced as the 'oo' in pool
ž	pronounced as the 's' in pleasure, or the French 'j' in janvier

Other letters are pronounced as they would be in English.

The complete Croatian alphabet is as follows: a, b, c, č, ć, d, đ, dž, e, f, g, h, i, j, k, l, lj, m, n, nj, o, p, r, s, š, t, u, v, z, ž. Note that there is no q, w, x or y.

Glossary

In the following list of vocabulary and basic phrases, 'Z' and 'D' have to indicate the Zagreb and Dalmatian dialects respectively. All other words and phrases are modern, standard Croatian. Alternative masculine/feminine/plural endings are given, where appropriate, as are some variations in meaning.

Greetings, introductions and basic phrases

English	Croatian
Hello/Good day	*Dobar dan**
Hi/bye! (informal)	*Bog! or Bok! (Z) (also used as a toast, from zbogom, 'go with God')*

English	Croatian
Good morning	*Dobro jutro*
Good evening	*Dobra večer*
Good night	*Laku noć*
Goodbye	*Do viđenja*
See you later!	*Vidimo se!*
Have a good trip!/Safe journey!	*Sretan put!*
Yes	*Da*
No	*Ne*
Please	*Molim*
Thank you	*Hvala*
Thank you very much	*Puno hvala/hvala vam lijepo*
I beg your pardon?	*Molim?*
Sorry!	*Oprostite!/Pardon!*
Excuse me (when about to request something)	*Oprostite*
Excuse me (when trying to get past someone)	*Samo malo*
Just a minute!	*Samo malo!*
Here you are! (when offering something)	*Izvolite!*
Cheers! (as a toast)	*Živjeli!*
Do you speak English/French?	*Govorite li engleski/francuski?*
I'm sorry, I don't speak Croatian	*Oprostite, ne znam hrvatski*
I only speak a little (Croatian)	*Samo malo govorim (hrvatski)*
I don't understand	*Ne razumijem*
I don't know	*Ne znam*
How are you? (formal)	*Kako ste?*
Fine, thank you	*Dobro, hvala*
Pleased to meet you!	*Drago mi je!*
Where are you from?	*Odakle ste?*
I'm English	*Ja sam Englez*
I'm from…	*Ja sam iz…*

English	Croatian
I'm a… (teacher/student/engineer…)	*Ja sam…(profesor/student/inženjer…)*
Mr	*Gospodin*
Mrs	*Gospoda*
I like/I don't like…	*Sviđa mi se/ne sviđa mi se…*
Great!	*Odlično!*
Let's go! (plural)	*Idemo!*
Please could I have…	*Molim vas…*
I'd like…	*Ja bih…*
Do you have…?	*Imate li…?*
I/we need…	*Trebam/trebamo…*
How much does it cost?	*Koliko košta?*
I've already ordered, thank you	*Već sam naručio, hvala (m)/ Već sam naručila, hvala (f)*
Can I order, please?	*Mogu li naručiti?*
Can I pay, please?	*Mogu li platiti?*
Can I have the bill, please?	*Molim vas račun?*
This is for you	*To je za vas*
Can I help you?	*Mogu li pomoći?*
I'm just looking, thanks	*Samo gledam, hvala*
One ticket to…, please	*Jednu kartu do…, molim*
What time does the train to Delnice leave?	*U koliko sati ide vlak za Delnice?*
Which platform?	*Koji peron?*
Which number?	*Koji broj?*
There is/there are…/is there?/are there…?	*Ima…/ima…?*
There isn't/there aren't…	*Nema…*

* The old Serbo-Croatian greeting Zdravo! (literally meaning 'healthy'), although still included in a number of guidebooks, is not used (and hasn't been for many years),

except occasionally for effect or in jest. Even in Belgrade, the preferred informal greeting is Ćao.

numeral	Croatian
0	nula
1	jedan
2	dva
3	tri
4	četiri
5	pet
6	šest
7	sedam
8	osam
9	devet
10	deset
11	jedanaest
12	dvanaest
13	trinaest
20	dvadeset
21	dvadeset jedan

numeral	Croatian
22	dvadeset dva
30	trideset
40	četrdeset
50	pedeset
60	šezdeset
70	sedamdeset
80	osamdeset
90	devedeset
100	sto
125	sto dvadeset pet
200	dvijesto
300	tristo
1000	tisuća
first	prvi
second	drugi
third	treći

Time, days of the week and months

English	Croatian
What time is it?	Koliko je sati?
9.25am	devet i dvadeset pet sati
2pm	dva sata (or četrnaest sati)
minute	minuta
hour	sat
day	dan
week	tjedan
month	mjesec
year	godina
Sunday	nedjelja
Monday	ponedjeljak
Tuesday	utorak
Wednesday	srijeda

English	Croatian
Thursday	četvrtak
Friday	petak
Saturday	subota
January	siječanj
February	veljača
March	ožujak
April	travanj
May	svibanj
June	lipanj
July	srpanj
August	kolovoz
September	rujan
October	listopad
November	studeni
December	prosinac
spring	proljeće

English	Croatian
summer	*ljeto*
autumn	*jesen*
winter	*zima*
today	*danas*
tomorrow	*sutra*
yesterday	*jučer*
in the morning	*ujutro*
in the afternoon	*popodne, poslije podne*
in the evening	*navečer*
General vocabulary	
after	*poslije*
and	*i*
beautiful	*krasan*
before	*prije*
big	*veliki*
black	*crni*
blue	*plavi*
closed	*zatvoreno*
cold	*hladno*
difficult/more difficult	*teško/teže*
easy/easier	*lako/lakše*
excellent	*odlično*
far	*daleko*
fast	*brzo*
from	*iz*
from...to...	*od...do...*
green	*zeleni*
here	*ovdje/tu*
hot	*vruće*
how?	*kako?*
in	*u*
later	*kasnije*
much/many	*puno/mnogo*

English	Croatian
near	*blizu*
now	*sada*
of	*od*
on	*na*
open	*otvoreno*
or	*ili*
red	*crveni*
slow	*polako*
small	*mali*
terrible	*strašan*
that	*ono/to*
there	*tamo*
this	*ovo*
to	*u (sometimes na is used instead)*
under	*ispod*
very	*jako/vrlo*
what?	*što? kaj? (Z) ča? (D)*
when?	*kad?*
where?	*gdje?*
white	*bijeli*
who?	*tko?*
with	*s/sa*
without	*bez*
In the mountains	
cascade, travertine fall	*buk*
cave	*špilja/pećina*
cliff	*stijena*
crag, bare limestone peak	*kuk*
dry-stone wall	*suhozid*
field/cultivated area between limestone ridges	*polje*

English	Croatian
forest	šuma
hill	brdo
lake	jezero
limestone depression	vrtača, doline, or (larger) duliba, dabar
limestone pit	škrapa
massif	gora/gorje
mountain	planina
mountain hut	planinarski dom, planinarska kuća
mountain range	planinski lanac
pass	vrata (lit. 'door'), prijevoj, sedlo
peak/summit	vrh
ridge	greben, hrbat, kukovi
river	rijeka
rock/rocky	kamen/kamenit
scree	sipar
shelter	sklonište
sinkhole	jama
small peak, hillock	glava (lit. 'head')
spring	izvor
steep	strm
valley	dolina
water	voda
waterfall	vodopad, slap

On the coast

beach	plaža
cape/headland/point	rt
coast	obala
island	otok
peninsula	poluotok
sandy	pješčan

English	Croatian
sea	more
stony	šljunčan

Directions and rights of way

Where are you going? (formal)	Kamo idete?
I'm/we're going to...	Idem/idemo u...
Excuse me, where's the path to...?	Oprostite, gdje je put za...?
How far is...?	Koliko daleko je...?
Is it marked?	Je li markiran?
I'm/we're lost!	Izgubio sam se (m)/ izgubila sam se (f)/izgubili smo se!
(on the) left	(na) lijevo
(on the) right	(na) desno
path	staza
road	cesta
way	put

Weather

It's raining/snowing	Pada kiša/snijeg
It's getting dark	Pada mrak
It's windy	Puše vjetar
weather	vrijeme
cloud	oblak
fog	magla
frost	mraz
hail	tuča
ice	led
lightning	munja
rain	kiša
snow	snijeg
storm	oluja

English	Croatian
sun	*sunce*
thunder	*grom*
Plants and animals	
animal	*životinja*
bear	*medvjed*
beech	*bukva*
bird	*ptica*
buzzard	*škanjac*
cat	*mačka*
common viper	*šarka* or *šarulja*
cow	*krava*
cypress	*čempres*
deer	*jelen*
dog	*pas*
dormouse	*puh*
eagle	*orao*
flower	*cvijet (not to be confused with svijet, 'world')*
fox	*lisica*
goat	*jarac*
grass	*trava*
griffon vulture	*bjeloglavi sup*
horse	*konj*
juniper	*borovica* or *smreka*
leaf	*list*
lynx	*ris*
mountain pine	*klekovina, planinski bor* or *bor krivulj*
nose-horned viper	*poskok*
oak	*hrast*
pine	*bor*
rabbit	*zec*
sheep	*ovca*
snake	*zmija*

English	Croatian
tree	*drvo*
wild mountain sheep	*muflon*
wild pig	*divlja svinja*
wolf	*vuk*
Towns and cities	
apartment	*apartman*
ATM	*bankomat*
bank	*banka*
bed	*krevet*
bookshop	*knjižara*
bridge	*most*
castle	*dvorac*
chapel	*kapelica*
chemist	*apoteka* or *ljekarna*
church	*crkva*
citadel/old town	*stari grad*
city walls	*zidine*
door	*vrata*
exchange office	*mjenjačnica*
garden	*vrt*
graveyard	*groblje*
hotel	*hotel*
house	*kuća/dom*
monastery	*samostan*
post office	*pošta*
restaurant	*restoran/konoba/gostionica*
room	*soba*
single room	*jednokrevetna soba*
double room	*dvokrevetna soba*
shop	*dućan, trgovina*
square	*trg*
street	*ulica*

English	Croatian
town/city	grad
village	selo
wall	zid
Transport	
aeroplane	avion
airport	zračna luka/ aerodrom
arrivals/departures	dolazak/odlazak
bus	bus
bus station	autobusni kolodvor
bus stop	stajalište
by train	vlakom
car	auto
main (railway) station	glavni (željeznički) kolodvor
on foot	pješice
platform	peron
taxi	taksi
ticket	karta
single ticket	u jednom smjeru
return ticket	povratna karta
train	vlak
Equipment	
book	knjiga
boots	čizme
crampons	dereze
gloves	rukavice
guidebook	turistički vodič
hat	kapa
ice axe	cepin
jacket	jakna
(mountain) map	(planinarska) karta

English	Croatian
mountain guidebook	planinarski vodič
rucksack	ruksak
sleeping bag	vreća za spavanje
sleeping mat	karimat
socks	čarape
tent	šator
Food and drink	
apple	jabuka
baked	pečeno
beef	govedina
beer	pivo
boiled	kuhano
bread	kruh*
breakfast	doručak
cake	kolač
carp	šaran
cheese	sir
chicken	piletina
coffee with milk	kava s mlijekom
coffee	kava
cucumber	krastavac
dessert	desert
dinner	večera
dried meat	suho meso
eggs	jaja
fig	smokva
fish	riba
food	jelo
fried/deep fried	prženo/pohano
fruit juice	voćni sok
grapes	grožđe
grilled	na žaru
ham	šunka
homemade	domaće

English	Croatian
ice cream	sladoled
lamb	janjetina
lettuce, green salad	zelena salata
lunch	ručak
mackerel	lokarda
main course	glavno jelo
meat	meso
milk	mlijeko
mullet	cipal
mussels	dagnje
octopus	hobotnica
orange	naranča
pasta	tjestenina
pear	kruška
pepperoni-type sausages	čajna
plum	šljiva
potato	krumpir
red wine	crno vino
rice	riža
rock melon	dinja
salami	salama
salmon	losos
sauce	umak/saft
sausages	kobasice
soup	juha
sour cherry	višnja
squid	lignje
strawberry	jagoda
strudel	štrudla
Swiss chard	blitva
tea with lemon	čaj s limunom
tea	čaj

English	Croatian
tomato	rajčica, paradajz (Z)
trout	pastrva
tuna	tuna
Turkish coffee	turska kava
veal	teletina
vegetables	povrće
venison	srnetina
watermelon	lubenica
white wine	bijelo vino

* Look for crni kruh (black bread), alpski kruh (alpine bread) and raženi kruh (rye bread), all of which keep much longer than the standard bijeli kruh (white bread).

Warnings, danger and emergencies

Danger!	Opasnost!
Be careful!	Pazi!
Help!	U pomoć!
doctor	doktor/liječnik
ambulance	hitna pomoć
Please call a doctor!	Molim vas pozovite doktora!
I fell/he fell/she fell	pao sam/pao je/pala je
sick/ill	bolestan (m)/bolestna (f)
hospital	bolnica
snakebite	zmijski ugriz
blood	krv
broken	slomljen
landmines	mine
abandoned military installation	napušteni vojni objekt

APPENDIX E
Other hiking areas in Croatia

Papuk

Papuk is a relatively compact range of wooded hills, just east of the towns of Kutjevo and Orahovica, reaching a height of 953m on the otherwise resolutely flat Slavonian plain. There are some interesting geological features, a number of endemic plant species and its slopes also bear the ruins of nine castles (the most impressive of them is Ružica grad, which can be reached on foot from the artificial lake and recreation centre above Orahovica).

Lonjsko polje

Lonjsko polje Nature Park (Park prirode Lonjsko polje, www.pp-lonjsko-polje.hr) stretches along the north bank of the river Sava, between the towns of Sisak and Kutina. While walking is fairly limited (and very flat!), this is a beautifully preserved rural part of Croatia, with distinctive traditional wooden architecture (many of the houses date from the 19th century). There are excellent opportunities for spotting birdlife: it is simply *the* place in Croatia to see storks. There are park offices in Lonja and Čigoć. The area is prone to extensive flooding in the spring and autumn. The southeastern areas of the park, near Jasenovac and around the Bosnian border, may still be unsafe due to landmines following the war of the 1990s; do not wander off the roads in this area.

Kopački rit

Kopački rit Nature Park (Park prirode Kopački rit, https://pp-kopacki-rit.hr, entry 10kn) is an important wetland area near the confluence of the Danube and Drava, around 10km outside Osijek, and is home to a huge amount of birdlife. The area is really best explored by boat – a combined ticket that includes a boat trip and a visit to the nearby Tikveš castle costs 70Kn. There are also dedicated ornithological tours in small boats.

Vransko jezero

Located midway between Zadar and Šibenik, Vransko jezero is Croatia's largest lake, a Nature Park (Park prirode Vransko jezero, www.pp-vransko-jezero.hr, entry 20kn), and one of the most important areas for birdlife on the Croatian coast, listed as an IBA and a RAMSAR site. Some 256 species of birds have been recorded here, 102 of which nest in the area, and over 100,000 waterbirds winter at the lake. A flooded karst valley and a cryptodepression, the lake's brackish waters are surrounded by reed beds. There are some short, signposted walking trails, and around 50km of cycle routes – the adjacent hill, Kamenjak, makes a good viewpoint, with a 4X4 road leading to the top.

The islands

Many of the Croatian islands – including Krk, Lošinj, Dugi otok, Vis – have excellent hiking trails, which make for some wonderful day walks. These are covered in a separate Cicerone guide, *The Islands of Croatia*.

APPENDIX F
Further reading

Hiking guidebooks

Islands of Croatia (Cicerone, 2013) Rudolf Abraham – detailed guide to hiking on the islands of Croatia's Adriatic coast

The Mountains of Montenegro (2nd ed; Cicerone, 2015) Rudolf Abraham – the most detailed English-language guide to hiking in neighbouring Montenegro

Guidebooks

Croatia: The Bradt Travel Guide (6th edn; Bradt, 2017) Piers Letcher & Rudolf Abraham – detailed general guidebook to Croatia

Istria: The Bradt Travel Guide (2nd edition; Bradt, 2017) Rudolf Abraham & Thammy Evans – the most detailed guide to the Istrian peninsula

National Geographic Traveler: Croatia (2nd ed; National Geographic, 2016) Rudolf Abraham

History

Croatia: A History (London, 1999) Ivo Goldstein

Croatia: A Nation Forged in War (Yale, 1997) Marcus Tanner

One Hundred Croatian Archeological Sites (ed. Aleksander Durman; Leksikografski zavod Miroslav Krleža, 2007)

Southeastern Europe in the Middle Ages 500–1250 (Cambridge, 2006) Florin Curta

The Byzantine Commonwealth: Eastern Europe, 500–1453 (London, 1971) Dimitri Obolenski

The Death of Yugoslavia (London, 1995) Laura Silber and Allan Little – account of the war in the former Yugoslavia based on the excellent BBC TV series

The Fall of Yugoslavia (London, 1992) Misha Glenny – another good account of the war in the former Yugoslavia

The Illyrians (Oxford, 1992) John Wilkes

The Uskoks of Senj. Piracy, Banditry, and Holy War in the Sixteenth-Century Adriatic (Cornell University Press, 2011) Catherine Wendy Bracewell – an excellent in-depth study of the Adriatic's most famous pirates

Plants and wildlife
Central and Eastern European Wildlife (Bradt, 2008) Gerard Gorman

Birds
Birding in Eastern Europe (Wildsounds, 2006) Gerard Gorman – covers the best birding sites in Croatia and several other countries in Eastern Europe

Birds of Europe (Princeton University Press, 1999) Lars Svensson, Peter J Grant, Killian Mullarney and Dan Zetterström – an outstanding field guide to European birdlife

Collins Birds of Britain and Europe Field Guide (Harper Collins, 2004)

Reptiles
Reptiles and Amphibians of Europe (Princeton Field Guides, 2002) E Nicolas Arnold and Denys W Ovenden, reprinted from the second edition of *Collins Field Guide to the Reptiles and Amphibians of Britain and Europe* (Harper Collins, 2002)

Invertebrates
Collins Butterfly Guide (Collins, 2009) Tom Tolman and Richard Lewington

Field Guide to the Dragonflies of Britain and Europe (British Wildlife Publishing, 2006) Klaas-Douwe B Dijkstra and Richard Lewington

Flowers
Flowers of Greece and the Balkans: A Field Guide (Oxford, 1987) Oleg Polunin

The Concise Flowers of Europe (Oxford, 1972) Oleg Polunin

Language
Colloquial Croatian: The Complete Course for Beginners (Routledge, 2007) Celia Hawkesworth with Ivana Jović

Complete Croatian: Teach Yourself (Teach Yourself, 2010) David Norris

Walking – Trekking – Mountaineering – Climbing – Cycling

Over 40 years, Cicerone have built up an outstanding collection of over 300 guides, inspiring all sorts of amazing adventures.

Every guide comes from extensive exploration and research by our expert authors, all with a passion for their subjects. They are frequently praised, endorsed and used by clubs, instructors and outdoor organisations.

All our titles can now be bought as **e-books**, **ePubs** and **Kindle** files and we also have an online magazine – **Cicerone Extra** – with features to help cyclists, climbers, walkers and trekkers choose their next adventure, at home or abroad.

Our website shows any **new information** we've had in since a book was published. Please do let us know if you find anything has changed, so that we can publish the latest details. On our **website** you'll also find great ideas and lots of detailed information about what's inside every guide and you can buy **individual routes** from many of them online.

It's easy to keep in touch with what's going on at Cicerone by getting our monthly **free e-newsletter**, which is full of offers, competitions, up-to-date information and topical articles. You can subscribe on our home page and also follow us on **Facebook** and **Twitter** or dip into our **blog**.

Cicerone – the very best guides for exploring the world.

CICERONE

Juniper House, Murley Moss, Oxenholme Road, Kendal, Cumbria LA9 7RL
Tel: 015395 62069 info@cicerone.co.uk
www.cicerone.co.uk

20 day walks and 7 short treks in Northern Velebit, Paklenica, Risnjak, Gorski kotar, Dinara, Plitvice Lakes, Krka, Zagreb, Istria and Central and Southern Dalmatia

Croatia's spectacular, diverse and remarkably unspoilt landscapes range from dense forest to dramatic karst scenery, rugged mountains, travertine falls and an exquisite coastline.

This guide describes day walks and treks in all of Croatia's main hiking areas and national parks on the mainland, from the forested hills around

Zagreb to the roof of Croatia on the Bosnia border, the national parks of Northern Velebit, Paklenica, Risnjak, Krka, UNESCO-listed Plitvice Lakes and more.

- routes range from easy 3km strolls to strenuous hut-to-hut mountain treks

- information on history culture, wildlife, public transport and accommodation

- useful glossary of Croatian terms and phrases

CICERONE

www.cicerone.co.uk

TREKKING | CROATIA

US $27.95

ISBN 978-1-85284-769-2

9 781852 847692